THE ILLUSION  REALITY

Books by Corliss Lamont

The Philosophy of Humanism, Seventh edition, Continuum, New York, NY, 1990.

The Illusion of Immortality, Fifth edition, Continuum, New York, NY, 1990.

Freedom of Choice Affirmed, Third edition, Continuum, New York, NY, 1990.

Freedom Is As Freedom Does: Civil Liberties in America, Fourth edition, Continuum, New York, NY, 1990.

Yes To Life: Memoirs of Corliss Lamont, Continuum, New York, NY, 1990.

Remembering John Masefield, Continuum, New York, NY, 1990.

A Lifetime of Dissent, Prometheus Books, 700 East Amherst St., Buffalo, NY, 14215, 1988.

Voice in the Wilderness: Collected Essays of Fifty Years, Prometheus Books, 700 East Amherst St., Buffalo, NY, 14215, 1974.

The Independent Mind, Horizon Press, New York, NY, 1951.

The Peoples of the Soviet Union, Harcourt, Brace & Co., New York, NY, 1946.

Russia Day by Day (Co-author with Margaret I. Lamont), Covici-Friede, New York, 1933.

Soviet Civilization, Second edition, Philosophical Library, New York, NY, 1952, 1955.

You Might Like Socialism, Modern Age Books, New York, NY, 1939.

Lover's Credo: Poems of Love, William L. Bauhan, Dublin, NH, 03444.

A Humanist Wedding Service, Prometheus Books, 700 East Amherst St., Buffalo, NY, 14215, 1970.

A Humanist Funeral Service, Prometheus Books, 700 East Amherst St., Buffalo, NY, 14215, 1977.

(Continued on last page of book)

THE ILLUSION
OF IMMORTALITY

Corliss Lamont

Introduction by John Dewey

Fifth Edition

HALF-MOON FOUNDATION, INC.

The Half-Moon Foundation was formed to promote enduring international peace, support for the United Nations, the conservation of our country's natural environment, and to safeguard and extend civil liberties as guaranteed under the Constitution and the Bill of Rights.

A Frederick Ungar Book
CONTINUUM • NEW YORK

TO
MARGARET I. LAMONT

1990

The Continuum Publishing Company
370 Lexington Avenue
New York, NY 10017

Fifth Edition

Printed in the United States of America

Library of Congress Catalog Card No. 65-25140
ISBN 0-8044-6377-8

Cover Photograph: "The Portal of Death" from Bartholomé's
Monuments Aux Morts

PREFACE TO THE FIFTH EDITION

I never expected to live to eighty-eight and to see *The Illusion of Immortality* printed in a fifth edition fifty-five years after its first publication in 1935. That fact indicates that the theme is of lasting interest to the American people. Yet it is surprising that both prior to and following the publication of my book, no similar work appeared in the United States concentrating exclusively on the denial of immortality. There have been chapters, yes; pamphlets, essays, lectures, broadcasts, and letters, but no entire volume.

In all of Great Britain's history, only one book entirely devoted to denying the hereafter has been published. That was *The Belief in Personal Immortality* by E.S.T. Haynes in 1913. Prior to that time, so far as I can discern, no volume in the West was printed concentrating wholly on death as the natural and final end of a human personality.

For the fifth edition, I wish to acknowledge the assistance of Dr. Gordon Stein, Editor of *The American Rationalist*.

CORLISS LAMONT

New York City
April 1990

PREFACE TO THE FOURTH EDITION

The Illusion of Immortality was first published some
thirty years ago. In its successive editions it has been
revised and rewritten to a considerable extent. I present this fourth edition with the continuing conviction
that the issue of personal existence after death remains
one of the most significant of all problems for religion
and philosophy. No man can work through to a mature
philosophy of life without coming to grips with this
agelong question.

I still believe that the probabilities against a future
life for the individual are so overwhelming that I am
fully justified in calling immortality an illusion. And
my main reasons for coming to this conclusion—reasons
based upon a study of science, philosophy and religion
—stand essentially unchanged.

Without being dogmatic about it, I take the position
that death is the end of the human personality. I would
welcome heartily any concrete evidence or valid reasoning tending to establish man's immortality. Indeed,
when I started my serious studies of the subject thirty-
five years ago, I both desired and believed in a future
life. Hence such bias as may have entered into my
analysis of theories of immortality was a bias in favor
of survival, not against it.

Now, in my sixties, I should be more than glad to
know definitely that there is an immortal realm beyond
death and that one day I shall awake there able to
enjoy again the company of beloved friends and relatives long dead. As the years have passed, I have found
life on the whole so interesting, so exciting and so rich

with happiness that I would very much like to go on indefinitely as a conscious individual.

In reaching my ultimate conclusions, however, about the final destiny of the human personality I have constantly tried to keep in mind George Santayana's saying that true wisdom "consists in abandoning our illusions the better to attain our ideals." Attractive as is the dream of immortality, I have attempted to follow faithfully where facts and logic have led. That is why I was compelled to change my mind and give up my early convictions. That is why I still hold that life after death is an impossibility.

At the same time it is theoretically possible that the science of medicine may eventually make such advances in curing the ills of old age that some individuals could live on century after century and rival the 969 years attributed to Methuselah by the Bible. Such prolongation of the life span would of course be based on the continuing partnership of body and personality, and would make particularly pertinent the original meaning of immortality as "non-death."

In preparing the four editions of this book I have utilized innumerable sources and have profited from the advice of many wise friends and associates. I am greatly indebted to John Dewey, one of my earliest teachers in philosophy, for the privilege of using as an Introduction his review of *The Illusion of Immortality* (*The New Republic,* April 24, 1935). I am also most grateful to Professor Frederick J. E. Woodbridge of Columbia University, who guided my early studies on human immortality and supervised my Columbia Ph.D. thesis, published in 1932 under the title of *Issues of Immortality.*

CORLISS LAMONT

New York City
August 1965

TABLE OF CONTENTS

INTRODUCTION

THE TITLE of this book, though fitting its contents, does not give an adequate idea of either its range or its depth. It is an extraordinarily complete and well-informed discussion of the various aspects of the problem of continuing personal life after death, surveying relevant arguments from historical, scientific, social and philosophical angles. While the conclusion is that belief in immortality is an illusion and upon the whole a harmful one, the book is pervaded with a strong sense, one may say a sympathetic sense, of the things in human life that, quite apart from arguments, have created the longing for personal immortality and built up the illusion. This fact, together with its command of the literature of the subject, gives the book a freedom from the *odium theologicum* in reverse that is not always found in books taking a negative position on matters of religious controversy.

The first chapter discusses the importance of the problem. Many persons and movements allied with historic religions have made immortality more important than the existence of God, and indeed have conceived God's existence to be important chiefly as a warrant for personal continuance. The insistent fact of death, moreover, has tended to give the problem of immortality a first place in human thinking. By way of opposition to such an attitude of mind, the author emphasizes at various places throughout his book the importance—biological, psychological and social—of mortality. His position is summed up in one of the later pages: "It is best not only to disbelieve in immortality, but to *believe in mortality*."

Having stated the problem, Dr. Lamont discusses the question of the relation of body to soul or personality in its bearing on a future life, bringing out with greater clearness than I have found anywhere else the inherent contradiction of religions—the tendency on the one hand to insist on the "resurrection of the body," and on the other hand to minimize the importance of the body, or else make a complete separation between body and spirit. Dr. Lamont also devotes a chapter to the discussion of the environment in which continuing life is carried on. He has no difficulty in showing that ideas of heaven have been conditioned by the cultures in which they were entertained, and makes a significant remark that strikes, I think, the keynote of the book: "What the religious liberals or modernists do is to abstract certain values and activities from the natural world and transplant them to a supernatural one." In another connection he shows the inconsistency of the argument for immortality that bases itself on the need for rectification of the ills of this life, on the futility and meaninglessness of this life without immortality, while at the same time deriving from this very mortal state all the values with which it endows a future existence.

In summing up the scientific grounds for disbelief provided by biology, psychology and medicine, the author is on ground made familiar by current discussion; but in the summary he brings out with great clearness the point already referred to, the difficulty in considering personality in heaven and hell as either immaterial or as associated with the material—a difficulty that affects also the nature of hell and heaven themselves. I have thought of only one consideration not dealt with. It may be argued, I think, that much of the current belief in immortality is not primary, but is the product of inculcation, from infancy throughout life, of the idea that persons are rewarded in heaven and punished in hell. If this is so, the waning of belief in the old theory of reward and punishment, together with increasing vagueness and dimness about both heaven and hell, is sure to lead to diminution of the importance of belief in future life.

I have space to touch upon but one further point out of many in the volume, the treatment of the social aspect of the belief. The author is on solid ground when he points out the fatal back-kick inherent in the position that life here loses all ethical meaning and basis if there is not personal immortality, and again when he shows the morally and socially injurious consequences of putting practical preoccupation with another world in place of active interest in this one. Of belief in immortality more than of any other element of historic religions it holds good, I believe, that "religion is the opium of peoples." The positive position of Dr. Lamont is summed up in the statement: "No single idea, such as that of immortality, is, in my opinion, all-important; what is of supreme importance is an inclusive and integrated philosophy of life and one that places the individual in a definite relationship to both society and nature."

The candor, the informed scholarship and the positive grasp of the various aspects and implications of the problem of immortality that are demonstrated in this volume make it worthy of the serious attention of all thoughtful persons, particularly of those associated with liberal religious thought.

JOHN DEWEY

CHAPTER I

IMPORTANCE OF THE PROBLEM

1. *Immortality and God*

"ALL MEN are mortal" begins the most famous of all syllogisms, and it proceeds to tell us that "Socrates is a man" and "therefore Socrates is mortal." The branch of philosophy known as logic has made much of this syllogism as an example of perfect reasoning; what is more significant is the prodigious amount of time and energy which philosophy as a whole has spent on inquiring into its true and complete meaning. On that meaning have been thought to hang the destiny of man, the fate of nations and even the existence of God. The real question has been: How seriously are we to take the proposition that men and Socrates are mortal? For there exists a well-known counter-proposition to the effect that men and Socrates are *im*mortal; or at least that what we call their personalities or souls are immortal. In fact, Socrates himself, if the *Dialogues* of Plato are to be trusted, was one of the first to advance the hypothesis of the soul's immortality.

To put the issue in another way, when men die, as everyone must admit they eventually do, do they *really* die, that is, do they stay dead? Or, as Job phrases it: "If a man die, shall he live again?" Now there can be no doubt that this problem—this mystery —of death was one of the first and foremost incentives to philosophical inquiry. It was Socrates again, according to Plato's *Phaedo,* who called philosophy a meditation on death, which in plain terms means a meditation on whether man is mortal or immortal. For various reasons it has become customary to refer to the problem of *immortality* rather than to the problem of death or of mortality. And with this in mind we can say that the history of philosophy has borne out to a great extent the saying of Socrates. For among philosophers, whether ancient, medieval or modern, the idea of immortality has bulked large, either explicitly as a definite promise or hope, or implicitly in the guise of metaphysical assumptions and epistemological trimmings. This is not surprising. For philosophers, after all, are but men and cannot help reflecting to a large degree the human cultures in which they live.

Now in those cultures, at least in the West, a study of history demonstrates that the idea of immortality may have played an even more important part than the idea of God. That discerning philosopher and acute psychologist, William James, has observed: "Religion, in fact, for the great majority of our own race, *means* immortality, and nothing else. God is the producer of immortality."[1] Miguel de Unamuno, the brilliant Spanish writer, relates that "Talking to a peasant one day, I proposed to him the hypothesis that there might indeed be a God who governs heaven and earth . . . but that for all that the soul of every man may not be immortal in the traditional and concrete sense. He replied: 'Then wherefore God?' "[2] To cite another American source expressed in characteristic American fashion: "Most men and women would rather be assured of eternal life than of anything else. If the privilege of living for ever were marketable, it would sell at the highest figure of anything offered to mankind."[3] Higher even than God, presumably. Luther evidently had something similar in mind when he indignantly cried: "If you believe in no future life, I would not give a mushroom for your God."[4] And even the poets follow suit with Tennyson proclaiming: "If immortality be not true, then no God but a mocking fiend created us."[5]

This line of thought, again, is not surprising. For all of these gentlemen have written in the Christian tradition. And probably no great religion has so emphasized immortality as Christianity. In the very earliest days of this faith St. Paul frankly and clearly expressed its central doctrine: "And if Christ be not risen, then is our preaching vain, and your faith is also vain. . . . If in this life only we have hope in Christ, we are of all men most miserable."[6] Later St. Augustine taught that the resurrection of the dead "is the special faith of Christians; this alone is the faith which divides off . . . Christians from all men."[7] While there have been many dissenters from the interpretation of Paul and Augustine, it can hardly be doubted that on the whole their viewpoint has prevailed.

The resurrection of Jesus to eternal life was not only the sure and unmistakable sign of his divinity, but a pledge that men in general would also rise from the grave. This decisive and dramatic victory over death, seemingly mankind's greatest enemy, proved not only that Jesus was the Son of God, but that *all* men were his sons. What surer or more lasting foundation could any religion wish than triumph over the tomb? In fact, one of the chief reasons why Christianity finally won out in the ancient Mediterranean world was that it appealed so strongly to the members of existing religious cults that stressed a future life. There can be no question that Christianity came into being first and foremost as a death-conquering religion.

As it developed, the Christian Church embellished and enlarged upon the simple fact of immortality testified to by Jesus. The hereafter became a complex and bewildering kaleidoscope of various heavens, hells and purgatories; while the here-and-now became an unending sequence of sacraments such as baptism,

confirmation, penance, extreme unction and the eucharist—all administered with the next world primarily in mind. The eucharist, or mass, most common
of all Christian rituals, is *par excellence* an immortaliz-
ing sacrament; for the faithful it is proof, through the
mystical experience of actually partaking of the nature
of eternal God, that the soul is immortal. "The chief
effect of a worthy Communion is to a certain extent
a foretaste of Heaven, in fact the anticipation and
pledge of our future union with God in the Beatific
Vision. . . . The Eucharist is the 'pledge of our glorious resurrection and eternal happiness' according to
the promise of Christ: 'He that eateth of my flesh and
drinketh of my blood hath everlasting life: and I
will raise him up on the last day.' "8

Preoccupation with the life beyond has also been
strongly stimulated by the Catholic practice of inter-
cession by the living on behalf of souls in purgatory,
whether through the requiem mass, the system of indulgences or individual prayers. "We have loved him
during life," said St. Ambrose. "Let us not abandon
him, until we have conducted him by our prayers into
the house of the Lord."9 The assistance may sometimes come from the other side, for there is considerable Catholic authority to the effect that the souls of
the dead can help the living with their prayers. The
celebration of All Souls' Day every year for the com-
memoration of the departed is a variation on the same
theme. Even in this twentieth century the peasants in
many Catholic countries believe that the spirits of the
deceased revisit their homes on All Souls' night and
partake of the food of the living. In the Tyrol milk
and cake are left for them on the table, while in Brittany the people flock to the graveyards at nightfall
and pour milk or holy water on the tombstones. Similar customs have been and still are prevalent on All
Saints' Day, a festival in honor of the saints of the
Church.

It is well known that in the realm of immortality the virtuous will enjoy a marvelous happiness and will find complete compensation for all the ills of this world. The highest joy possible in paradise is to see God face to face, to be united with him in that Beatific Vision described so rapturously by Dante in the final Canto of *The Divine Comedy*. This is what the faithful mean when they talk ecstatically of enjoying God forever and ever. But even in this connection it is to be doubted if God, for the great majority, is primary. What is primary, we suspect, is the eternal bliss of saintly souls. God is the supreme pleasure-giving object of the other world. And though men have claimed that they would willingly suffer damnation for the glory of God, they have been conscious, when they said this, that such devotion would almost surely win for them just the opposite.

God is also the supreme pleasure-having person of the other world. He is pure and perfected personality liberated from all earthly checks and balances; and as such he is free, happy and immortal—the divine exemplar of all that man could wish to be. Though he is a most necessary part of heaven, only in heaven could he exist. Indeed, we can agree with Ludwig Feuerbach that "God is heaven spiritualized, while heaven is God materialized"; and that "there is no distinction between the absolute life which is conceived as God and the absolute life which is conceived as heaven, save that in heaven we have stretched into length and breadth what in God is concentrated in one point."[10] But in this fundamental identity between God and immortality priority still belongs to immortality. God would be dead if there were no immortality. And it is plain that survival after death was a commonplace notion long before the idea of a monotheistic God had become widespread.

In modern times the priority of immortality has become so insistent that more openly and frequently than ever before the existence of God has been deduced from the existence of a future life. We have already quoted Luther and other moderns who hew close to this line. But the prime example is Immanuel Kant. With Kant the categorical imperative, the great moral law, demands immortality for its proper fulfilment. God is then introduced in order to guarantee the immortality which the moral law makes necessary. The Reverend Harry Emerson Fosdick, most prominent of the Modernist group in the Protestant Church, follows the reasoning of Kant and makes it more explicit. "The goodness of God," says Fosdick, "is plainly at stake when one discusses immortality, for if death ends all, the Creator is building men like sand houses on the shore, caring not a whit that the fateful waves will quite obliterate them. . . . The universe distinctly is not friendly, if it has reared with such pain the moral life of man, only to topple it over like a house of cards."[11] In the same vein Dr. George A. Gordon tells us that on the question of immortality depends "the ultimate reasonableness or unreasonableness, the intelligence or brutality, of the Power that is responsible for our existence."[12] In other words, to paraphrase Dr. Fosdick and Dr. Gordon, the very existence of God, who is by definition good and intelligent, depends on man's having immortality.

The evolution of modern religion goes far to explain the expression of such sentiments. That keen student of religious psychology, Professor James B. Pratt, penetrates to the heart of the matter when he writes: "As the belief in miracles and special answers to prayer and in the interference of the supernatural within the natural has gradually disappeared, almost the only *pragmatic* value of the supernatural left to religion is the belief in a personal future life."[13] To an increasing number of moderns God, if he is not actually "an unnecessary hypothesis," *has* become a kind of God Emeritus, retired peacefully in his old age to the pleasures of professorial contemplation; or an Absolute, an Infinite, a One, a mystic Formula as abstract as the Theory of Relativity and still less intelligible. God no longer has, as with Newton, even the duties of regulating the more distant stars and comets.

Thus, in the modern world, little else remains for God to do but to function as the benevolent purveyor of man's immortality. With his personality becoming increasingly vague and empty, the old sense of warmth and intimacy associated with him disappears. And the most popular supernatural substitute proves to be intercourse with the departed. In the modern cult of Spiritualism we find an extreme example of these observations. Dr. George Lawton, in his able study of this sect, observes: "God . . . plays a very minor part in the belief system as well as in the daily life of the Spiritualists not simply because of his inaccessibility, but because they are not interested in him. They *are* interested in spirits and all the details of the after-life. Communication with the spirits, their 'saints,' they find far more desirable than communion with God, and easier, I may add."[14]

As a matter of fact, it is perfectly clear that only immortality can provide definite compensation for the ills of this still very imperfect world and especially for the loss of loved ones. If an awakening into a blessed hereafter were as much a law of Nature as our daily awakening to a far from blissful morrow, no God would be required to play cosmic philanthropist to a suffering humanity. Nor, with human personalities going on to the end of time, would any God be necessary to preserve the great ethical and social values. But realizing that a future life demands the saving intervention of more than natural forces, the dealers in celestial securities have had to call in God to guarantee that paradise preferred is a safe and sound investment. Again God is secondary.

Although the Lord may be given credit now and

then for the turning of some earthly ebbing tide, the great masses of mankind end their days very much in need of a new world to redress the balance of the old. From the viewpoint of ethics the experience of Job has proved to be almost universal: so far as this earth is concerned obviously neither the righteous nor the unrighteous receive, on the whole, their just deserts. It is for this reason that both Catholics and Protestants still argue that even taking the existence of God for granted, the end of belief in the hereafter would mean the end of ethical conduct in this life. As things turn out, the Almighty as the regulator and enforcer of morals can do little without the realm of immortality; and he seems to be a good deal more at home there than on earth.

There are other reasons, deep in human psychology, that help to account for the possible priority of immortality. First, we have the distinction, discernible to common sense as well as to subtle philosophy, between the body and the personality or soul. Dreams and trances reinforce here the testimony of everyday life. And death comes to give the most convincing and dramatic of verifications: the personality disappears, whither is a mystery, but the body remains, solid and real. Second, we find that it is extremely difficult to imagine ourselves as non-existent. We may envisage our own death and even our own funeral, but it is *we* who do the envisaging. *We* are there witnessing the events *after* our death. No matter how far forward we reach with our imaginations into the future or how far back into the past, we ourselves inevitably remain the audience at the passing pageant. The egocentric predicament holds us fast in its clutches; and it lures on the unsophisticated to a spontaneous belief in unending life. Then, third, there is the innate animal impulse to cling to life and flee from death with all the accumulated determination of the species' age-long struggle to survive. Other emotions may now and then force this will to live into the background, but in ordinary circumstances it is a ruling passion. Under its impulsion the conscious man, seeing ultimate death written indelibly on the horizon, attempts to dodge his fate by taking refuge in a transcendental self-preservation beyond the grave.

It is such characteristics of human nature—and these by no means exhaust the motivations that encourage the idea of a future life*—that help to make the *desire* for immortality, potentially present in every human heart, easy to awaken and develop, so that it very often becomes a more or less permanent mental attitude in a particular person or a particular civilization. These characteristics, too, render the belief in immortality a *natural* one in the sense that it might easily emerge without indoctrination; certainly it would be more likely to do so than belief in an all-seeing Divine Providence. Children and primitives seem to take the continuity of life for granted; it is the fact of death that has to be taught them. But children and primitives obviously do not take for granted the existence of God, especially the more highly developed God of monotheistic religions. Anyone can understand the simple meaning of personal survival after death; but it is a wise man indeed who can comprehend the Christian doctrine of the Trinity.

It would be foolish to deny that most men have considered the ideas of God and immortality to be inseparably connected and to stand or fall together. But inseparable connection, either in ideas or things, does not necessarily imply equal significance. If, on the one hand, the existence of God is taken to mean in and of itself the existence of a future life or the non-existence of God the non-existence of a future life, it is because part of the very definition of God has implicitly been *the guarantor of immortality*. Now a guarantor is, of course, of immense significance, but

* See Chapter VI.

in the last analysis the main thing is *what* is guaranteed. This is what people are after, whether security before death or after death is trembling in the balance. Thus, immortality remains primary. If, on the other hand, the existence of survival is thought to imply in and of itself the existence of God or the non-existence of survival the non-existence of God, the same conclusion is reached even more easily, because it is crystal clear that here the actuality of God was in the first place a deduction from the assurance of immortality.

There are, of course, both people and peoples for whom the idea of God has been of far more importance than the idea of immortality. The Jehovah of the Old Testament Hebrews was immeasurably more significant to them than their feeble after-existence. In fact, wherever and whenever immortality has not been considered clearly worth-while, its importance in relation to God or the gods has necessarily been less. And in all times there have undoubtedly been a certain number of persons, professional philosophers and others, who have had faith in God but not in immortality. For such persons, it should be noted, the *problem* of immortality as distinct from *belief* in immortality has unquestionably been of great consequence. Confronted with the fact of death they had to come to some conclusion about it; they had to decide whether they were mortal or immortal. They decided that they were mortal. The ancient Hebrews decided that there was an after-existence, but that it was of a very unattractive nature; and this had far-reaching implications for their whole philosophy of life.

On the relative importance, then, of God and immortality we have two main points to make. First, for believers in both God and immortality there is a good deal of evidence, particularly in the Christian West, to show that immortality has been and is primary. Second, for *everyone*, whatever his beliefs about God and immortality, the problem of immortality or mor-

tality or death, however the matter be phrased, is of at
least equal importance with the problem of the existence of God or, indeed, with any other religious or
philosophical problem whatsoever. The way in which
this problem of immortality is settled affects most
seriously almost every other religious and philosophic
issue. And without a settlement of it no religion or
philosophy can pretend to offer a complete and satisfactory way of life.

2. Insistence of the Question

It is not necessary, however, to establish definitely
the relative importance of the idea of immortality and
of other religious and philosophical ideas in order to
show how fundamental is the problem of a future life.
Its immeasurable significance for mankind becomes
apparent upon the slightest analysis. It is true that no
less a person than Benedict Spinoza wrote: "A free
man thinks of nothing less than of death, and his wisdom is not a meditation upon death, but upon life."[15]
But Spinoza, be it remembered, had already concluded
that there was no personal immortality. For him the
most significant problem connected with death was
settled. It was comparatively easy for him, therefore,
to lean back in his chair with the satisfying consciousness that he was free from the need of cogitating about
his fate beyond the grave.

Such free men cease to meditate on death because
they come to understand its meaning and its place in
the world that is their home. But the necessary pre-
lude to this understanding must be for everyone long
and careful reflection on this inescapable event which
comes to all human beings. At some time or other
every mortal must intellectually look death in the face
and decide what is to be his attitude towards this all
too familiar stranger. Even the agnostic with his plain-
tive "I don't know" takes a position. If the inevitability

of his own earthly end does not cause a man to think seriously about mortality and immortality, then the death of friends, of family, of utter strangers, of the human race (which some scientists prophesy for the distant future) must surely lead him to ponder upon this subject.

Civilizations, economic systems, migrations, war and peace may come and go; but the question of death insistently remains. And it links together in one common humanity—perplexed and distressed—all the thousand upon thousand generations of men, all the myriad tribes, races and nations, all the varying groups, types and classes of mankind. But in our modern machine civilization the need for a sane and sober analysis of this problem is perhaps greater than ever before. In the twentieth century sudden death through accident, adventure or premeditated violence, often taking the young and innocent, is so frequent and so widely broadcast that few can avoid a certain sombre impact from it all. Automobile, airplane and railway take so heavy a toll that you can hardly escape the feeling that it may be your turn next. And there is always the danger, whether you are a fighter or a non-combatant, that the far-flung ferocities of modern war will claim you as a victim. This possibility has enormously increased since the invention of nuclear weapons which, when exploded, spread throughout the world radioactive fall-out dangerous to health and to life itself.

Then, finally, there is the ordinary incidence of disease and old age. The grand totals of death are formidable. In the United States, which has a comparatively low death rate, more than one and a half million persons die every year; for the whole world the figure is in the neighborhood of fifty millions, with no less than one hundred thousand deaths per day. As the Book of Common Prayer so accurately phrases it, "In the midst of life we are in death."

In the face of these various considerations it is curious to find thinkers like the Oxford philosopher, F. C. S. Schiller, claiming that the alleged importance of the question of immortality is only a "literary tradition" foisted on the public by a few writers who have chosen to play up the subject. The mass of men, he says, have not really been interested in the problem and so have not produced books about it.[16] Of course, the average person does not write books about anything; but he does know that some day he is going to die and he does see his friends and family die about him. Only an individual emotionally insensitive and intellectually stolid can fail, in the kind of world in which we live, to ask himself whether death is the end of the story or merely the introduction to a new chapter.

This does not mean that the ordinary citizen, immersed in the manifold activities of daily life, is or should be constantly preoccupied with the question of man's final destiny. Nor does it imply that it is one of his favorite topics of discussion. The event called death, bound up as it is with very personal feelings, memories and associations, is far too intimate a thing —and for most men too sorrowful a thing—to enter a great deal into general, everyday conversation. As the pious churchwarden said to a questioner: "Of course I believe in eternal bliss, but do let us talk about something less depressing." Also those religious believers for whom the assurance of a future life is an unquestioned and cardinal conviction may well maintain comparative silence on the matter, rather than stirring it up continually as do those who are doubtful and who therefore strive to produce new arguments in support of their waning faith.

The general pragmatic effects, for good or for ill, of belief in a future existence are writ large in the history of the race, whether we examine the practices of ancient primitive tribes or modern civilized nations.

In China ancestor worship has been for ages a domi-
nating and conservative influence; in India the laws
of karma and reincarnation have century after century lent support to the rigid caste system and helped
to suppress the initiative of the masses to better their
lot; in the Mohammedan countries the legions of
Allah have gone forth to battle again and again with
the promise of paradise spurring them on; and in the
West the idea of immortality has been, as we have suggested, perhaps the most important single element in
the Christian religion, affecting directly the lives of
millions through hope and fear, ritual and dogma, and
working indirectly on the minds of the people through
philosophy, literature, education and other cultural
media.

While not the only factor making for the metaphysical and ethical dualism so characteristic of Christianity, the concept of life everlasting has here been
outstanding in its influence. It has probably been the
most basic assumption of that ethical view which op-
poses the spirit to the flesh and regards the instincts
and desires of the natural body as evil, degraded, and
to be suppressed. It has been the underlying premise
of the whole Christian philosophy of other-worldliness
which sees man's true destiny as belonging to another
realm beyond this earthly vale of tears. Dr. John
Baillie, himself an eloquent defender of the idea of
immortality, writes: "It was as the old preoccupation
with eternity began to disappear and the traditional
eschatological picture—that vast triptych of hell, purgatory and paradise—to lose its power over the imagination, that the cry for social reform was first clearly
heard in the land. . . . The desire for political freedom, the movement towards the emancipation of the
disinherited classes, the abolition of slavery, the advent
of universal education, the gradual emancipation of
womanhood and, as one born out of due season, the
movement to make an end of war—these are all typi-

cal products of our modern period and are definitely associated with the modern shifting of the imagination from the eternal to the temporal prospect."[17]

But this shifting of the imagination has not meant that the influence of the former viewpoint has come to an end. For it "has left its impress on the commonly accepted moral codes of the West to this day, and seems even yet to make impossible the whole-hearted and simple enjoyment of the goods of a natural existence that men now envy in the Greeks of old."[18] In addition, the idea of immortality has helped to start and stimulate unhappy and still-existing theories of knowledge which have as their fundamental assumption, to quote Professor John Dewey, "that experience centers in, or gathers about, or proceeds from a center or subject which is outside the course of natural existence and set over against it," thus making the bearer of experience seem "antithetical to the world instead of being in and of it."[19] This has encouraged the regrettable tendency to partition the mind off from the outside world which is its natural sphere of application, and has promoted that deplorable separation between theory and practice which has ever been such an obstacle to human progress.

Immortality doctrines probably have their widest effect indirectly rather than as an ever-present incentive. It is doubtful if their direct effects are ever as great as, for instance, the official tabulations of religious groups professing belief in a hereafter would lead us to suppose. This is because so many listed members of the Church, especially in modern times, do not really take stock in the theory of survival; or they only half-believe or merely hope, preferring to keep the notion in the vague, uncertain limbo of partly settled difficulties, on tap for purposes of consolation but in the main neglected. Where, however, the theory is in actuality strongly and sincerely believed, we cannot question that it makes a difference in the lives of the believers. For instance, in 1933 a member of the United States House of Representatives, Samuel A. Kendall, committed suicide some four months after his wife's death and left a note for his children reading in part: "Mother has been calling me to join her and little Van in heaven and I can no longer resist the call and am going to join them. Good-bye."[20] The Kendall tragedy dramatically accents numerous cases of the same kind in America and abroad.

If the establishment of immortality as a basic fact in the minds of men is of crucial importance for supernatural religion, then the establishment of *mortality* is of equal significance for Humanist, materialist or naturalist philosophies. So Lucretius, the great materialist and philosopher-poet of ancient Rome, writing *On the Nature of Things*, was far more concerned with disproving a future life than with putting a complete quietus on the gods. In fact he reserved certain far-off regions of the sky in which the gods might go on perpetually enjoying themselves, a notion remindful of the status which God has today for many modern minds. But these distant deities of Lucretius' did not intervene in human affairs and, above all, they could not touch a man whom death had taken. For death was the final and complete end of human beings as self-conscious personalities. Death was really death in the opinion of Lucretius. There was nothing to fear beyond death because there was nothing there to fear, not even the consciousness of nothingness. For Lucretius the assurance of mortality meant the liberation of man from all those awful apprehensions traditionally connected with the after-existence. It meant the finish of the dual terrorism of priests and gods. It meant a new courage in the eyes of the human race, a new nobility in its step and a new dignity in its philosophy.

It can scarcely be denied that the history of Christianity has borne out the views of Lucretius. The Church in its palmiest days maintained its sway over the multitudes chiefly through appealing to fear of *post-mortem* punishment. While occasionally the hand of God could be discerned smiting the wicked right here and now, the most terrible part of divine retribution was reserved for the after-life. There the vast majority of the human race would suffer tortures so excruciating and long-enduring that the most frightful of terrestrial sufferings paled into insignificance beside them. And the Church heightened the natural aversion to death by teaching that it was a punishment introduced into the world, afflicting everyone, the virtuous as well as the wicked, because of the original sin of Adam.

Whether fear and punishments are stressed, as in the Middle Ages, or hope and rewards, as in the last century or so, it is clear that in either case God's power and a very large proportion of the Church's power rest in the last analysis on the existence of another world. To take the economic sphere, for example, the religious ceremonies connected with the departed have meant untold wealth for the Church. Particularly has this been true in the Roman Catholic and Eastern Orthodox faiths where much stress is laid upon masses, prayers and other good offices on behalf of the dead, the dying and all those in any way concerned over their future state.

Since the early Middle Ages the Catholic Church has obtained, through the granting of indulgences alone, huge sums from rich and poor alike. These indulgences, given in return for money payments, almsgiving or other kinds of offerings, provide that one's own soul or the soul of a deceased relative or friend be spared all or part of its destined punishment in purgatory. It was controversy over the extent and propriety of this practice that was the immediate cause of the Protestant revolt in the sixteenth century. In Russia the Orthodox Church accumulated enormous wealth through similar intercessions on behalf of the dead. Besides the steady income from workers and peasants anxious to mitigate divine retribution, many members of the nobility and upper class endowed monasteries and churches on condition that daily prayers be said for their departed souls.[21]

The dependence on a hereafter of God's authority over human beings is especially apparent in modern times when the growth of science and the extension of natural law have made the earthly interventions of the Lord very few and far between. With God and other supernatural agents becoming less and less of a factor in daily life, the idea of immortality takes on relatively greater importance. Faith in the far-away, academic God of the modern age does far less to distract men's minds from their earthly conditions and tasks than does reliance on an after-existence. For if men give up belief in a life beyond, then all but a few mystics who think that they can unite their being with the mind of God must of necessity devote themselves to the affairs of this world; and the modern God being one who hardly ever gets into action here below, men must also rely on their own powers and potentialities. As long, however, as a future life is conceived to exist, people will devote to the thought of it much time and attention that could be used for earthly enterprises.

To the average reader, whatever his attitude towards the idea of immortality, it may well seem, as it does to me, that the problem of a future life is on the face of it sufficiently significant to need no justification for its analysis. But the truth remains that a considerable number of persons today take the position that to examine the issues centering around the fact of death is irrelevant and a waste of time. It will be found, however, that such persons, like Spinoza, have usually made up their own minds concerning these issues. For them further inquiry may indeed seem useless. And if their particular conclusions happen to fall on the socially unpopular side of the main question at stake, the labeling of the whole problem as essentially unimportant is a very convenient way to avoid the risk of taking a public stand. This is the present-day attitude, it would seem, of not a few professional philosophers, especially in the universities.

Another favorite way of sidestepping the issue of mortality versus immortality is to claim that human reason is impotent to deal with it. The whole subject, it is said, is too much in the realm of speculation to be susceptible of definitive treatment. A friend of mine asks: "Why not, like Goethe, 'reverence the mystery' and leave it alone? For myself I am frankly bored when people begin on it, for I know they don't know—not one whit more than Plato or Plotinus or Shelley or those other great minds who have gone in search."[22] Survival after death, the argument continues, is one of those hypotheses which because of their very nature are incapable of conclusive investigation by the human mind. This perhaps sounds well until we reflect that in this class of hypotheses would be such remarkable ones as that invisible fairies tend the flowers at night, that the valleys of the moon are filled with an invisible substance, and that angels helped the French to turn back the Germans at the Battle of the Marne. A sane science and a serious philosophy cannot abdicate before the million and one fantasies of this kind which the superstitious are ever bringing forward as the latest revelation.

Then there are those who do not wish to have the problem of death too rigorously looked into for fear of hurting people's feelings. Sir Arthur Keith, a former President of the British Association for the Advancement of Science, telling of his "strange reluctance" to reveal his unorthodox opinions concerning religious issues, frankly admits that "the real explanation . . . is fear—cowardice, if you will. By nature I am of the common herd. I fear ostracism. . . . We cannot discuss our innermost beliefs openly and candidly without

committing an assault on persons whose comradeship
we desire to retain. Hence most of us choose to be
silent; wrangling is painful, and the paths of peace
pleasant."[23] What Sir Arthur so outspokenly states is
the actual attitude, though often not consciously formulated, of many persons well equipped to furnish
light and leading on the matter of death. Professor
C. D. Broad of Cambridge University, who tends to
disbelieve in a future life, even goes so far as to say
that "it is quite possible that the doctrine of human
immortality (whether it be in fact true or false) is one
of these socially valuable 'myths' which the State
ought to remove from the arena of public discussion."[24]

It is undoubtedly true that frank and open treatment of the issues centering around the subject of
human mortality is likely to offend many people. Professor Schiller is probably right in stating that all but
the most inevitable mention of death "is tabooed in
polite society."[25] This holds for the United States as
well as England. "Most Americans," writes Mary Austin, "are even more reticent, and possibly more dis-
honest about their attitude toward death and the hereafter than they are toward any other personal concern.
. . . Americans in general, it seems, suffer a glandular
resistance to the idea of death which makes them not
only averse to talking about it, but anxious to evade
its mention by every sort of diddling phraseology."[26]

In the face of such a situation it is understandable
why those who have thought through the problem of
immortality, especially when their conclusions are contrary to prevailing opinion, should often keep to themselves their ultimate judgment. Yet this position is not
one that we can approve, least of all for the reasons
given. For the history of intellectual progress reveals
nothing more clearly than that every new truth must
deeply wound the feelings of those with vested emotional, ideological or economic interests in outworn
ideas. It is strongly to be suspected that those who ob-

struct the exposure of religious superstitions, regarding either death or other matters, are, whether knowingly or not, special pleaders for the maintenance of some such vested interest. "The mission of philosophy," asserts Professor Morris R. Cohen, "is to bring a sword as well as peace."[27] And nowhere is this excellent precept more applicable than to the traditional religious theories that concern themselves with the meaning of death.

CHAPTER II

THE FUNDAMENTAL ISSUE

1. *Immortality Defined*

BEFORE STATING what I consider the fundamental issue involved in the question before us it is necessary to define carefully *immortality*. It should have already become apparent that I mean *personal* immortality, that is, the literal survival of the individual human personality or consciousness for an indefinite period after death, with its memory and awareness of self-identity essentially intact. In other words, one will awaken in the life beyond in very much the same sense as one wakes up here on every new day. And in that other world the awakening, as here, will be to fresh activities and in the midst of friends and family. The memory there will not hold all the particulars of one's past life any more than from day to day or decade to decade on earth, but it will retain enough to provide a definite sense of identity and continuity. This is fundamental, for a personality that had no conscious links with anything that has gone on before would to all intents and purposes be another personality.

As Liebniz asks: "What good, sir, would it do you to become King of China, on condition that you forgot what you have been? Would it not be the same as if God, at the moment he destroyed you, were to create a king in China?"[28] Special psychological and metaphysical definitions of individuality or personality, while they may bear importantly on the case for or against immortality, do not alter seriously the *meaning* of immortality. The personality may be thought of in the last analysis as pure atomic force, pure spirit, pure mind, pure or impure anything at all; and yet it will be accurate to define immortality as above.

All this is not to say that *immortality* has not had other noteworthy meanings, among Christians as well as others. The word has sometimes signified the attainment here and now of a certain eternal quality in life and thought, with "eternal" meaning that which is independent of time and existence. This view has been held by such philosophers as Spinoza and Santayana and is frequently called *ideal* immortality, or, with questionable accuracy, *Platonic* immortality. Often this ideal immortality is combined with the primary meaning of actual personal survival. *Immortality* has likewise designated the survival after death of an impersonal psychic entity which is absorbed into some kind of All or Absolute or God. Akin to this is *material* or *chemical* immortality through the reabsorption by Nature of the elements of the body. Then there is *historical* immortality through the irreversibility of the past and the permanent place that every life necessarily has in the simple truth and succession of existence; *biological* or *plasmic* immortality through one's children and descendants; and *social* or *influential* immortality through enduring fame or the unending effect of one's life on the minds and acts of succeeding generations.

More foreign to Western minds is the concept of immortality through *reincarnation* on this earth in future human or other living forms. This doctrine is often known as metempsychosis or transmigration, and postulates a pre-existence as well as an after-existence. Influential among ancient peoples such as the Greeks and Egyptians and always the very core of the Buddhist and Hindu religions, the theory today maintains its sway over large sections of the East and has in recent times penetrated to Europe and America through the Theosophists. Perhaps least important and least known of all is the idea of immortality involved in the return of all things over and over again in their precise detail, the *eternal recurrence* theory urged by the Stoics in ancient times and revived in the nineteenth century by the German philosopher Nietzsche.

It is logically possible to believe simultaneously in several of these vicarious forms of immortality. There is no inconsistency, for example, between social, biological and material immortality. No reasonable person would deny the actuality of material immortality, or of social and biological immortality as long as the species man continues to exist. But whether they be true or not, we are not vitally concerned with the eight secondary types of immortality mentioned above. It is immortality as signifying the continuation of the individual personality after death that is the chief and central concern of this book. That is the meaning of immortality that has so moved mankind in the West and throughout a large part of Asia and Africa. It is the meaning which has been sanctioned by the teachings and practices of the Christian and other important religions. For these various reasons I shall, when referring to the secondary senses of immortality, use the proper qualifying adjectives.

2. *The Issue Stated*

While there are manifold approaches to the question of immortality, the fundamental issue lies, I believe, in the relationship between body or the physical organism on the one hand and personality or soul on the other. Other synonyms or near-synonyms for personality are consciousness, mind, self, spirit, psyche and the ego. In order to avoid controversy and confusion I shall ordinarily use the word *personality* as the definitive term to denote the characteristic mental and emotional activities of a human being. A number of thinkers have reacted strongly against the traditional psychological and philosophical associations of *soul* and *consciousness* and have gone so far as to deny that these terms are applicable to men at all. But no one has yet had the audacity or folly to assert that there is no such thing as *personality*. I shall, however, employ the word *soul* interchangeably with *personality* when discussing those theories which themselves habitually refer to *soul*. And I shall utilize the term *mind* when talking about the intellectual activities which constitute such an important part of the life of the personality.

Whatever words are used, it is necessary to admit the distinction between body and personality. As we noted in the first chapter, death is here the unimpeachable witness. For in death there is still a body—cold, silent, inert—but the personality has completely disappeared. A dead body is indeed very different from a living body. If it were not, there would be no problem of immortality. And also a living sleeping body is quite different from a living waking body. The sleeping body is always active to a certain extent, but what we know as the personality is, except in the case of dreams, quiescent and temporarily in a state of unconscious repose. When a living body is under an anesthetic, the same condition prevails. But men do not have to die or sleep or undergo an operation in order to make plain the distinction between body and personality; they simply need to think and feel. There is surely a difference between the physical state of a bad tooth, on the one hand, and the feeling of pain it causes and the thoughts of a curative it stimulates, on the other. If there were not this difference, there would be no such thing as conscious experience.

Now however naturally common sense, as well as sage philosophy, differentiates between body and personality, at the same time it links the two together in the most intimate fashion. It is all but impossible to imagine a disembodied personality. When we are thinking of absent persons, whether they be dead or alive, we invariably visualize their natural forms, their bodies through which alone we have known them and been aware of their personalities. Pictures are our favorite and most vivid reminders. The workings of association are so strong that for a time at least we tend towards identifying a dead man with his body. Indeed, we find it very hard to say farewell to the lifeless forms of our loved ones; and we do not like to think of their bodies being mutilated, dissected or resting in a noisy, strange or unbeautiful place. If a person dies away from home or drowns, every effort is usually made to bring back or recover the body. The relatives of thousands of American soldiers killed abroad in the First and Second World Wars insisted that the bodies be shipped back and interred in the United States.

After a burial our first instinctive thought in recalling the departed may well be that the man himself is in the coffin and the cemetery. For this reason graveyards are notoriously the favorite haunts of ghosts. Even the most hardened unbeliever might feel some misgivings about spending the night in a cemetery. When we are thinking of our own death rather than someone else's it is even more difficult to dissociate the personality from the body. As Lucretius said long ago: "When in life each man pictures to himself that it will come to pass that birds and wild beasts will mangle his body in death, he pities himself; for neither does he separate himself from the corpse, nor withdraw himself enough from the outcast body, but thinks that it is he, and, as he stands watching, taints it with his own feeling."[29]

We know from ordinary experience, furthermore, how closely the personality is actually tied up with our body. Bodily changes almost invariably carry with them mental and emotional changes. Coffee stimulates the mind; codeine normally relieves pain; alcohol generally removes inhibitions. A hard knock on the head may result in unconsciousness or even in mental abnormality. The personality is well when the body is well; sick when the body is sick. A walk, a ride, a skate— any sort of exercise—in pure and bracing air can give life a new zest in short order; sitting in one position too long in a crowded and stuffy room will try the temperament of the most cheerful and dull the mind of the most keen. Conversely, it is well known that, under certain circumstances, one's state of mind can affect one's bodily state, either for better or for worse. The obvious truth of the mind's influence on the body has been stretched by Christian Science beyond all reason and made the basis of a new religion. But we need no religion, either new or old, to tell us that body and personality are interlocking directorates affecting each other in every move they make.

Those thinkers who have emphasized the distinction between body and personality, and the personality's power over the body, have insisted that the personality is a substance of a different order, an immaterial or non-physical soul that inhabits the body and uses it as its instrument. When the body dies, this soul departs and may go on existing elsewhere; and, according to some, it existed before its earthly body came into being at all. In philosophical and psychological terminology this theory of the personality's independence has been called *dualism* or *Platonism*. It has usually been associated with a far-reaching metaphysical Dualism that divides the whole of existence into the two realms of matter and spirit. But I intend to use *dualism* mainly with a small "d" and in its psychological sense.

Other thinkers, while admitting a distinction between body and personality, have claimed that the personality is the life or function or activity of the body. It is the body acting, the body living; and, to be exact, the body acting and living in certain definite ways closely associated with the brain and the rest of the central nervous system. For purposes of convenience we talk and write about an abstraction, *personality*; but it can in actuality no more be abstracted from the human body than can the activities of breathing and digestion. This personality is, then, a quality of the body, not an independently existing thing, just as redness is an inseparable quality of a red rose. The mind, as part of this personality, has the same kind of relationship to the body; and indeed a wise man has been defined as one who does not know the difference between his mind and his body and cannot tell which is which. Such a personality would have the same difficulty in existing without its body as the flame of a candle would have in burning without its wax base.

This theory of the personality was in ancient times presented most persuasively by Aristotle and Lucretius. It has been variously known as the Aristotelian psychology, the naturalistic psychology, the organistic psychology and the monistic psychology. Most accurate and meaningful, in my opinion, is this last-mentioned term, the *monistic* psychology*, signifying that man is an inseparable oneness comprising both body and personality. Psychological monism must not be confused with the philosophical meanings of *Monism* as a great metaphysical or cosmological system.

It now becomes clear what is the basic issue that faces us. Is the relationship between the body and personality which we know in this life so close, deep-reaching and fundamental that their indissoluble unity appears to be the most reasonable conclusion? Or is that association so vague, loose and unessential that the personality may be considered as a separable and ultimately independent entity? In a word, is the human self built and nurtured only on the basis of living flesh and blood; or can it somehow, like the captain of a ship that sinks, continue its existence after the dissolution of its life partnership with the bodily organism?

* From the Greek *monos,* meaning single.

This issue, which is in essence that of a monistic versus a dualistic psychology, is not, of course, the only important one involved in the study of death's meaning. But it seems to me the most crucial of all. Metaphysical and ethical arguments for immortality may be offered without end, but they must appear unsubstantial as long as this issue is not faced. For it cuts across and illumines all other issues connected with a future life. No matter what changes occur in the fashions and terminologies of philosophy and science, this issue endures. It is as real today as 2,400 years ago in the time of Plato and Aristotle. It cannot be circumvented, except verbally, by any out-of-the-way definitions of the body or of the personality. Both may be defined as ideas in the mind of God or both as rhythms in the realm of matter, but the exact relationship between these ideas or these rhythms remains fundamental. Likewise the ideas that make up the mental life of the personality may be defined as pure and immaterial essences or as particles of physical energy in its most refined form, but the essential point for the question of immortality is still how binding is the partnership between the personality which has ideas, however described, and its body.

The central issue as stated, furthermore, involves points about the hereafter that at first glance might seem to be independent of that issue. Outstanding among these derivative issues is the question whether the personality will function in the life beyond as a pure, discarnate soul with no cooperative organ through which to work; or whether it requires there as well as here a bodily instrument—a resurrected natural body, for instance, in accordance with traditional Christianity, or some kind of supernatural "celestial," "spiritual" or "etheric" body. Even God, assuming for the moment that he exists and has the power of ensuring human immortality, must decide whether the spirit of man is to be, in St. Paul's language, "unclothed" or "clothed upon." As a matter of fact all those who write or talk in favor of immortality do take a position on this issue of an after-life body. And, as will be seen, the defenders of immortality or *immortalists,* as I shall call them, provide the surviving personality, either explicitly or by implication, with some sort of body.

This body of immortality is in no instance the natural body that we know on this earth. For even in the case of the resurrection, while it is the old, this-worldly body that supposedly rises from the tomb, it is at the same time this former body radically transformed, made incorruptible, immortalized. In short, the natural body becomes at the resurrection a supernatural body. Since, however, neither the resurrection body nor any other body of the hereafter is the same body with which the personality is associated on this side of death, the immortalists do not really carry through the monistic principle. Yet—and this is the significant thing —most of them surreptitiously recognize and pay tribute to this principle by insisting on *some* kind of after-life body and by creating it in the image of the natural body.

There are good reasons why they should do this. For—and this is another important issue—it is essential to ask what *kind* of existence the individual is to have in the world beyond. Is he to enjoy a vigorous and happy life, or is he to pursue a thin and melancholy career midst feeble imitations of his former glory? In other words, is the hereafter to be desirable or undesirable? This question is inseparably bound up with the attribution of a moral significance to the after-life. For it cannot and does not have such significance unless it offers the virtuous of this earth an opportunity for what we have called *worth-while* immortality. Only then is it possible to talk seriously of rewards and consolations, of heaven and eternal bliss.

Again and again, however, those who have spun

prophecies about the land beyond the grave have been unable to make that place appear desirable without endowing the spirit with a corporeal helpmate as similar as possible to the body of this terrestrial globe. But that is not all; for just as in the here-now the body and personality that constitute the complete man must have a suitable environment in which to function, so in the thereafter the same law has been discovered to apply. Existence *in vacuo* seems neither intelligible nor profitable. And, accordingly, the immortalists have usually given their imaginations free rein in assigning to the future life surroundings ample for the most varied employments, whether hell, purgatory or heaven be concerned.

That the personality in the after-existence should have a body and the resulting body-personality a many-sided environment is explainable in terms of a general law which may be formulated as follows: If any idea of immortality is to be wholeheartedly believed and acted upon, it must possess the three attributes of emotional efficacy, imaginative reality and intellectual acceptability. This holds as true of primitive tribes as of civilized peoples, of backward peasants as of urban intellectuals. By emotional efficacy I mean the ability to awaken a deep emotional response, whether it be of fear, joy or moral approval. Such a response may be strongly stimulated through the use of certain rituals definitely connected with the idea of a future life. But in the last analysis emotional efficacy must depend on the second attribute of imaginative reality, since for most people the unimaginable cannot possess emotional power. Intellectual acceptability for the conception at issue implies a certain degree of consistency, varying according to the individual, with those ideas which a man has accepted as true— whether they be ideas of common sense, of science, of philosophy or of other branches of knowledge. It becomes an increasingly important factor with the rise of science and the life of reason; but in the form of ordinary common sense it has undoubtedly been an element in the attitude of primitive peoples.

Ideas having emotional efficacy, imaginative reality and intellectual acceptability obviously differ according to the total culture and environment of the group concerned. It is readily seen, therefore, why descriptions of immortality should vary so widely and in terms of the time and place of their origin; and why in addition they should go into such extensive and concrete detail. Especially is it understandable why the personality in the future life should possess a body. For that personality must be imaginable; it must be recognizable to both its former earthly self and to others; it must have a form definite and substantial.

This necessity turns out to be a demand of the intelligence as well as of the imagination. For the intelligence, seeing the great importance of the body in earthly life, deduces from this that the personality, if it is to have an adequate immortality, needs something of the same kind as its aid and accessory in that other realm. Hence, although almost all theories of a future life accept the fact that a man's mortal and dissolving body is left behind on earth—and this implies a species of dualism in psychology—the additional fact that the surviving personality must at once or soon acquire another body to take the place of the one discarded is a most important concession to the monistic principle. The immortalist, realizing the impossibility of the personality's retaining its natural body in eternity, does the best he can under the circumstances to be a sensible monist and gives the personality a body closely resembling the old one. And he assumes that the relationship in the next world between the personality and its new body will be almost exactly the same as the relationship in this world between the personality and its mundane body. Thus the immortalist tries to carry over natural monism into a supernatural sphere, but in spite of heroic efforts he perforce becomes a dualist in the process.

No further discussion seems necessary to demonstrate how fundamental and far-reaching for the idea of immortality is the issue revolving around the relationship between body and personality. I now propose to trace the fortunes of this issue in the after-life conceptions of different peoples and periods, beginning with ancient and primitive cultures, going on to traditional Christianity and then examining the views current in the modern age. Finally, we shall consider what science has to say about the central issue that confronts us.

3. *Among Ancient and Primitive Peoples*

Among ancient peoples in general there prevailed a profound inability to imagine or believe in a full and happy after-existence without the survival of the natural body. As persuasive examples of this fact we can point to the Old Testament Hebrews with their Sheol, the Homeric Greeks with their Hades, the early Romans with their Orcus and the Babylonians with their Aralu. It may be stated with few qualifications that all of these peoples supposed that the souls of the dead, their bodies discarded and in decay, would go to a grim and shadowy underworld, devoid of ethical significance, to wander sadly, aimlessly and indefinitely, poor feeble ghosts of their former selves. That the most convenient and customary way of disposing of dead bodies was to bury them beneath the earth was without question the most fundamental factor in locating the beyond in a subterranean realm. Indeed, it was often thought that the shades of the departed actually inhabited the very tombs or graves where the bodies had been placed. Where the bodies of the dead went, there the souls went too. Here at the very outset, then, we find testimony to the close

association between body and personality in the beliefs of early culture groups.

It is not generally realized that throughout the
greater portion of the Bible, the Old Testament, a
rather gloomy view is taken regarding the prospects
of a worth-while immortality. In the writings which
have been preserved the old Hebrew prophets seem
vastly more concerned with the future welfare of
the tribe or nation on this earth than with a happy
hereafter for the individual. God would in due course
mete out the proper rewards and punishments, but
their point of application would be in this world.
And the final sign of God's partiality to the Israelites,
the chosen people, would be their deliverance into
a heaven or New Jerusalem in this mundane sphere.
But the decisive point for the main issue under discussion is that the prevailing psychologies of the Old
Testament discourage, to say the least, belief in a
desirable future life.

Indeed, the first one of these psychologies to be
considered points with remorseless logic towards the
personality's extinction at death. It is based on the
account of man's creation in the first part of Genesis:
"And the Lord God formed man of the dust of the
ground, and breathed into his nostrils the breath of
life; and man became a living soul."[30] Here the soul
is a function of the material body which has been
quickened by the breath of life. At death this breath
of life survives, but since it is only an impersonal force
common to all men and animals, it goes back to God;
while the personality which it had cooperated to produce simply fades into nothingness and the body which
it had informed returns to dust. On the basis of this
semi-monistic psychology such an ending is inevitable,
unless there is a resurrection of the body or a bodily
translation, before death, to another world, as in the
cases of Enoch and Elijah.

Accordingly, the idea of the annihilation of the

personality at death constitutes a strong undercurrent running through the books of the Old Testament. "The living know that they shall die," says Ecclesiastes, "but the dead know not any thing, neither have they any more a reward; for the memory of them is forgotten. Also their love, and their hatred, and their envy, is now perished; neither have they any more a portion for ever in any thing that is done under the sun. Go thy way, eat thy bread with joy, and drink thy wine with a merry heart; for God now accepteth thy works. . . . Live joyfully with the wife whom thou lovest all the days of the life of thy vanity. . . . Whatsoever thy hand findeth to do, do it with thy might; for there is no work, nor device, nor knowledge, nor wisdom in the grave, whither thou goest."[31] "A man hath no preeminence above a beast: for all is vanity. All go into one place; all are of the dust, and all turn to dust again."[32] And the psalmist cries out to his God: "Thou turnest man to destruction. . . . Thou carriest them away as with a flood; they are as a sleep: in the morning they are like grass which groweth up. In the morning it flourisheth, and groweth up; in the evening it is cut down and withereth."[33] "O spare me, that I may recover strength, before I go hence, and be no more."[34] There are a number of other passages to the same effect; and the Sadducees, who constituted an important and influential branch of Judaism, supported such views as a considered part of their religious doctrines.

The other chief psychology of Old Testament literature, though not implying extinction at death, does not indicate either a satisfactory survival. According to this psychology, man is a composite made up of the body on the one hand and the spirit or soul on the other. Spirit or soul are really one and the same in essence and origin, but the term *spirit* came to mean the stronger aspect of the soul. At the dissolution of the body the spirit passes out of existence and

the soul goes down alone to Sheol greatly enfeebled
because of no longer being united with the spirit.
Naturally, therefore, the soul is no longer able to lead
its former full and vigorous life, as accounts of Sheol
so adequately inform us. "Let me alone," bewails Job,
"that I may take comfort a little before I go whence
I shall not return, even to the land of darkness and
the shadow of death; a land of darkness, as darkness
itself; and of the shadow of death, without any order,
and where the light is as darkness."[35] The very word,
Sheol, betrays the nature of this underworld, for the
term at first designated simply the collective graves
of the tribe or nation. And in fact Sheol never lost
the sad and sombre imagery associated with the tomb.

While especially towards the end of the Old Testament period the writers and prophets, spurred on by
God's repeated failure to establish for Israel a this-
earthly paradise and by the growing sense of individual worth and responsibility, mention occasionally
the hope of a happy immortality, this is decidedly not
the tone of the work as a whole. And such hints of a
decent future life as do occur postulate what eventually becomes the orthodox position, namely, a
resurrection. In view of the predominant psychologies
of the Old Testament, which I have described, this
outcome is perfectly understandable: the body is so
vitally important to the life abundant of the personality that it can be no better spared in the hereafter
than in the here-now.

When we turn to the Homeric Greeks, we find
much the same story as with the Hebrews. "In the
moldering house of chill Hades," as Hesiod calls it, the
sickly phantoms of the departed flit about forlorn and
futile, with faint voices and nerveless limbs. They are
so bereft of strength that only the energizing effect of
natural animal blood enables Ulysses to talk to them
during his visit to the underworld. It is no wonder that
the shade of Achilles tells Ulysses on this same occa-

sion: "Better to be the hireling of a stranger, and serve a man of mean estate whose living is but small, than to be ruler over all these dead and gone."[36] Plato, it will be recalled, suggested that this passage, and others like it, be deleted from the poets, lest such descriptions make the warriors of the ideal state less willing to sacrifice their lives in battle.[37]

When Homer wishes to ensure for his heroes a really worth-while immortality, he has them take their bodies with them to the great beyond. Thus Menelaus and Ganymede are carried bodily and alive with their this-worldly equipment and attributes to Elysium and Olympus, respectively, where they assume the status of minor gods. To Homer and to many other ancient Greeks of all periods this seemed entirely logical, since immortality for them held its pure and original meaning of *not-death*. For them, therefore, to be immortal meant not to die, to go on living like the gods who were alone "the immortals." Ordinary humans, however, whether ancient Greeks or modern Americans, leave behind them, when they depart this world, their very solid but unmistakably very dead bodies. And this inescapable fact has led from time immemorial to the most distressing embarrassments and complications for the theoreticians of the future life.

Without examining in detail the underworld conceptions of the early Romans and the Babylonians, which are quite similar to those of the Hebrews and Greeks, I shall proceed to take up the interesting and instructive case of the ancient Egyptians. The afterworld beliefs of these Egyptians offer a curious variation on the theme we have been following and illustrate remarkably well the part which the body is thought to play in a satisfactory future life. While these beliefs vary from period to period, there can be no doubt that for a time, at least, a desirable immortality is considered possible for both the kings of Egypt and their subjects. But such an immortality is indissolubly connected with the practice of mummification and the proper preservation of the natural body.

To this fact the great pyramids of Egypt, built primarily to shelter the bodies of the kings, bear imposing witness. Members of the nobility and the wealthy class set aside enormous fortunes for the expert embalming of their bodies after death and for the meticulous and lasting care of these bodies. The mummies are elaborately swathed in bandages and often given the benefit of two or even three coffins, so constructed as to fit precisely into one another. In an effort to preserve permanently the dead man's personal identity his features are often painted on the outer wrappings of the body, or a mask made in his image is attached to the head. Before final burial painstaking attempts are made to give back to the body, so far as is possible, what it has lost at death.

In the reanimation ceremony, by means of magical instruments and incantations, the mouth, eyes and ears of the deceased are opened in order that he may once more see, speak, eat and hear. The use of his limbs is stimulated so that he may move and walk, while moisture and warmth are restored through incense and libations. Sometimes this life-giving ceremony is extended to a statue of the dead man which has been placed in the tomb as a further help in sustaining his personal identity. The immense amount of time, energy, and thought which the Egyptians devoted to mummification and supplementary observances shows clearly that they could not conceive of a desirable beyond without the cooperation of the old, this-earthly body. And I could cite beliefs and practices very much like theirs among many other peoples and, in the case of the great Inca civilization of Central and South America, in a different hemisphere.

Turning to more primitive peoples we are able to observe persuasive illustrations of our central thesis.

The supposed close connection between the personality and the natural body, even after death, is fundamental in giving rise to the widespread belief that the soul, restless and unhappy, will return to haunt or trouble the living unless the body is buried, cremated or otherwise disposed of properly. To get rid of the bodies of the dead is the best way to get rid of their ghosts as well. It is customary among numerous tribes to carry a corpse out of a dwelling by some exit other than the ordinary door so that the spirit will not be able to find its way back. The general principle assumed in a great variety of such customs is that doing something to the dead body will seriously affect the surviving soul in one way or another.

This principle finds extreme exemplification in the deliberate mutilation of corpses by many primitive peoples. Fearing harm from the dead, they will bind the limbs of the body, bury it under a high mound of earth and place heavy stones on top. Some tribes tie the toes of the dead body together and the thumbs behind the back, or put thorns in the feet so that the spirit will not be able to walk. If the corpse happens to be that of an enemy, they are likely to resort to the most extravagant measures. In order to disable the ghost for fighting they will break the spinal column of the body or chop off its hands and feet or cut away its eyes and ears. Some savages think that they can completely annihilate the soul of an enemy by eating the body or destroying its bones. Certain tribes extend similar precautions to the animals they have killed, lest the ghosts of these victims take revenge on them in some unpleasant way. These ingenious practices are reminiscent of the century-long methods of protection against vampires, reanimated dead bodies that issue forth from the grave and get sustenance through sucking the blood of the living. The commonest way of dealing with a vampire has been to drive a stake clear through the heart and body. It is evident that all these various sorts of mutilation presuppose that the condition of the dead body will influence to a large degree the condition of the surviving spirit.

For the same reason some tribes have had the habit of killing individuals before they arrive at the age of decrepitude, since otherwise they will not be able to lead healthy and active careers in the after-existence. Among the Chinese at one time there was a distinct preference for execution by strangling or shooting rather than by decapitation, since a headless body will result in a headless soul. Returning for a moment to the Old Testament Sheol, we learn that the shades of those who have been slain with the sword carry with them the marks of a violent death, while the shades of those who have died from grief bear forever the traces of it. And in Virgil's *Aeneid* Dido wanders through the woods of Hades with "her wound still fresh." In general, then, ancient and primitive peoples regard the inhabitants of the next world as reproducing more or less exactly the same features that marked them at the instant of death.

As already indicated, the reasons are complex for casting the natural body in such a significant role as regards the drama of the after-life. Some critics lay much emphasis on methods of burial as an explanation. In this connection Professor Pratt suggests that the Western custom of burying the dead body intact and in a definite, visitable place is of great importance. In India, he says, a different usage prevails and strongly affects the psychology of the Hindu. "The body of his lost friend is burned within a few hours after death, and the ashes swept into the river and forever dispersed. There is no body left and no grave around which he may center his thoughts of the departed. If he is to think of him at all it cannot be of his body and must be of his soul."[38] We grant that this method of disposing of the corpse is likely to weaken the natural association between the personality and the *dead* body, but memory of the long-enduring association between it and the living body is sure to persist. And the proof of this is that when we try to think only of the soul of a deceased person, we inevitably objectify our lost one in the familiar form and visage that we knew and loved on earth.

Furthermore, in the case of the Hindus, while according to their religion they leave behind irrevocably their former natural bodies, they soon enter and possess other natural bodies. For their souls become reincarnated in the future generations of men and of every sort of animal, bird, reptile, insect and fish. For the Hindu it is better to inhabit the frame and flesh of a cow, a crow or a cobra than to have no body at all. The Hindus, then, make available for the after-existence the easily imaginable and surely existent environment, including bodies, of the natural world. In doing this they give added support to our claim that no matter what disposal is made of the dead it is highly necessary to furnish bodies in the beyond in order to give that realm both imaginative reality and intellectual acceptability. And while the ancient and primitive peoples whom we have considered certainly did not, for the most part, make the matter intellectually clear to themselves, they seem to have possessed a kind of intuitional or common-sense recognition of the monistic principle that the personality and its body are inseparable accompaniments of each other.

4. *The Christian Resurrection*

Of all the doctrines that any religion has offered to the world that of the Christian resurrection most conclusively reinforces the idea of a close and inseparable union between body and personality. As indicated in the last section, the nature of man set forth in the Old Testament necessitates the promise of his resurrection in the New, if he is to enjoy a worth-while immortality. And accordingly the New Testament proceeds to give with a flourish this most remarkable and influential of all pledges, climaxing the life of its hero, Jesus, with his resurrection from the tomb and ascension unto heaven.* Even the personality of Jesus, the greatest, according to the gospels, and strongest and most god-like ever known on earth, has need of a body in the realm beyond. But this need becomes quickly and easily a splendid triumph, with the rising of Christ seeming to assure to all men their own conquest of hateful death.

As to the nature of the resurrection body, there can be no doubt that when the crucified Jesus rose from the dead he possessed the same body with which he had formerly walked the earth, although it was also and at the same time different through having become incorruptible and glorified. The most certain proof that the Son of God has passed into eternal life is the empty tomb. "He is not here," announces the angel at the sepulchre, "for he is risen, as he said. Come, see the place where the Lord lay."[39] And Jesus himself declares, "Behold my hands and feet, that it is I myself: handle me and see; for a spirit hath not flesh and bones, as ye see me have."[40] "Reach hither thy hand," he tells doubting Thomas, "and thrust it into my side."[41] The risen Christ ate, spoke, walked, was visible, could be touched; yet he also made sudden appearances inside rooms with shut doors and would sometimes vanish instantaneously. Finally "he was received up into heaven, and sat on the right hand of God."[42] Thus his immortal body was miraculously endowed with both natural and supernatural powers

* Acording to Catholic doctrine, the Virgin Mary at her death also ascended body and soul into heaven.

that enabled it to feel at ease in both this-worldly and other-worldly environments.

Though there have been from time to time heretical divergences of opinion, the mainstream of Christian thought right up to the present day in the Roman Catholic Church, the Eastern Orthodox Church and the Protestant Church, has interpreted the resurrection, both of Jesus and all other men, in terms of a transformed and glorified natural body. The Church has viewed in the same light St. Paul's distinction in the famous fifteenth chapter of I Corinthians between "natural" and "terrestrial" bodies on the one hand and "celestial" and "spiritual" bodies on the other. The latter are taken to mean transfigured natural bodies, and there is little question that Paul himself considered the matter in this light. When he asserts that "flesh and blood cannot inherit the kingdom of God,"[43] he is condemning the works of the flesh, not its substance. The claim that is sometimes put forward to the effect that Paul disbelieved in a literal resurrection seems to carry weight because he did stress the difference rather than the identity between the immortal and the mortal body. Conversely, other Christian thinkers have tended to emphasize the identity. But their emphasis, like that of Paul, has taken place within the accepted outlines of a common doctrine.

The Apostles' Creed of the second century A.D. explicitly states that there will be a resurrection of the flesh; the Council of Trent in the sixteenth century asserts that the "identical body" shall be restored "without deformities or superfluities"; Pope Pius X in our own twentieth century declares that "God wishes the resurrection of the body in order that the soul, having done good or evil when united with the body, may now, together with it, receive reward or punishment"; and the chief creeds of the Protestant

Church, such as the Westminster Confession of the Presbyterians, have held fast to the traditional conception of the resurrection. St. Augustine, answering some of the more obvious objections, declares: "In the resurrection the substance of our bodies, however disintegrated, shall be entirely reunited." For, "Far be it from us to fear that the omnipotence of the Creator cannot, for the resuscitation and reanimation of our bodies, recall all the portions which have been consumed by beasts or fire, or have been dissolved into dust or ashes, or have decomposed into water, or evaporated into the air."[44]

This recall will be complete and absolute. Not a hair or a finger-nail will be missing. When it was asked of what use teeth could be in the hereafter, since there would be no eating there, one early Church Father replied that they would serve to illumine the smiles of the blessed and another that they would permit an appropriate gnashing of teeth on the part of the damned. The resurrection will include, too, the distinctions of sex, without which the body would lack full integrity, though these distinctions will be "adapted not to the old uses, but to a new beauty." St. Thomas Aquinas, who accepted with certain qualifications Aristotle's dictum that the soul is naturally united to the body as its form, writes: "We cannot call it resurrection unless the soul return to the same body, since resurrection is a second rising. . . . And consequently if it be not the same body which the soul resumes, it will not be a resurrection, but rather the assuming of a new body."[45] To this day the general position set forth above has been, in the main, the accepted doctrine of the Christian Church. And it has also been the orthodox view of Judaism and Mohammedanism.

The seriousness with which the Christian Church has taken this matter of the resurrection is demonstrated, among other things, by its constant and deep-seated opposition to cremation of the dead. The burning of the bodies of the departed was a widespread practice among the Greeks and Romans of the early Christian era, but by the fifth century A.D., owing to the rise to power and influence of Christianity, it had become very greatly reduced in extent. In the early days of the faith the hostile pagans used to cast the corpses of Christian martyrs into the flames in order to destroy the belief in a resurrection. The attitude of the Church has always been that such ways of disposing of the body make no difference in the efficacy of the resurrection. But while abstractly, as Augustine says, God should have no more difficulty in restoring a body that has been reduced to ashes than one which has been buried intact, the Church well knows that practically and psychologically faith in a resurrection is likely to be weakened by cremation. For this practice is liable to nullify the natural habit of associating a dead man with his dead body and to stimulate ordinary common sense into asking awkward questions about the resurrection.

If the doctrine of the resurrection points convincingly to the never-ceasing reliance of the personality on the body, the theories invented to explain the state of human souls between death and resurrection support the same principle with almost equal force. Fortunately for their ease of mind the early Christians did not have to trouble with this problem of the intermediate state. In the first place, they anticipated the end of this world at any moment in conjunction with the second coming or Advent of Christ. The resurrection of the dead, the Last Judgment and the establishment of the Millennium would immediately follow. Those living at the time of this marvelous occasion would continue in their natural and now glorified bodies, while the dead would rise in their former and now incorruptible bodies. Since, however, those in their graves would not have long to wait, the question of the intermediate state did not come to the fore. In the second place, the first Christians worked out the mechanics of immortality chiefly on the basis of what occurred in the case of Jesus; and since he rose from the tomb almost immediately after dying, again the problem of the intermediate state was not compelling. But as time passed and Christ did not return and the world showed no signs of coming to an end, the matter became embarrassing.

Ultimately the Church evolved what seemed to it a satisfactory solution. While neither the happiness of the blessed nor the misery of the damned could be complete until after the recovery of the old, this-worldly body, the soul would nevertheless pursue, between death and resurrection, an exciting and varied career in divers hells, purgatories and heavens. Indeed, Christian theologians and great writers like Dante assigned to this supposedly disembodied spirit even more remarkable and colorful adventures than to the reunited soul-body following the resurrection. And if we carefully examine their accounts, we find that by either implication or explicit statement they actually provide this spirit with a body. To begin with, their descriptions give to it activities, functions and environments usually pertaining to earthly existence and natural bodies. The immortal personality in the intermediate state both enjoys and suffers a great many experiences that would simply be impossible without the cooperation of something very much like the body of this world.

The immortalists in question often seem to recognize or half-recognize this point. Dante, for example, through the words of an inhabitant of purgatory, tells us that there "the neighboring air shapes itself in that form which the soul . . . virtually imprints upon it. . . . Since thereafter it has its aspect from this, it is called a shade; and thence it organizes every sense even to the sight; thence we speak, and thence we laugh, thence we make the tears and sighs, which thou mayst have heard on the mountain."[46] Clearly this "shade" constitutes a special supernatural body temporarily called into being to take the place of the natural one. The Catholic Church of the present day, rephrasing statements by Augustine and Thomas, upholds a position similar to Dante's when it argues: "It is urged: How can a material fire torment demons, or human souls before the resurrection of the body? But if our soul is so joined to the body as to be keenly sensitive to the pain of fire, why should the omnipotent God be unable to bind even pure spirits to some material substance in such a manner that they may suffer a torment more or less similar to the pain of fire which the soul can feel on earth?"[47] Again, it is evident that "some material substance" is assuming the role of the body in the intermediate state.

This matter of the intermediate state brings out very well the difficulties involved in any idea of immortality that attempts to escape entirely from the monistic principle by postulating the survival of a "pure" soul. This position relies, we find, on the fundamental premise of the basic dualism between body and personality. Death terminates an uneasy partnership between the two and, far from being detrimental to the personality, sets it free to pursue its essentially noble and spiritual life. According to this view, the final liberation of the soul from its bodily prison-house gives to immortality its chief worth and meaning. Some religious sects, such as the Greek Orphic and Dionysiac cults, destroyed the dead body by fire lest the soul should re-enter it and again become imprisoned. Thus a resurrection of the natural body, or any other connection of the supernatural self with it, becomes both unnecessary and undesirable. Gone, at least formally, is the belief in the unity of man, of body and personality living in the completeness of human nature.

But as soon as the supposedly uncompromising

dualist begins to talk of what the bodiless spirit does
in the future life he runs into the same troubles that
the orthodox Christian meets in trying to describe the
intermediate state. For it turns out that there is well-
nigh nothing of importance that a spirit can do without a body being implied in the doing. And to develop
the framework of the after-life simply in its most
general aspects leads inevitably, through the laws of
inference, to the necessity of a bodily support for the
activities of the personality. Indeed, the dualist who
purports to believe in the survival of the self as a
thoroughly independent and immaterial entity is likely
to betray himself in the very first words he uses. For
he often defines the soul as a *substance*, a term which
has its natural and original application to material
things and which inevitably carries with it spatial and
corporeal considerations. Apparently, what our in-
flexible dualist is really trying to do is to portray an
immortality in terms of a visual image of the body that
is entirely dissociated from the tactile image, to preserve the form of the earthly body without its solidity.
But this is an impossible feat, except, of course, in a
Wonderland like that of Alice where the grin of the
Cheshire Cat has the astounding faculty of lingering
on after its feline creator has completely disappeared.

The enthusiastic dualist may claim that the ordinary laws of thought do not hold for the hereafter, that
consistency is no necessity there, and that intuition is
to be relied upon rather than reason. Or he may argue
that what now appear to be inconsistencies in his immortality ideas will not prove to be so in the light of
more complete and perfect knowledge. Such fine-spun
subtleties, however, are not likely to appeal to a great
proportion of mankind. The only other escape from the
result we have noted is for the dualist to maintain an
almost absolute silence in regard to the beyond, to say
nothing more than that there is some sort of after-
existence. But to refrain from all description of the

other world is an impracticable course in view of the need for making the future life seem real, intelligible and worth-while.

Suppose, however, the surviving soul is itself conceived of as a physical thing, as a highly subtle and attenuated order of air, breath, fire, matter, electricity or energy. Does not this view, perhaps most accurately described as materialistic dualism and held in many different times and places, including twentieth-century America,* avoid the dilemma we have been describing? It does, but only to confirm quite clearly our central argument. For as soon as the death-conquering spirit becomes itself a material thing, it then and there receives a body. But in this case it is not possible for the soul to be simply what might be termed a "pure" body, because this entity proceeds to perform functions and activities characteristic of the personality as well as of the body. In other words a fully functioning human body, or a material soul that is equivalent to such a body, can no more exist without a personality than a personality can exist without a body. Thus the essential unity of the body-personality is again demonstrated. And this principle cannot be thwarted by loosely calling something that does the work of *both* body and personality either just "soul" or just "body."

Returning now to the matter of the resurrection, we discover that the obvious difficulties in the traditional Christian position regarding the intermediate state of the dead have led a number of religious thinkers to deny any conscious existence whatsoever to the personality between death and resurrection. We find heretics being reclaimed from this error as far back as the third century. Every now and then the heresy has reappeared. Perhaps the most acute and careful reasoning on the problem of the intermediate state

* See William Pepperell Montague, *The Chances of Surviving Death,* Harvard University Press, 1934.

took place during a controversy which raged in England at the beginning of the eighteenth century. Such writers as Coward, Hallet, and Dodwell argued that man was naturally mortal, but that God, by his pleasure and will, would restore him at the day of the general resurrection. But previous to that occasion the departed soul was temporarily dead, asleep or unconscious. Later in the century the well-known philosopher and theologian, Joseph Priestley, supported the same views. The idea lived on at the beginning of the nineteenth century in the work of Samuel Drew. This writer claimed that there is a germ in the natural body which slowly ripens and prepares the resurrection body in the grave. As a seed must be buried for a season in order to spring up in perfect life, so must the human body be buried till the Day of Judgment.

Today in the United States the religious sects known as Russellites and Seventh Day Adventists adhere to the same general notion of a sleeping or unconscious soul between the death and resurrection of the body. In spite of the fact that this solution has never gained any large or important group of converts, it must be conceded that it has the advantage of a certain heroic consistency. And its defenders, of all those who have called themselves Christians subsequent to the earliest days of the faith, come nearest to admitting monism in its pure and simple form. For they not only ultimately provide the personality with its former body, but also, by eliminating the intermediate state as a time of activity, do away with all need for the supplementary body which orthodox Catholics and Protestants must postulate for this period. It would, however, be rather tragic for these stalwart dissenters if the long-promised and long-heralded resurrection never took place after all. For then, according to their own theory, neither they nor anyone else would ever taste the joys of immortality.

5. *Immortal Bodies: Modern Style*

Until the nineteenth century, Protestant theologians as well as Catholic had with few exceptions accepted the orthodox meaning of the resurrection as signifying the literal rising and glorification of that very flesh or body which had once trodden the earth. Then an accumulation of various factors began to cause doubts concerning this doctrine among certain elements in the Protestant fold. In general it was undoubtedly the progress of modern science that was most responsible for the weakening of faith in the resurrection of the dead, cast-off body. Under the influence of biology the dissolution of the body had come to be regarded as a natural event subject to regular causes rather than as a penalty inflicted upon man for original sin; death was coming to be accepted as an integral part of the natural machinery of evolution.

Most influential of all, however, was the emphasis of science on law and its consequent discouragement of reliance on miracle. Orthodox Christians had always admitted, and indeed proclaimed, that the resurrection was a miraculous event depending on the special intervention of God. But modern science caused a number of the devout to think of God as working through law rather than miracle. And they naturally grew skeptical concerning that perhaps most radical and remarkable of all miracles—the resurrection from the tomb. To support these considerations there was, finally, the growing feeling that the resurrection of the flesh was, after all, a rather gross and unspiritual sort of thing.

Now while modern science undermined belief in a resurrection, at the same time it demonstrated with increasing force the extraordinarily close association between the body and the personality. Especially did biology, physiology, psychology, medicine and their related sciences disclose a multitude of facts showing an apparently inseparable linkage between physical and psychical activities. Hence the more alert and informed Protestant churchmen, when they started to question the possibility of men's rising from the grave, did not take refuge in a pure discarnate soul that survived death, but chose to make their bow to the monistic principle and to reinterpret the concept of the resurrection and immortal life in a way which made room at least for *a* body. And these reinterpretations, they claimed, were consistent with the progress of modern thought.

As the first example of this tendency I shall cite Bishop B. F. Westcott of the Church of England, one of the most noted of the theologians who, towards the end of the last century, led the way in trying to reform the traditional ideas of a hereafter. "I believe in the resurrection of the flesh," he says. "But in shaping for ourselves this belief we need to use more than common care lest we allow gross, earthly thoughts to intrude into a realm where they have no place. The 'flesh' of which we speak as destined to a resurrection is not that material substance which we can see and handle, measured by properties of sense."[48] A later authoritative statement further clarifies Bishop Westcott's position. "We believe for certain in the resurrection of the body," writes Bishop Charles Gore. "This does not mean that the particles of our former bodies, which were laid in the grave and which have decayed into all sorts and forms of natural life, will be collected together again; but it means that we in our same selves shall be re-clothed in a spiritual body which we shall recognise as our own body, probably because it will, as it were, take the form and impress of our own unchanged selves."[49]

What Bishops Westcott and Gore have indicated in general terms, Dean W. R. Matthews, also of the

Anglican faith, has expounded more explicitly. "It is not easy," he writes, "to see how any distinctness of selves can be supposed to continue unless they are clothed with some body. The body is both our instrument and our boundary. . . . On these grounds, therefore, we are led to affirm the essential truth of the resurrection of the body. . . . In the days when the body was supposed to consist of minute particles, the idea of the collection of these particles at the resurrection caused discomposure in the minds of even the most determined theologians. But the physicists themselves have, if the phrase may be allowed, dissolved the materiality of matter. A body is, in the last resort, I suppose now regarded as a complex system of energy. We have moved some way towards a position where there can be no theoretical objection to the hypothesis that the activity of the soul builds up a body which shall hereafter be the vehicle of its life, a body which differs indeed from the present body, but is nevertheless continuous with it."[50] This position, claims Dr. Matthews, is hinted at by St. Paul in his declaration, "It is raised a spiritual body."

Canon B. H. Streeter also cites Paul to support a similar conception. Thinking and action in the hereafter, he argues, demand "a center of consciousness"; and such a center "must be conceived of as associated with or attached to some entity which is at any rate on the way to having a claim to the title 'body' in more than merely a symbolic sense. . . . We cannot deny the attribute 'material' in its strictly philosophic sense to the 'body' of the future life; though in the popular sense of the word 'material' we assuredly must do so—and that with emphasis, since we must suppose it to be normally invisible and impalpable to earthly senses, though probably both visible and palpable to the acuter perceptions of the next life. . . . We may suppose that during our life on earth we are, although we know it not, building up an unseen celestial body which is a sort of counterpart of our earthly body but more exactly adapted to the expression of the character which our thoughts and conduct are all the while developing. Or again, we may hold that the death of this body is the very act of birth of a new body. . . . In either case we may expect the body to reflect the nature of the self far more clearly than it does in this world. It will be fair and vigorous when the character is good, mean and weak when the character is bad. And in either case, if there is any growth or change of our character in the next life, it would be reflected and accompanied by a corresponding growth in the 'spiritual' body." [51]

In America Dr. Fosdick, most able and influential of the Modernists, sets the problem. He affirms "the persistence of the personality through death,"[52] and maintains that without this belief death would mean "mental confusion" and "the triumphant irrationality of existence."[53] At the same time Dr. Fosdick rejects completely the resurrection of the flesh or any kind of survival of the physical person, admitting, however, that he does not "easily imagine a completely disembodied existence."[54] Dr. Fosdick stops there. Dr. William Adams Brown in his book, *The Christian Hope*, ventures a little further. Early in this essay he admits, referring to St. Paul, that "this conception of a spiritual body presents difficulties to our thoughts. . . . Spirit we can understand. It is that which thinks and feels and wills. Body we can understand. It is that which has extension, location and motion. But a spiritual body is a union of opposites which conveys no clear meaning to our imagination."[55] Later on, however, he finds himself compelled to say: "Like Paul we 'would not be unclothed but clothed upon,' furnished, that is to say, with whatever instrument we need for the effective execution of our social purposes. *Body* is the term which lends itself most readily to the expression of this vital faith."[56]

Dr. S. D. McConnell, long prominent in the Episcopal Church, becomes more explicit: "Now suppose that before that ruin [death] befalls, the soul shall have been able to build up, as it were, a brain within a brain, a body within a body, something like that which the Orientals have for ages spoken of as the 'astral body.' Then, when the body of flesh shall crumble away, there would be left a body, material to be sure, but compacted of a kind of matter which behaves quite differently from that which our sense perceptions deal with. . . . It moves freely among and through ordinary matter without let or hindrance. . . . 'There are celestial bodies and bodies terrestrial' and each has its own modes of action. Such ethereal bodies compacted with living souls would of necessity inhabit a universe of their own, even though that universe should occupy the same space that this one does."[57]

The Reverend Robert Norwood informs us: "Even as matter enters into our conscious selfhood by digestion, so gradually is the spiritual body forming within the physical body for the soul's use when it passes through the gate of death to another plane of life."[58] "We are not to think that the soul is provided with a new body the moment death has destroyed the old, for there is a natural body and there is a spiritual body. They exist together. We have them now. Death is only a discarding of that exterior flesh body, so admirably adjusted to our present material environment. We no longer need that body when we pass into the blessed state of the departed. We go on with the spiritual body which we have now, though it is not manifested as it will be after death destroys the physical body."[59] Bishop James De Wolf Perry promises that in heaven people will know each other better than on this earth because "the masks of flesh" will be off; yet there is no doubt in his mind that immortal spirits must have "some form of body."[60]

Bishop William T. Manning's attitude is particularly revealing. From the pulpit of the Cathedral of

St. John the Divine he tells us: "I do not know with what body I shall come. I do not need to know. God will give me a body as it pleaseth him, a body suited to the glorious conditions of that other life." In spite of this indefiniteness as to the sort of body that is to be forthcoming in the after-existence, Bishop Manning is very sure that "when I enter there I shall be myself. This personality, these tempers and tastes, this character that I am forming here will be mine there. . . . I shall be seen as myself and shall be judged by what I am, I shall know my dear ones in the other life. I shall see and be seen. I shall speak and be spoken to."[61] This statement and its implications clearly reveal that the body of immortality is to be, after all, of a quite definite variety; indeed, that it is to be just about as definite as indicated in William Blake's "The Meeting of a Family in Heaven," a drawing in which age, sex and other distinctions are portrayed.

This is far from astonishing. For the Blake etching, which deserves study for its meaning as well as for its beauty, truthfully represents one of the chief hopes of those who desire or believe in a hereafter. An essential and central feature of a worth-while immortality is reunion with loved ones from the circle of friends and family. And this longing is one of the prime motivations leading to faith in a future life. But how are the departed to know and communicate with one another in the beyond? Moral characteristics and ideal qualities are very important, but they are elusive, general, and almost useless as identification marks when severed from their appropriate expression in the looks and actions of embodied personalities.

This man was good, that man was brave, another was brilliant, but so were hundreds and thousands and even hundreds of thousands who have passed out of this life. This woman—this mother, this wife, this daughter—was beautiful, that one was tender, another markedly unselfish, but so were many, many others who have died. And what distinguished their beauty, their tenderness, their unselfishness when they lived was the concrete and constant embodiment of these qualities in specific acts, in characteristic little gestures and in all the details of day-to-day existence. We want to see those whom we have liked and loved in the great beyond, but as Blake's drawing demonstrates, we want to see them again very much as we knew and loved them on this earth. And, indeed, if we do not see them that way, we shall probably not know them at all. As George Santayana puts it, "To recognize his friends a man must find them in their bodies with their familiar habits, voices and interests; for it is surely an insult to affection to say that he could find them in an eternal formula expressing their idiosyncrasy."[62]

Yet it should be noted that even granting the availability in the after-life of bodies closely resembling those of this earth, the difficulties of recognition do not end. How, for instance, are parents to recognize their long-lost babies amongst great multitudes of other departed babies all looking, as they did on earth, very much alike? Or how will small children who died when their parents were young and vigorous recognize them when, having become aged and decrepit, the parents cross over to the other world? Of course an easy answer to this last question is that in the realm of immortality no one will look or be aged or decrepit. In Blake's picture the parents are represented as being full of health and in the prime of life. Persons with old and decrepit bodies or with crippled and deformed bodies expect that somehow death will cure them of all those ills which life could not overcome. One of the favorite ideas of Christians has been that in the hereafter they will find themselves possessed of splendid bodies similar in appearance and vitality to natural bodies at the ideal age of thirty— ideal not only because of the obvious advantages of

that age, but also because Jesus Christ was supposed
to be about thirty when he triumphed over death and
ascended to everlasting glory. But even this wonder-
fully convenient solution would by no means solve all
the problems of after-life recognition.

I could continue indefinitely citing, and showing
the implications of, statements by modern Christian
immortalists in England and America. Those I have
quoted are typical of one important and influential
group of contemporary Christians who are trying to
work out an adequate substitute for the old idea of
the resurrection of the original physical body. Their
solutions are fundamentally the same whether they
speak of the spiritual, the celestial, the astral, the
ethereal, the etheric or the crystalline body. It is also
revealing to note how close in essence their interpretations are to the survival theories of certain esoteric
modern cults in the West.

For example, the Spiritualists believe in a form
intermediate between the material body and the conscious spirit. After physical death this becomes the
body of the eternal spirit, which needs an instrument
for individualizing itself and for realizing a separate
existence and personality. To quote Sir Oliver Lodge:
"The body of matter which we see and handle is in no
case the whole body; it must have an etheric counterpart to hold it together, and it is this etheric counterpart which in the case of living beings is, I suspect,
truly animated. In my view, life and mind are never
directly associated with matter; and they are only
indirectly enabled to act upon it through their more
direct connection with an etheric vehicle which constitutes their real instrument, an ether body which
does interact with them and does operate on matter.
. . . An etheric body we possess now, independent of
accidents that may happen to its sensory aggregate of
associated matter, and that etheric body we shall continue to possess, long after the material portion is dis-

carded. The only difficulty of realizing this is because nothing etheric affects our present senses."[63]

In a two-volume work showing the identity between primitive Christianity and modern Spiritualism, Dr. Eugene Crowell sums up the matter as follows: "All spirits agree in stating that their spiritual bodies are of the same general form and feature as their earthly; complete in every member and organ; in the main subject to like emotions, feelings, and desires, and like us requiring food for nourishment. Sublimated nerves convey impressions to their brains; and sublimated blood circulates in their veins."[64] The existence of such after-life bodies even makes it possible, we are told, to obtain the fingerprints of deceased persons from "the other side."

Theosophists make provision not only for an otherworldly body, but for no less than four such bodies: the etheric, the astral, the mental and the spiritual bodies. These are, as it were, encased within one another; when one body disintegrates, there is another to take its place. When in his other-worldly form a man leaves the physical body there is no break in consciousness; he merely shakes off the heavier vessel and is unencumbered by its weight. Likewise the Swedenborgians postulate an undecaying and incorruptible inner body, an ethereal organism which is the instrument of the spirit in the other world. When one wakes up in the realm beyond, "one finds himself in a body and world as complete in every respect as the body and world here. All is substantial and real. . . . So natural is it all that one does not realize, until he is told, that he has changed worlds."[65]

Plainly the Spiritualists, the Theosophists and the Swedenborgians are facing the same problem as the modern Protestant clergymen I have quoted and are meeting it in much the same way. The solution that all of these groups offer, including the Protestants, is a far cry from the original and orthodox doctrine of the Christian resurrection. Their after-life body resembles in substance the shadowy nether-world duplicate of ancient and primitive peoples, though in function it is like the resurrection body since it provides the surviving personality with an adequate basis for full and vigorous activity. But while orthodox Christians may strenuously object to these modern theories, they themselves, as we demonstrated in the last section, must accept something of the kind. For whether or not they definitely say so, they are compelled to give the soul in the intermediate state a body which, when analyzed, is very like the spiritual or etheric or otherwise described body of the modern revisionists. This is a thoroughly logical outcome, because the modern immortalists who completely rule out the old-time resurrection idea in effect give to the personality forever the same general status which it was once supposed to have only during the temporary intermediate state. And it stands to reason that the soul will have the same needs whether this status is eternal or transitory.

Looking back over this sketch of outstanding and representative immortality ideas, we see that without exception the undying human personality has been endowed, either explicity or implicitly, with an active and versatile body in order to make the future life seem worth-while and intelligible. Some culture groups have insisted upon the old body's resurrection, some have filled the gap with spiritual or etheric bodies of various sorts, some have postulated the survival of a pure soul, the activities of which imply a species of body, and some have believed in an immortal soul which is material and therefore includes in itself the equivalent of a body. Peoples like the ancient Hebrews and Greeks, who had no faith in a desirable after-existence for ordinary mortals, were unable to imagine even their forbidding underworlds without granting to the departed souls pale and feeble dupli-

cates of their this-worldly bodies. This is why Lucretius, who was a careful student of such beliefs, tells us
that in no other way "can we picture to ourselves the
souls wandering in the lower world of Acheron. And
so painters and the former generations of writers have
brought before us souls thus endowed with senses."[66]

It has not been, then, primarily skeptics or unbelievers who have insisted on the necessity of a body
for the soul's career in the other world; it has been
the immortalists themselves, of all ages and cultures.
And in so doing they have very definitely paid homage
to the monistic principle that the human personality
and the human body are basic and inseparable accompaniments of each other. For not only have they given
the surviving self *a* body, but one as similar as possible to the body of this earth; and, in the case of the
resurrection, that very body refashioned for immortality. We need not labor the point. He who is determined to be immortal must decide which one of
the various sorts of bodies offered he will posit. He
who is determined to follow the truth about death
wherever it may lead must decide whether *any* of the
bodies offered seems rationally possible or adequate.

CHAPTER III

THE VERDICT OF SCIENCE

1. *Biology and Physiology*

As I have shown in the preceding chapter, the close relationship between personality and body was understood, both inside and outside the Church, long before the rise of modern science. Ancient philosophers as well as ancient theologians worked out this relationship in some detail, Aristotle, Epicurus and Lucretius being noteworthy in this respect. For Aristotle the soul or personality is the form or actuality or function of the body; it is the inseparable accompaniment of the body and indeed its very life. The soul is to the body, he says, what seeing is to the eye and cuttingness to the axe. Body and soul are together yet different, like wax and the imprint upon it.[67] Though Aristotle, unlike Epicurus and Lucretius, mars the purity of his monism by claiming that something called "the active intellect" is immortal and survives death, he is careful to explain that all the rest of the soul, including memory and love, perishes with the dissolution of the body. Thus he definitely rules out a worth-while personal immortality, which clearly demands both love and other emotions; and which depends above all on memory, in order that there shall be in the hereafter a sense of identity and the ability to recognize self as well as others.

The general position of Aristotle on the intimate co-existence of the personality and body has been steadily and strongly reinforced by the progress of modern science, although modern science as such has not attempted to draw from its findings inferences regarding the idea of immortality. Biology, first of all, has definitely established man—mind and body—as a part of Nature, knit by ties of origin and kinship to the other animals of the earth and evolved like them through countless ages of time. In the process of evolution body has been prior and basic, whether we consider the first manifestations of life, from which all other living forms have sprung, or the higher orders of reptiles and mammals. In all the lower forms of life and in most of the higher we certainly cannot discern anything which can rightfully be called mind. And I tend to agree with those scientists and philosophers who argue that mind—that is, the power of abstract thought—emerged only with the appearance of man on this planet.

The development and integration of mind and personality in men have clearly been dependent upon the infinite complexity of the human body and especially of the nervous system centering in the brain, the spinal cord and the sense-organs. We find that the greater the size of the brain and its cerebral cortex in relation to the animal body and the greater their complexity, the higher and more versatile the form of life. The relative size and complexity of the brain, as well as the scope of its powers, reach their present culmination in man. And it is probable that if ever a species more advanced than man appears upon the earth, it will possess a brain, and therefore a mind, more highly developed than that of human beings.

For the human body to evolve from the lowest forms of life has taken, according to the most reliable estimates, at least two billion years. The result has been an organism of the most marvelous intricacy, with its manifold parts a hundred times more delicately adjusted to one another and to the external world than the different sections of the most involved machine ever invented. It is difficult to conceive anything more remarkable than the actual functioning and interfunctioning of the nervous system, the digestive system, the respiratory system, the blood and circulatory system, the reproductive system and the system of ductless glands. It is extraordinary how these key systems (not to mention the rest of the human organism) operate under just ordinary circumstances; in addition, they have a self-regulative capacity of rapid and sensitive adjustment to all sorts of abnormal conditions, both internal and external, that are constantly threatening man with varying degrees of distress and danger. Very appropriate it is that Professor Walter B. Cannon of the Harvard Medical School should entitle one of his books on physiology *The Wisdom of the Body*.[68]

As for the actual physical make-up of the body, some 200 bones and 260 pairs of muscles form its major bulk. In one muscle of a man's arm, the biceps, there are 600,000 fibers; and each fiber is composed of many smaller units called fibrils. The basic unit of the body, however, is the cell, a microscopic speck of living matter or protoplasm surrounded by a membrane. Competent biologists judge that there are as many as 265,000,000,000,000,000 of these cells cooperating in nearly perfect harmony in the normal life of a human organism. And even the simplest cell is an intricate whole composed of many interfunctioning parts. A single act of thought involves great multitudes of brain cells; a single movement of the arm or leg brings into play millions of muscle cells; a single beat of the heart—and there are normally over seventy beats a minute—sends literally billions of blood cells whirling through the long, winding passages of the arteries and veins.

The most extraordinary body section of all is the vast and labyrinthine network of nerve cells and their intercommunications which constitutes the brain and the rest of the nervous system. Without describing this part in detail here, it is no exaggeration to say that all in all man's body, whatever its imperfections, ranks as one of Nature's supreme accomplishments. And it does not seem surprising that such a body has proved able to create and support the human personality and, together with it, subdue the wild forces of Nature, build great cities and skyscrapers, think out prodigious systems of science and philosophy, produce magnificent art, literature and music, and invent all the thousand and one things that go to make up a mature civilization.

The ancient and medieval cultures, and even a people as intelligent as the Greeks, looked down upon the matter out of which the human body or anything else is constructed as base, inert and uncreative. Today, however, we know that matter, even at its most elementary atomic levels, is a thing of the most amazing complexity, dynamism and versatility. It no longer appears anomalous that life and finally human beings should have arisen out of such altogether remarkable stuff. Indubitably the creative matter become protoplasm of which living bodies are composed provides a sufficient foundation for the human organism, with its manifold powers and potentialities.

The natural human body is not only itself incredibly complex, but has evolved and functions in a very complex and particular kind of environment. Life as we know it is confined to the surface of the earth and to a few miles above and below. Living things can exist and flourish only under certain specific conditions. The most vital for men are temperature limits and the availability of those elements—oxygen from the air, water and food—that are transformed through the most diverse and devious mechanisms into energy and tissue. Our existence is adapted to a very narrow range of temperature variation. Without clothes or shelter human beings would probably succumb in a prolonged temperature only as low as fifty degrees Fahrenheit. On the other hand, when the thermometer rises to ninety degrees or above we are liable to become, especially if there is much humidity, depressed, unfit for strenuous activity and even feverish or sick. When 100 or over is reached, distinct danger to life begins; and under normal circumstances no one can endure for long a steady temperature of 113 or more. It is well known that the general state of the temperature can and does affect the personality of man and, indeed, the behavior patterns of whole peoples.

As for oxygen, none of us could survive even a temporary failure of it for more than a little while. This applies to the embryo as well as to the full-grown adult. Water is also a necessity for life. Living protoplasm is a watery substance and its constitution is disrupted if it is deprived of water. A human being can do without food far longer than without water, the complete absence of which in some form leads to death after a few days. But frequent nourishment is, of course, essential for the normally functioning man. Faulty or insufficient nutrition is almost bound to have at least a temporary adverse effect on personality; and when the malnutrition is serious enough, especially in the case of children and embryos, the bad effects are likely to be permanent. These various considerations point towards the conclusion that the body-personality, dependent on a most delicate equilibrium of natural forces, is inseparably linked up with its earthly environment.

There is every reason to believe, not only that body was prior in the long evolution which resulted in the species man, but that it is also prior in the production and growth of every human individual. It is not two particles of mind or consciousness that meet to create a new human being, but two purely material germ cells, the ovum from the mother and the spermatozoon from the father. At the moment of conception there is nothing present that can legitimately be described as personality or mind. And these terms are simply not applicable to the early stages of the embryo, if to any stage.

There are those, of course, who take exception to our definition of mind as the power of abstract reasoning and apply the word not only to the behavior of embryos and the lower forms of animal life, but also to atoms and electrons. This does not, however, really alter the issue. It is obvious that the lower forms of "mind" exemplified in the amoeba and the atom bear only the most far-fetched and superficial resemblance to that infinitely higher form of mind characteristic of the mature man. In short, no matter what words are used, the various differences in the functioning of atoms, amoebas and human beings still remain as great as ever. And we are able to reformulate our central point by showing how man's higher form of mind has evolved from a lower form and in what ways this evolution and the evolution of each individual human mind depend on bodily processes.

Returning now to our own definition of mind, we see that the exact point at which it is accurate to say the human organism has mind and personality is not important. The important thing is to observe that the mind and personality develop and expand as the body develops and expands. Any father or mother who carefully watches the growth of a child from birth through adolescence to maturity can make innumerable commonplace observations that convincingly testify to the continuing unity of mind and body. It is an intimately correlated association in which the psychic and physical functions advance together all along the line, in interaction with the economic, social and cultural influences of the environment. And this correlation is on the whole manifest throughout adulthood and old age as well as during childhood and youth. In the words of Lucretius:

Again, feeling doth prove that mind is born
Along with body, and with it step by step
Doth grow, and equally must waste with age.
For e'en as children totter with a weak
And tender frame, so doth a slender wit
Attend thereon; but as with riper years
Their strength doth wax, wisdom will grow apace
And force of mind gain increase. And at last,
When time's stern strength hath sapped the frame, and
*   loosed*
Are all the limbs, their powers benumbed, anon
The wits are lamed, tongue raveth, mind is shaken,
All things give way and in one breath are fled.
'Tis meet, then, that the nature of the mind
Should all be scattered likewise, e'en as smoke
Into the high-flung breezes of the air;
Since side by side with body do we see
It brought to birth, and side by side they grow,
And worn with age together droop and fade.[69]

Of course Lucretius' statement requires qualification. Men can grow very old and remain quite alert and clear in their minds until the very end. However, some slowing down in the mental processes does take place in practically all persons during advanced years; and definite personality changes usually occur beyond middle age if only for the reason that the human organism then no longer possesses the same physical strength and recuperative powers as in the days of youth. Thus as a rule athletic champions are not found among the older generation.

The laws of heredity also point to the close dependence of the personality on the body. The sciences of biology and genetics have shown that it is the multitudinous and extremely minute genes, transmitted through the germ cells of each parent in threadlike group structures known as chromosomes, that largely determine the inherent bodily characteristics and mental capacities of every individual. The genes are the decisive units of inheritance in human beings as in all living things, although there is evidence that other physical factors can affect or supplement them. Some combinations of genes produce imperfect specimens of man—feeble-minded, deformed, monstrous. Dr. Gardner Murphy, Menninger Foundation Director of Research, estimates that deficient heredity accounts for about 90 per cent of all mental defectives, thus pointing conclusively to the decisive effect of the gene patterns on the mind. Most gene combinations, however, give rise to normal and healthy individuals, some decidedly superior to others. But no two combinations are the same (except in the rare cases of identical twins), and that is why all men are different. Of course, when there are identical twins their separate bodies entail distinct and separate selves, even though these selves are very much alike.

No other mixture of genes except that from which my personality sprung could possibly have produced the particular unit of consciousness that I know as *me*. Other mixtures originated by my own parents do not result in *me*, but in brothers or sisters. So if my special synthesis of germ cells had not been made during the adult life of my father and mother, the possibility of my existence would have been cut off forever, no matter how many millions of other syntheses were produced till the end of time. When we look into the matter carefully, we discover that the chances are very slim for the coming into being of any particular *me*. During the act of procreation any one of the 300 to 500 million spermatozoa of the father may unite with the ovum of the mother. Each such possible union would result, of course, in a different combination of genes and in a different individual. During his life a man may produce, at a conservative estimate, the staggering total of 500 billion or more germ cells[70] and a woman some 17,000 cells or ova, though only about 400 of hers come to maturity.

In these estimates we have been taking for granted the existence and union of the parents. But the odds against this particular marriage were probably fairly high. And the odds against the existence of each parent were just as great as in the case of *me*. The same holds true of *their* parents, and so on back through endless generations. Thus, not only does the personality of a man depend on a unique combination of genes, but also the occurrence of this combination in the first place hangs on a unique concatenation of circumstances stretching far into the past. There is an infinitely complicated pattern of events behind the appearance of every human being in this world. And in view of these facts the religious view that a soul, bearing the main determinants of personality, is through a specific and separate act of God created to fit each embryo as it enters the realm of existence, becomes the most gratuitous of theories.

Among the most important characteristics determined by the genes is that of sex. Sex differentiation originated at an early stage of evolution and gradually developed to the advanced state in which it is found among men and higher animals. It is obvious that some of the fundamental differences between the male and the female personality depend primarily upon different bodily organization and functions. And everyone knows the varying but always powerful and sometimes paramount influence of sex and sexual emotions upon all human beings. It follows naturally that abnormalities closely connected with sex development will drastically alter the personality.

For instance, there are certain pathological conditions of the adrenal glands which may cause a woman to develop a deep voice, a beard, and masculine tastes and instincts in general. Many examples exist, too, of people born physically malformed in such a way that they are neither truly male nor female, but bodily a sort of intersex or hermaphrodite with personality to match. Again we see that the kind of personality one has is conditioned to a substantial degree by the kind of body one has. The pattern of every human personality is so inextricably interwoven with sexual characteristics that we are unable to imagine a sexless individual; even the gods have sex.

Biology has one final word to say. Just as mind and sex and sense organs have their definite and useful place in the evolutionary process, so has death. Death is not necessary or universal and made its appearance only after living things had advanced some distance on the path of evolution. There were and are various single-celled organisms, such as amoebas, fungi and seaweed, in which senescence and death are not inherent and which perish only through external accident, attack or extreme environmental adversity. These tiny organisms reproduce by division of the body, one individual becoming two with nothing left behind in the process corresponding to a corpse. Such division may continue indefinitely. Likewise the sex cells or germ-plasm of man and other animals, so long as passed on to new generations, divide and grow but do not die. Thus the whole chain of animal life, reaching through hundreds of millions of years, is really one unbroken continuum of deathless protoplasm.

Moreover, single cells or groups of cells can be separated from the animal or human body and preserved from death indefinitely. Isolated nerves, muscles, hearts, kidneys and even a spinal cord have been kept alive in laboratories which provide them with a carefully regulated environment and special nourishment. There was a famous bit of tissue taken in 1912 from the heart muscle of a chicken embryo by Dr. Alexis Carrel and maintained in a robust state of life for thirty-four years. On its thirtieth anniversary this chicken tissue, which was nicknamed "Old Strain," had lived three times the average lifespan of a chicken and was at the age equivalent of 200 human years. Its cells were as healthy and young as ever. "Old Strain" could have been kept living as long as scientists were willing to tend it, but the experiment was concluded in 1946 as having fully served its scientific purpose. It seems that the individual cells in a body do not die because mortality is inherent in their structure, but because they are parts of a very complicated system which is constantly making great demands on them and of which one section, small or large, sooner or later lets the others down.

Actually, the occurrence of death, inevitable through the laws of Nature for all but the lowest forms of life, has enabled life to push on to ever more impressive heights of efficiency, brilliance and self-awareness. Nature sets a limit to recuperative powers in the individual; the old organisms finally break down and die, making room for more vigorous ones and opening the way for the continuous development that we know as the evolution of species. In this process of ringing out the old and ringing in the new, Nature, which cares nothing for human values, is terribly cruel and inordinately wasteful. From the lowest to the highest of living forms she produces untold numbers of seeds or cells of generation, of which only a tiny proportion come to fruition and then survive the initial hazards of existence. Yet this immense prodigality guarantees the onward march of life: when an all but infinite supply of seeds are scattered over the earth, some are bound to take root and some of these are bound to mature.

The fresh human machines that Nature brings forth are, like the old ones, in the first place, bodies; and all the feats of strength or skill that they may perform are necessarily bound up with these bodies. Biology does not strictly rule out immortality for human personalities, but it insistently indicates that any immortality must be based on natural bodies. It is theoretically possible that at some far-off day the science of medicine will discover how to prolong indefinitely the life of human bodies, except in cases of serious accidents or acts of violence that injure or crush the physical organism beyond all chance of repair. Then there would be immortality in its original sense of *not-death,* for people would simply not die at all. And there would be no question of a life *after* death. But these are speculations which do not vitally concern our central issue. The significant point is that, biologically speaking, natural death is not in the least mysterious, but is as understandable as birth itself. Both occurrences are part of a biological process that provides for a perpetual fountain of youth. Remarkable as human bodies are, Nature eventually discards them for fresh ones; and it ought not to be surprising if, remarkable as human personalities are, Nature adopts the same policy towards them.

2. *Psychology and Medicine*

Psychology and medicine, together with their associated sciences such as abnormal psychology and psychiatry, offer the most weighty evidence of all in support of the unity of body and personality. If we turn to the processes of conscious experience, we immediately reach the crux of the matter. It is our nervous system that makes it possible for us to have the vast range and number of experiences that fill a normal life. Were it not for the functioning of the nervous system, we could be burnt to death without ever knowing it. This system is made up of billions of complicated cells called neurons distributed principally throughout the brain, the spinal cord and the sense organs, but extending in the form of thread-like fibrils or nerves to all parts of the body.

The brain and the spinal cord, which are usually designated as the *central* nervous system, play a role analogous to that of the exchange in a telephone system. A physical change in the environment acts upon the nerve endings in a sense organ and causes them to transmit impulses to the spinal cord or brain. Then one of these two, depending on how complicated a reaction is called for, responds by giving, as it were, an order, which is transmitted through outgoing nerve processes and causes thereby the appropriate functioning of muscles or glands. This cycle of incomings to the switchboard of spinal cord and brain and outgoings from it is known as the reflex arc. And it repeats itself daily in the life of the normal individual in a thousand different ways. It is no exaggeration to state that if we had a complete map of every circuit in all the telephone, telegraph and cable lines in the world, it would be far simpler than a chart of the ordinary nervous circuits in a single human being.

Coming now to the extraordinary experience and activity of thinking, it is true, in a way, that the whole body thinks just as the whole body, every cell of which needs and takes in oxygen, breathes and just as the whole man walks. Of course, ordinary thinking no more goes on without the stimuli and experiential impressions transmitted to the brain by means of the sense organs and nervous system than breathing goes on without the air carried to the lungs through the nose, mouth and internal passages of the respiratory system. But just as lungs are the specific organs of breathing and legs the specific organs of walking, so in the same sense the brain, and especially that part of it known as the cerebral cortex, is the specific organ of thinking.

The cortex is a thin, outer layer of wrinkled and

convoluted gray matter that grows around and over most of the rest of the brain, enfolding it like a cloak or mantle. It comprises approximately half the total weight of the brain; the brainstem and the cerebellum, which take care of less complicated functions, make up the other half. There is no well-developed cerebral cortex in the lowest animals, but with the reptiles it begins to assume a mature form and increases in size and complexity as the higher animal species evolve. In man it attains its culmination, the human cortex being twice as big and more than twice as complicated as that of the nearest animal, the ape.

It is estimated that in the infinitely complex human cerebral cortex there are about 14,000,000,000 nerve cells or neurons[71]; and each of these is enmeshed in a tangle of very fine nerve fibers coming from many different parts of the body. These vast quantities of neurons are related in so intricate a pattern that the total number of ways in which they are and may be linked is staggering and almost beyond comprehension. According to Professor C. Judson Herrick in his *Brains of Rats and Men*,[72] a few minutes of intense thought probably involves interneuronic connections as great in number as the total of atoms—10^{56}—in the entire solar system. If only one million of the billions of neurons in the cortex, he tells us, were combined among themselves in all possible patterns, the total aggregate of such connections would far exceed $10^{2,783,000}$. It is no wonder Professor Herrick concludes that the figure of potential associations among the neurons of the cortex may be regarded for all practical purposes as approaching infinity.

It does not seem astonishing that with such a remarkable and complex instrument at our disposal we should be able to perform with considerable efficiency and success the characteristic human activities of reasoning, willing, imagining, remembering and the like. At the same time it is hard to see how these activities of the personality, bound up as they are from the very start with the cerebral cortex, could possibly get along without it. The proper functioning of memory, for instance, clearly depends in the first place on the associational patterns laid down as enduring structural imprints through means of interneuronic connections. And the functioning of reason itself depends to a large extent upon the facility with which the patterns of memory and past knowledge can be recalled and reactivated in new and useful combinations to fit new situations. However ideas may be defined, it seems certain that awareness of or use of them requires as a condition the cooperation of the neuronic pathways in the cortex. But these pathways, these memory patterns, these records—millions and billions of them— are all imbedded in the gray cortical matter of the brain. And it is difficult beyond measure to understand how they could survive after the dissolution, decay or destruction of the living brain in which they had their original locus.*

By these remarks it is not meant that memory is a function of the cerebral cortex alone. The whole brain and the whole body, with all of those stored-up memories known as habits, take a part in the process of remembering. What, for example—if his hands suddenly forgot their skill—would become of the artist, the sculptor, the surgeon, the wielder of any complex or delicate instrument? And where would any of us be if the involved mechanism which makes possible speech and language should all at once lose the power to function? We cannot utter a syllable without the complicated cooperation of the lungs, the larynx, the throat, the tongue and the lips. We cannot write a word without the aid of arms, hands and fingers. And while we need not go to the extreme of

* Certain physiological functions of a destroyed part of the brain may, however, be taken over by another part. See p. 80.

claiming that all thought and memory involve talking subvocally to oneself or vocally to someone else, it is clear that intellectual activity does depend to a very great extent on conscious or unconscious verbalization. Without the employment of the multitudinous symbols which language brings into being, it is more than doubtful whether there could be such a thing as reason. Anyone who has ever tried to learn a foreign language realizes very well that memory is the all-important tool in its acquisition. And if a man suddenly lost, for some reason, the memory of all words (or other signs that serve for symbolization), it seems most probable that he would lose his mind at the same time.

This matter of memory is crucial not only because of its importance for thought and language, but also because it is fundamental to the sense of personal identity that we have in life. If after a severe fracture of the skull John Smith finally recovers consciousness with all memory of past events totally and permanently obliterated, in a very real sense it will be a new self that goes on living. To the new John Smith the old John Smith will be dead and gone, except for such reports of him as can be gathered from written and pictorial records and from the anecdotes of other persons. Now it can be undeniably maintained that something like this happens to all of us in the natural course of events. As adults we cannot recall a thing about ourselves when we were one year old; and precious little about what we did or what we looked like when we were five or even ten, though we may find out to some extent by rummaging through the diaries and photograph albums of our relatives. But we can also refer to records concerning our parents and grandparents, and indeed totally unknown persons, and make their childhood, before we were ever born, almost as real to us as our own. For our own early youth is to us only a faint and hardly discernible echo that occasionally comes through to us out of a distant past.

In fact, a great deal of what we did barely a year or a month or a week ago is already entirely finished and forgotten. Thus the feeling of personal continuity and identity rests not only on the faculty of memory, but on the memory of only a comparatively small slice of our past. The amount of that remembered part varies from man to man and from period to period during life. But from minute to minute, from day to day, from year to year, there is enough recalled to guarantee an unbroken sequence of identity. When we are forty-five years of age, we do not remember much of our existence at ten; but at fifteen we remembered a good deal about it and even at twenty a considerable amount. In this manner there occurs the gradual and uninterrupted transition of the personality from youth to maturity to old age. There is no sharp and total break as in the case of the John Smith whose skull was fractured. The very fact, however, that we can and do forget such large portions of our experience indicates the tenuous hold of our sense of self-identity on existence and suggests that some day—at death, for instance—it might well disappear entirely through our forgetting *everything*.

What William James called the "stream of consciousness" would be simply a chaotic and unorganized rush of experience were it not for the aid of memory in uniting, relating and ordering its quickly coming and quickly going flow. The self is, as someone aptly put it, primarily a "memory-synthesis." Indeed, the vital necessity of memory for the integration of the mind and personality should be apparent no matter what general psychological or philosophical theory one accepts. For our experiences and thoughts obviously do swiftly succeed one another in time, and only memory or an equivalent can bridge the durational gap between them. One may purport to discover through introspection all sorts of marvelous things about the self, but whatever discoveries may be claimed or established, memory will still remain essential. It is not everything in the life of the personality, but it is indispensable. And if a transcendental self or a supernatural soul holds sway behind the empirical curtain, it too must make use of memory; but the logical and apparently only available remembering mechanism for it to work through is the maze-like material organization of the cerebral cortex and associated centers.

This conclusion receives convincing corroboration through the study of various types of mental abnormality and insanity. It is a commonplace that a severe blow on the head may so affect the brain through actual destruction or injury of tissue, that temporary or permanent insanity sets in. Sometimes a fracture or concussion causes complete or partial loss of memory —for days, for months and even for years—of everything that preceded the accident. Even a blow that has no lasting bad effects may make a man totally lose consciousness for a time. On the other hand, a person who is born insane or becomes so through an accident may be completely cured by an operation on the skull to remove the abnormal pressure of bone on the cerebral cortex. But if the brain of a man is too far under the average weight, he will be feeble-minded or worse and no operation can make up for his defect. The pinheaded microcephalics, with their diminutive brains, usually attain at most a mental level comparable to that of a child two or three years old.

Some injuries affect a specific area of the brain and through it specific functions of the man, thus demonstrating that certain activities of the body are definitely associated with certain portions of the brain. For instance, an injury to the frontal lobe of the left cerebral hemisphere disturbs the powers of speech by causing motor aphasia, while one to the temporal lobe affects a person's hearing. Though most of the charts drawn up by phrenologists and their ilk assigning definite functions to definite parts of the brain are false or misleading, it is true that the sciences of psychology and physiology have correlated a number of functions such as seeing, smelling, hearing, limb movements and speech coordination with generally identifiable sections of the cerebral cortex. The center for vision, for example, is in the posterior part of the cortex, while that for hearing is near the middle.

It is to be noted, however, that these cortical centers or fields fade away diffusely into adjacent areas and so cannot be sharply defined anatomically; that they are connected directly or indirectly with all other parts of the cortex through an intricate network of association fibers; and that they are incapable of performing any function independently, but always act together with the cortex as a whole. In some cases of serious damage to a certain area of the cortex other sections may take over the duties formerly allocated to the injured segment. This fact has been cited to show that some kind of supernatural entity is at work, but it rather proves the amazing plasticity and educability of the very sensitive brain tissue.

Diseases have just as distressing an effect on the brain and mental functions as external injuries. The worst brain disease of all is probably paresis, a form of paralysis, which is caused by syphilis germs from other parts of the body invading the cerebrum and destroying the brain cells. It is characterized by progressive mental and physical deterioration eventually leading, unless arrested, to death. The disease usually results in profound changes of the personality. The afflicted individual tends to lose his judgment and self-control; to become reckless, indulgent and morally irresponsible; and to neglect his obligations to family and community. In the final stages his cerebral decay may be so far-reaching that he leads an almost purely vegetative existence, as helpless as a new-born babe. This last condition is also typical of senile dementia, which is caused by deterioration of the brain tissue due to old age in general, to interference with the cerebral circulation from hardening of the arteries and to other such hazards of senescence. Tumors within the brain are also likely to lead to dementia. And if a blood-vessel bursts within the cerebrum, the result is apoplexy and often outright death.

Another common trouble is caused by the failure of the thyroid gland in the neck to secrete sufficiently. In a child this results in a stoppage or distortion of growth, and ordinarily in feeble-mindedness or imbecility. This disease is called cretinism. In combating it the administering of thyroid extract from sheep can produce remarkable results and bring physical and mental normality to the child. A similar though less serious ailment in adults is known as myxedema and responds to the same treatment. Here, then, we are able to cure a grave sickness of the mind by giving medicine, as if we were dealing with a bad liver or an upset stomach.

The dependence of mind on body is further illustrated by the importance to mental activity of a proper quantity and quality of blood for the brain. A large proportion of the body's total supply of blood is constantly traversing the brain. If the flow of blood to the brain wholly ceases, certain cells necessary to normal functioning quickly ·become irreversibly damaged. When the brain becomes tired, its energy diminishes and the flow of blood to it becomes less. So during sleep when the brain, and the mind with it, is resting, there is relatively less blood passing through. The common experience of feeling sleepy after a heavy meal is due to the fact that the digestive processes are making extra demands on the blood supply and are drawing blood away from the brain. It is primarily through the blood stream that drugs and stimulants, poison and starvation, influence in their various ways the mind of man.

Too much alcohol adversely influences the mind

through a depressant effect on the higher nerve centers. More than two thousand years ago Lucretius gave an all but perfect description of intoxication:

> . . . When once the fiery potency
> Of wine hath stolen into a man and spread
> Abroad through all his veins its liquid fire,
> Why is it there doth follow in the frame
> A heaviness, as the uncertain limbs
> Stagger and stumble, tongue becometh thick,
> The mind is sodden, eyes are bleared; meanwhile
> Shouting, sobbing, and quarreling grow apace
> And all the signs that go along therewith?
> Why come all these to pass, except it be
> The mastering might of wine is wont to throw
> The mind in turmoil, e'en within the frame?[73]

Of course, if the use of alcohol be excessive and long-continued, there results the dangerously over-excited and hallucinatory condition of delirium tremens or, finally, the general deterioration of all mental functions known as alcoholic dementia.

The ordinary functioning of sleep well illustrates several of the points we have been making. As the body grows tired, the mind grows tired with it. And though it is possible to fight off fatigue and sleep for no little time, the natural thing is for the whole man as a unit to want and take repose. During slumber a person remains unconscious, except in the sense of occasionally having dreams. Were it not for the connecting links that memory provides between each fresh day and the one before, we should arise each morning with no consciousness of the past and without the knowledge of continuing self-identity so essential to human selfhood. In sleep, as in all other periods of unconsciousness, it is undeniable that the mind, whether a natural or supernatural entity, loses its sense of awareness. And it may be argued that this furnishes us with a hint of what happens when we die. Certainly it is proper to infer that if so often during life a person temporarily loses consciousness, he may at death lose that consciousness permanently.

Coming now to the natural processes of death itself, we find additional light thrown on the relationship between body and personality. As at the beginning of an individual's life—during gestation, birth and infancy —the body is controlling, so at the end of life. Just as no personality can enter the world until some body issues, as it were, a passport, so no matter how desirous a personality may be of leaving the world, no matter how terrible its anguish through the ravages of disease or man-inflicted torments, no matter how noble it may be or how much favored of God, it cannot depart this life until the body gives leave by ceasing all vital functions. The only known method of committing suicide is to bring about the death of the body. Though during the final stages of dying men are frequently unconscious, they may at any point regain consciousness, for a moment or considerably longer.

And they can be recalled from what is almost equivalent to a state of death, as when they are revived from drowning, suffocation, electric shock or carbon monoxide poisoning through various types of artificial respiration, such as the use of a pulmotor or the administration of oxygen; through the injection of powerful stimulants such as adrenalin or caffein; or through radical therapy concentrating directly upon the heart. So-called "clinical death," which begins when heart action and respiration cease, can sometimes be reversed by drastic measures before true biologic death sets in. These considerations do not point to personalities or souls which are as independent of bodily processes as dualists claim. They demonstrate how intimately personalities are bound up with their this-earthly bodies and that in such situations as we have been discussing they come and go according to the expert medical treatment of those bodies.

This citation of facts showing how physical states affect the personality and its mental life does not in the least imply that mental states do not affect physical. All of us are constantly altering our bodily motions according to the dictates of mental decisions. Everyone is familiar with the far-reaching results that optimism or worry, happiness or sadness, good humor or anger, may have on the condition of the body. Good digestion makes for cheerfulness, but the converse is also true; and scientific research has definitely shown that pleasant emotions favor the secretion of the digestive juices, while unpleasant emotions hinder this process. Anger increases the production of adrenin by the adrenal glands and this secretion, in greater quantities than usual, sweeps through the blood vessels, raises the pressure and sugar-content of the blood, speeds up the heart beat, delays muscular fatigue and prepares the whole body for strenuous action such as fighting or fleeing. A man during rage may feel no pain from injury until after his wrath has cooled. Intense fear has very much the same effect as anger. And every other emotion has its physiological reverberation, however slight.*

Morale is as necessary to the effectiveness of an army as food. Mental depression or irritation can produce many kinds of bodily ills. And if one's state of mind does not actually bring on some organic trouble, it is always of importance in the extent and rate of recovery. A physical process such as the knitting of a broken leg can be prevented or delayed by faulty nu-

---

* The famous James-Lange theory claims that the physiological reaction is prior and primary. Thus we do not cry because we feel sorry, but we feel sorry because we cry. The acceptance of this extreme theory, however, is by no means necessary for our argument.

trition resulting from anxiety. Extreme terror may paralyze a man, strike him dumb, or cause palpitation of the heart; after earthquakes men and women are found dead who show no signs of injury. Without accepting all the conclusions of Freud and other psychoanalysts, we can safely say that repressions connected with sex may adversely affect an individual's health. Love-sickness is a real disease which can afflict both men and women. There can be no doubt, either, that what is termed the subconscious plays an important part in the general functioning of the personality.

The remarkable effects sometimes achieved through the acquisition of ordinary self-confidence through auto-suggestion and hypnotism, work, it is thought, primarily through the subconscious. Not long ago in the United States hypnosis saved an eminent citizen from death by putting an end to hiccoughs that were causing grave hemorrhages after a throat operation. Hypnotism can apparently make a receptive mind do almost everything from the trivial and harmless to the serious and violent. The disease of the imagination called hysteria also functions to some extent through the subconscious. The hysterical patient, though organically sound, may suffer paralysis of a limb, lameness, blindness, dumbness and at least the outward symptoms of many other bodily disorders.

It is also appropriate to mention the appearance on the bodies of religious devotees of the stigmata, that is, marks corresponding to the wounds inflicted on Jesus at the crucifixion. St. Francis of Assisi was the most noted of those who are said to have received this supposed mark of divine favor; but there have been many well authenticated and quite recent cases, mostly of women, in modern times. While in this matter conscious or unconscious impostures are sure to have taken place, a certain residue of cases is probably genuine. In every instance, stigmatization has come about only after prolonged meditation upon the passion and crucifixion of Jesus. Modern psychologists believe that the phenomenon of the stigmata can be explained in entirely naturalistic terms and that it is due to as yet undiscovered mechanisms of the subconscious or unconscious. The attempts, however, to smuggle back the supernatural soul through the subconscious would appear to follow the old and exploded procedure of resorting to the supernatural to explain the relatively unknown.

Such examples as these of the mind's control over the body are often interpreted as conclusively proving that the mind is independent of the body. But they point with at least equal force to a connection between the two so exceedingly intimate that it becomes inconceivable how the one could function properly without the other. Furthermore, it is to be remembered that many of the mental states that exercise an influence on the condition of the body are set up in the first place by phenomena primarily physical. Sex neuroses, for example, follow upon the suppression or thwarting of physical desire and then proceed to react unhappily on the whole being. A bilious attack may make a man mentally depressed, and this psychic condition may then help to bring on insomnia. In short, there is a constant interplay between the mind and body.

If we take the position that the mind is a function of the brain, there is no mystery here. For the brain is part of the body and accordingly what it does naturally affects the rest of the body just as what the stomach or what the heart does affects the rest of the body. At the same time what is going on in the rest of the body naturally affects the brain and sometimes, as we have pointed out, rather thoroughly disrupts its activities. But not everything that goes on in the rest of the body has immediately important consequences for the brain and its powers of thought. And this is why persons may have serious, long-drawn-out and often fatal diseases, such as cancer or tuberculosis, without their mental faculties being substantially impaired—at least until the very end. Cases of this kind do not, as some people believe, yield much of an argument for the complete independence of the mind. They simply show that while the human organism is a closely integrated system, some parts of it in some ways are relatively independent of other parts; and that as long as the brain remains comparatively unaffected, the intelligence will remain so, too, and may considerably outlast other bodily powers.

Perhaps the most easily accessible indication of the pervasive unity between personality, soul or mind on the one hand, and body on the other, is the way in which the physical exterior of a man may reflect his essential being. If "the apparel," as Shakespeare says, "oft proclaims the man," how much more so do the gait, the bearing, the hands, the voice, the face. In fact, as any professional actor or teacher of dramatics knows, it is the whole body acting as a unit that brings out the character. While there is some disagreement as to what special portion of the body most completely expresses the mood of a man,[74] the face is by common consent an excellent example of our general principle. In its habitual cast or in its fleeting expressions it frequently mirrors a person's inmost feelings. A barely perceptible quiver of the mouth, a passing smile upon the lips, a slight wrinkling of the forehead, a faint knitting of the brows or a sudden lighting of the eye all tell their particular story. While we sometimes speak of laughing eyes and gloomy eyes, honest eyes and shifty eyes, eyes that look daggers and eyes that look love, careful experimentation has brought out that it is the expression of the mouth which reveals most of all. John Donne, the English poet and divine, puts our whole point beautifully in describing the animated countenance of a high-spirited young girl:

Her pure and eloquent blood
Spoke in her cheeks, and so distinctly wrought
That one might almost say her body thought.[75]

The so-called science of physiognomy has traditionally been a favorite stamping ground for charla-
tans, who have puffed it up with false pretensions and
over-extended it to the point of absurdity. I do not intend to follow suit by claiming that it is possible to
learn everything about a man from his features or that
people's faces cannot be very misleading and indeed
quite inscrutable. Marked inability to read a face, however, is often due to inexpert interpretation, to unfa-
miliarity with some sectional or foreign type, or both.
There is good reason to believe, for instance, that the
supposed inscrutability of the Oriental countenance
holds only for non-Orientals.[76] The conventionalized,
stereotyped expressions native to one culture group are
under ordinary conditions likely to convey a minimum
of significance to members of another. Finally, when
conscious volition steps in to control facial reactions,
as in the case of the well-known "poker face," much in
the way of deception can be accomplished. But the
very fact that in such cases the will must interfere
shows how intimate is the natural integration between
personality and physical expression. And the additional
fact that in spite of all effort our facial reactions often
reveal a state of mind which we wish to conceal reinforces the point.

Finally, let us note the extent to which the personality is moulded by the human environment. All of
us are born into a family and into a society. The kind
of family and the kind of society that nurture us make
a very great difference in the kind of personalities we
develop. Our parents, our teachers, our nationality, our
language, our economic condition and many other social factors influence enormously the growth and cali-
ber of our characters and minds. Weighty and dramatic

evidence here is the recent well-authenticated discovery of two "wolf-children" in India, as recounted in the scholarly study, *Wolf Child and Human Child*, by Dr. Arnold Gesell of the Yale Medical School. Dr. Gesell's book is based on the diary of the Reverend J. A. L. Singh of Midnapore,[77] who tells how he and his helpers found, in the year 1920, two female human children, one aged about eight and the other about one and a half, in a wolf-den on the edge of the jungle. Several wolves fled at the time of capture, but the mother-wolf stood her ground and was killed. Evidently this mother-wolf had suckled and cared for the two girl children for a considerable time. The natives of the district, having glimpsed them occasionally in the forest, had come to believe that they were "man-ghosts."

Kamala, the older girl, and Amala, the younger one, had been able to survive by acquiring characteristic wolf habits and adapting themselves as best they could to wolf "culture." Kamala walked and ran on all fours, seized her food by mouth, insisted on nudity, preferred darkness to daylight, and howled at night in a piercing half-animal, half-human wail. She knew no human ways or words. The Reverend Singh put Kamala and Amala into the Orphanage at Midnapore and, with his wife, undertook to train them as normal human beings. Amala, being still a baby, learned more quickly than Kamala, but survived only a year in her new environment. Very slowly the Singhs were able to teach Kamala how to stand upright, how to walk, how to wear clothes, how to talk. In 1924 Kamala had six words in her vocabulary; in 1927, forty-five. Gradually she came to enjoy human association and to lead an essentially human existence, though a retarded one. Unfortunately she died in 1929, at the age of seventeen, nine years after leaving the wolf-cave.

This story cogently illustrates, it seems to me, the point that the personalities of human beings do not

enter ready-made into this world, but are the product
of culture and circumstances as well as heredity. One
of the most striking things about Kamala was that her
wolf-life and conditioning prevented her from even
learning to walk upright while she was with the
wolves. The significance of this fact for the monistic
psychology is well brought out by Dr. Gesell in his
analysis of the wolf-children. He reminds us that "the
basic framework of the action-system of all vertebrates
is posture. Even in man the finer and subtler patterns
of behavior are grafted on postural sets and postural
attitudes. Kamala had basic ways of squatting, reclin-
ing, inspecting, sniffing, listening and of locomotion
acquired in the wolf era of her developmental career.
These motorsets constituted the core of her action-
system and affected the organization of her personality.
. . . Even after several years of sojourn with upright
human beings, quadrupedal locomotion was resorted
to whenever speed was necessary. On two feet she
never learned to run at all; on four feet she ran so fast
it was hard to overtake her."[78]

In short, even a normal human body does not automatically produce a characteristic human personality,
but only when that body is subject to certain environmental and social influences. The remarkable case of
Kamala, in conjunction with a multitude of other scientific data, logically leads to the crucial statement that
not only do our individual minds depend upon the accumulated intellectual and cultural heritage of the
race, but that mind as we know it is in its very origin
a social product. For the human mind matures and attains its distinctive powers of abstract thought only
through the symbols of speech and language. Men are
born with brains; *they acquire minds.*

Now articulate speech came into existence only
through men associating together and developing—
from elementary movements, grunts and cries—definite, recognizable, rememberable signs which served

as a medium of communication. The faculty of speech is admittedly not an original, but a derivative function of the human organism; and the organs necessary for it—the mouth, the teeth, the tongue, the pharynx, the larynx and the lungs—had biological and survival value in the first instance because of their physiological role in eating, tasting or breathing. The human brain itself was to begin with an organ for the greater coordination and efficiency of behavior and not primarily one for reasoning and knowing. Speaking, language and abstract thinking, then, are a social outgrowth of prior animal functions.

We can add the further point that moral standards, like the categories of mind, originate and evolve in the course of human association. Hence morality, too, is a social product. The notion that a supernatural soul enters the body from on high, already endowed with a pure and beautiful conscience, runs quite counter to the findings of anthropology, psychology and ethical science. It is possible, then, to summarize the entire situation by saying that, in addition to the indissoluble union between body, on the one hand, and mind and personality, on the other, there is also an indissoluble connection between the body-mind-personality, that is, the whole man, and the sustaining and conditioning environment, both human and physical.

3. Dualism in Distress

Our short and necessarily far from inclusive review of scientific considerations bearing on the point at issue indicates why psychological dualism finds itself today in a decidedly weak position, with increasing troubles and decreasing support. Further insight into the matter may be acquired by analyzing the specific doctrines of some outstanding thinkers of recent times who are persuaded that the dualistic psychology is sounder than the monistic. We may take as representative ex-

amples of this standpoint Henri Bergson, a French-
man, Hans Driesch, a German, and William McDougall, an Englishman who taught during the latter years
of his life in America.

Bergson, the most distinguished philosopher of
twentieth-century France, believes that it is impossible
to correlate completely mental activities with the
brain, that the mental life overflows the cerebral life,
and that the survival of consciousness at death accordingly "becomes so probable that the onus of proof falls
on him who denies it rather than on him who affirms
it."[79] Professor Driesch's approach is primarily through
biology, in which field he is known as one of the most
prominent Vitalists. He tells us that "the essential
agents responsible for the formation of an organism are
not agents working in space and having their starting
points in particles of matter, but agents working *into*
space, if a paradoxical expression may be permitted.
May such agents not also come from 'outside time,' we
may ask, and go into 'outside time,' when the phenomenon of death occurs?"[80]

Professor McDougall, a noted psychologist, calls his
view Animism and claims that there is an animating
principle operating within man that is of a nature different from that of the body, "a psychic or mental
structure that is not extended in space, but may rather
be described, in Driesch's terms, as a qualitative manifold which, while not spatial, yet acts into space." Mc-
Dougall bases his position chiefly on the proposition
that the functionings of life and of mind are only par-
tially correlated with material structure. In reference
to the operation of the brain, he states: "As was to be
expected on any informed view of the possibilities,
there seems to be close correlation between, on the one
hand, experiences of the various sense-qualities and of
various bodily movements and, on the other hand, certain parts of the brain structure. But all attempts to
carry the correlation farther have broken down. . . . In

general, it may be said, the evidence supports the view that in some sense the brain functions as a whole; and that when one part is destroyed, other parts can in a surprising manner take over, as it were, the impaired functions."[81]

McDougall seems to provide the answer to his own argument when he says that "in some sense the brain functions as a whole." Of course it does, especially when it is carrying on the higher intellectual processes such as reasoning and memory. Such processes have never been definitely localized in any one section of the brain and almost certainly never will be. In all probability the more involved mental activities always utilize interneuronic connections running over a very large portion of the complex cerebral cortex. As McDougall himself notes, it is certain physiological functions such as seeing and hearing that have been correlated with particular parts of the brain; these cortical areas act as specialized switchboards for certain incoming and outgoing nerve processes. But they do not do their work in isolation, particularly when, as is true most of the time, the seeing or hearing or other function is associated with and cooperating with actual thought. The limited possibilities of correlation between different *parts* of the brain and different functions of consciousness hardly justify McDougall and Bergson, who also employs similar reasoning, in claiming that consciousness can get along without the brain *as a whole*. For the limitation in question seems quite natural in view of the structure of the cortex and the mechanism of thought.

Very pertinent to this discussion is what Professor Cannon calls the body's "margin of safety."[82] Cannon finds, in agreement with other physiologists, that our bodies are not built on the principle of niggardly economy but on the basis of generous superabundance in order to allow for all sorts of contingencies. The active tissues of most organs in the human body greatly exceed in quantity what is needed for normal functioning of the organs. In some cases the surplus amounts to five, ten or even fifteen times the actual requirement. Many human organs, such as the kidney, are paired; and in such instances the body often maintains comparative efficiency with only one of the paired organs working.

In the brain, as in other parts of the body, there is a wide margin of safety. And this helps to explain why various portions of the brain can go permanently out of commission without mental activity and bodily control being permanently impaired. There are, however, certain indispensable sections of the brain whose destruction inevitably brings about death. In his stimulating essay, "The Energies of Men," William James, by showing what immense reserve capacities human beings possess, gives in graphic language striking support to Dr. Cannon's principle.

The fact that the function of a destroyed part of the brain can sometimes be taken over by another part testifies to the remarkable versatility and reserve potentialities of the cortex rather than to the presence of a supernatural soul. And there is no reason why such a soul should be able to educate a small section of the cortex to a new responsibility any more easily than the natural body-personality with its infinitely complicated brain and nervous system and its unparalleled powers, known and unknown, conscious and unconscious. Similarly, the immense complexity and versatility of the brain and body, functioning together beautifully as a united whole, provide an adequate answer to McDougall's further point that "the fact of psychical individuality . . . cannot be rendered intelligible . . . without the postulation of some ground of unity other than the brain or material organism."[83]

McDougall also tells us that if the dualistic view, of which his Animism is one form, is discarded, "the belief in any form of life after the death of the body will continue rapidly to decline among all civilized peoples, and will, before many generations have passed away, become a negligible quantity." It is "highly probable that the passing away of this belief would be calamitous for our civilization. For every vigorous nation seems to have possessed this belief, and the loss of it has accompanied the decay of national vigor in many instances."[84] This debatable statement raises in a very frank manner the question of to what extent the defenders of the dualistic psychology are consciously or unconsciously motivated by a desire to save for mankind the belief in immortality. And it leads to the additional question, mentioned in the first chapter, of how much the great metaphysical Dualisms, which usually are associated with the dualistic psychology, owe to the same motivation.

Science itself casts a good deal of light on why the dualistic theory is so frequently advanced. For scientific analysis does make a number of valid distinctions in describing the human organism. Breathing, after all, is not the same as digesting; nor does one eat ideas. Furthermore, there are certain natural divisions within the human brain itself. On the one hand we have the cerebral cortex, the thin, outer, upper layer of gray matter that carries on a man's conscious thinking and coordinating. On the other hand we have the thalamus, the cerebellum and the brain-stem which together constitute the lower half of the brain, which function to a large extent as the seat of the emotions, and which govern automatic processes like respiration and the circulation of the blood.

This lower half of the brain developed first in evolution and is often in conflict with the upper half known as the cerebrum. Modern psychologists and psychoanalysts attribute many of the neuroses so characteristic of civilized life to discoordination between the two main parts of the brain; to the subconscious or unconscious working at cross-purposes with the conscious. This wholly *natural* dualism within the brain that we have been discussing is the basis for numerous arguments claiming a *supernatural* dualism, in which the functioning of the cortex is explained in terms of a super-physical soul. The point to keep in mind is that whatever distinctions we make within the human brain or body, they are always distinctions within the same natural body; and that whatever distinctions we draw between man and other things, animate or inanimate, they are always distinctions within the same realm of Nature.

The dualists are led into further error by their misinterpretation of the profound difference between thinking as a process and any other process in man or Nature. The faculty of reason lifts man so immeasurably above all other things in the world that the dualists pay it homage by elevating it to a superhuman and supernatural plane. The monistic psychology, while recognizing the uniqueness of mind, holds that human thinking is as natural as walking or breathing, that it is indivisibly conjoined with the functioning of the brain, and that ideas, far from existing independently in some separate realm, arise and have reality only when a complex living organism such as man is interacting with the environment and is intellectually active. When ideas, which are non-material meanings expressing the relations between things and events, occur in human thought, they always do so as functions or accompaniments of action patterns in the cerebral cortex of a thoroughly material brain.

For the individual who is thinking to himself ideas are private and to that extent subjective. But ideas are also objective in that human beings can communicate them to one another and can understand one another's meanings, when these are adequately defined. The objectivity and non-materiality of ideas has been a strong factor in impelling philosophers of a dualist bent to set up a realm of ideas or mind apart from and above Nature. The monistic and naturalistic position is that ideas, whether simple or complex, trifling or noble, true or untrue, are not apart from but are *a part of* Nature. The experience of thinking or having ideas is *distinguishable* from men's other activities, but not existentially *separable*.

It is important to note that a dualistic psychology does not in itself guarantee a satisfactory immortality. A spiritual soul may do our thinking and constitute our personality, yet dissolve completely when it ceases to be associated with the body. Or, as Bergson himself has suggested, this soul, individuated through particular material bodies, may return to a vast impersonal ocean of consciousness where personal immortality would have no meaning and no status. Or it may return to the mind of God, but enjoy there no separate and individual self-conscious existence. The poet Shelley has exquisitely expressed such possibilities in his famous lines:

> *Life, like a dome of many-colored glass,*
> *Stains the white radiance of Eternity.*

But most of those who adhere to dualism also believe in the survival of the personality after death. And it is interesting to analyze the various ways in which they deal with such indubitable scientific facts as I have presented earlier in this chapter. These facts compel the greater portion of them to admit that the soul somehow uses, manipulates and expresses itself through the bodily organism. Sooner or later they are forced into a position similar to that proposed by William James, in his lecture on *Human Immortality*,[85] with the explicit purpose of making survival seem intelligible. James, accepting the general correlation of thought with brain activity and the general proposition that thought is a function of the brain, goes on to state that this function might be considered as *transmissive* rather than *productive*.

Steam is a productive function of the tea-kettle and light of the electric circuit, because the kettle and the circuit actually create these effects. A colored glass, however, a prism, or a refracting lens have only a transmissive function in respect to the light that shines through them, since they do not themselves create the rays. The same may be said of an organ, which transforms already existing air into music. In a similar fashion the human body may act as a transmission apparatus for the supernatural soul, which reveals itself in the tones and colors appropriate to earthly existence. In one form or another all immortalists who rely on dualism must come to a theory very close in essence to this, though they may differ with James as to the extent of brain-thought correlation.

However modern may be the terms in which such a theory is formulated, it does not escape certain fundamental difficulties that have always characterized the dualistic psychology. In the first place, it is impossible to understand how an immaterial soul can act upon and control a material body. In the seventeenth century Descartes tried to solve this problem by assigning to the soul, which was for him a separate immaterial and spiritual substance, a definite spatial locus in the pineal gland of the human brain. From that seat of vantage it was supposedly able to alter the direction of the animal spirits and thus determine the body to act in one way or another. But critics were quick to point out that if the soul physically touches and influences the body at one point, then at that point it must be extended and material. As might be expected in a world where apparently only a physical thing can act on a physical thing, the soul then itself becomes corporeal. And we find on our hands the doubtful blessing of a material soul like those ancient conceptions of it as an invisible and very subtle air, breath, fire or pneuma. Of course, those few dualists who frankly describe the soul as a form of matter or physical energy are exempt from the main criticism of this paragraph, though plainly enough there is plenty of mystery in their position.

If, however, one must be a dualist, it may be more intelligent to be a *materialistic* dualist. For if we ask *where* the soul is at any moment, we must admit that it is where the body is. When a ship carries our body across the ocean, when a train takes it across a continent, when an airplane flies with it into the clouds, our soul invariably goes along too. If a man is kidnapped and transported against his will to a distant place, his soul is not able to stay behind with friends and family, except in a metaphorical sense. And no matter how far we may travel in our dreams or how high we may soar in our imaginations, we know well enough that these are the dreamings and the imaginings of a particular self attached to a specific body situated in a definite place. Most of us have an unmistakable common-sense feeling that our self is somehow and somewhere within our body. At all events, whether the whole or a special part of the body is the seat of the soul, the soul has a spatial locus: it is very decidedly wherever the body is. But it does not make sense for an immaterial and separable soul to have a material and spatial locus.

Akin to the insoluble riddle of how the immaterial can be associated with and work together with the material is the question of how the immortal can be joined with the mortal, a soul that is by nature undying with a body that is by nature sure to die. "To link the mortal with the everlasting," says Lucretius, "and to think that they can feel together and act one upon the other, is but foolishness. For what can be pictured more at variance, more estranged within itself and inharmonious, than that what is mortal should be linked in union with the immortal and everlasting to brave raging storms?"[86] Even if the supposedly immortal soul can somehow enter into and achieve control over the body, will it not inevitably, through its close association with the corporeal and with the vicissitudes of temporal existence on earth, become tainted with mortality? It was such considerations as these, no doubt, that led Santayana to pen his epigram: "The fact of having been born is a bad augury for immortality."[87]

But the greatest trouble with the dualistic conception arises when, taking the living man just as he is, an effort is made to distinguish between those characteristics which belong to the soul and those which belong to the body; between those which will survive death and those which will not. The attempt to divide up in this manner either the emotional or intellectual faculties meets insuperable obstacles. A severe injury to the head, for instance, may change an ordinarily cheerful and amiable man into a sullen and morose one subject to sudden fits of homicidal mania. If the brain and body are simply the instruments of the soul, we have to say in such a case that this personality is really still brimming over with joy and benevolence, but that unfortunately these sentiments can only express themselves in dark glances, in peevish complaints and in violent attacks on people with canes and carving knives. On this basis it is quite possible that our best friends, who have always displayed the greatest affection and consideration, are actually boiling with hate and malice which some kink in their brains prevents them from putting into word or action.

Suppose now that a man becomes definitely insane, that he is convinced he is Napoleon and that he gives military orders to all whom he meets, and demands that they salute him. Are we to say that his real personality is still normal, that his soul is still thinking clearly and healthily, and that as soon as he gets rid of his body by dying he will come to his senses and realize that he is John Smith again? Can we accept the touching optimism of Mr. Feeble-mind in Bunyan's *Pilgrim's Progress* when, about to leave this earthly existence, he declares: "As for my feeble mind, that I will leave behind me, for that I have no need of in the place whither I go"?[88]

The dualistic defender of immortality holds with Bunyan, of course, that insane or feeble-minded persons would not continue in that condition in the afterlife. On the other hand, the immortalist would claim that others, such as great geniuses, who have deviated considerably from the average human mentality, *would* go on in the future existence bearing all their genius with them. In other words, if the intellectual powers of a man are far above the norm, the dualist gives full credit to the immortal soul; but if they happen to be far below the norm, then he blames the body and says that the mental defects in question disappear with death. Or if he goes so far as to admit that the body may permanently affect the mind, it is the good effects and not the bad effects of the body that are lasting.

On the other hand, where the emotions are concerned, the dualist is likely to condemn the poor soul for the natural needs and desires of the body. In religious circles this has been particularly true in regard to the matter of sex and has led to the most unhappy and unhealthy suppressions. Some dualists have tried to solve this problem of the emotions by making a distinction between those feelings engendered in the soul by the body and those which belong to it in its own right and will therefore survive death. But such an arbitrary separation seems to rest on no valid or workable principle and, if seriously put to a trial, results in unutterable confusion.

Let us take the example of a man who is born incurably blind as a further test of the transmissive theory. Is it reasonable to suppose that in this case the soul which is using the body as its instrument still has the potentiality of vision and that it will suddenly see perfectly when released from its earthly limitations? And if a man is deaf and dumb as well as blind, will the supposedly *real* personality that is ever lurking mysteriously behind the bodily screen all at once hear and talk in the realm beyond the tomb? In this connection we must ask why, if the soul carries over to that future life the advantages and experiences accruing from keen and healthy sense organs, it does not also carry over the disadvantages of deficient and diseased ones. Here again we cannot permit the dualist to have his cake and eat it too. It must be admitted that to ordinary common sense it does not occur, when a man goes blind or deaf, that he continues somehow to see and hear with spiritual eyes and spiritual ears in a supernatural realm. We deplore the unfortunate blindness and deafness of the man and leave it at that. Yet if instead of the senses being destroyed separately and gradually by disease or accident, they are all simultaneously destroyed by death, the dualistic immortalist asks us to believe that they will go on in some other state with unimpaired, if not greatly improved, capabilities!

The phenomenon of dissociated personality provides another good test for the transmissive hypothesis. It is a commonplace that human individuality never functions as a complete and perfect unity. We are all of us more or less split personalities, seldom wholly consistent in our attitudes and actions and continually falling below our own ideals and aspirations. Thus we talk, and with some justice, of our "better" self and our "worse" self. When the lack of integration becomes serious enough, there occurs what is called *dissociation* of the personality, in which part of the mental life exists independently of the rest. We receive hints of this phenomenon during fits of absent-mindedness, during dreams and during daytime reveries. It may become so far-reaching, however, that two or more entirely separate selves appear to be associated with the same bodily organism. In the famous "Doris Case of Multiple Personality,"[89] Dr. Walter F. Prince found that one woman possessed no fewer than five different personalities to whom he gave the names of Real Doris, Margaret, Sick Doris, Sleeping Margaret and Sleeping Real Doris, each of whom had her own characteristic behavior and consciousness. In the light of such phenomena Robert Louis Stevenson's fascinating story of *Dr. Jekyll and Mr. Hyde* takes on added significance.

But in such cases the dualistic transmissive idea is far from helpful. For it implies either that the "real" personality has broken up into different parts, thus destroying the unity and simplicity that was one of its proudest boasts; or that the dissociation is all the fault of the material brain tissue, the real personality remaining intact behind it with the assurance of regaining complete integrity of expression in the after-life. On the latter hypothesis the dualist is again, it seems, loading the dice for himself. That is, when the personality is functioning with normal integration, he attributes its unity to the supernatural soul (witness McDougall); but when there is serious dissociation, he absolves this soul from all blame and pins the entire guilt on the brain and the body. In instances of extreme and lasting dissociation it is also necessary to ask the dualist *which* personality is going on at death to immortal bliss. With the monistic psychology no such complications arise. The cause of dissociation may be primarily physical, primarily psychical, or a mixture of both. All of the personalities are equally real, though one may be predominant. And the reality of the once unified personality is not that it remains normal behind an abnormal brain, but that it has temporarily or permanently become separated into different parts, each depending on the same bodily organism.

These various test cases, which by no means constitute simply straw men set up to be toppled over, make very plain the hopeless entanglements into which the dualistic transmissive theory inevitably leads. The weakness of this theory also reveals itself in the very analogies employed to make it intelligible. If the human body corresponds to a colored glass or to a church organ, then the living personality corresponds to the colored light that is the result of the glass or to the music that is the result of the organ. Now while light in general will continue to exist without the colored glass, and air in general without the organ, the specific red or blue or yellow rays that the glass produces and the specific notes and music that the organ produces will certainly not persist if the glass and the organ are destroyed. But it is these specific rays and this specific music that correspond to the specific personality which is supposed to be immortal. And if we are strict with the analogy, the dissolution of the body implies just as complete an ending of the individual personality that was associated with it as the destruction of the colored glass and the organ entail an ending of the individuated rays of light and notes of music formerly transmitted through them. Of course, colored light and organ music will come into being again if a new lens or organ is provided and personality will do the same if a new body is supplied. But whereas a new lens or another organ will produce practically the same effect as the old, a new or different body will, as we know, result in a quite different and uniquely individual personality.

Other favorite analogies are to compare the soul and the body to music and a violin which may be broken, or to music and a radio that may be shut off. "Look at your radio set," one preacher seriously tells us. "Perhaps there is the clue to the mystery of life and death."[90] All such analogies, I believe, are misleading and prove specious on the slightest analysis. Indeed, if they demonstrate anything, it is the mortality rather than the immortality of the personality. For these musical analogies really define the soul as an attunement or harmony of certain material conditions. And as Simmias said long ago in Plato's *Phaedo:* "If the soul is only a harmony dependent on the proper admixture of bodily elements, it follows clearly that when the body (like the lyre) is either slackened or tightened out of due proportion by sickness or other mishap, then the soul, however divine it may be, like other harmonies in music and other works of art, must at once perish, although the bodily remains may last for a considerable time, until they are decayed or burnt."[91]

Thus a closer examination of the dualistic position only serves to reinforce that monistic view which the positive facts of modern science have already tended to establish. The more the psychology of dualism attempts to solve the obvious difficulties inherent in it, the more it raises problems that seem insoluble. But the monistic psychology, so much more simple and natural, while not purporting in its present stage to be able to describe in exact detail all the workings of the body-personality, does give on the whole a clear and satisfactory account of the activities of the complex human organism. And it does not run into or give rise to any irresolvable dilemmas. The implications of the monistic concept are very sweeping and far-reaching and touch many different fields of human knowledge and endeavor. Into the supporting pillars of traditional eschatology they cut very deeply and offer, to say the least, many intimations of mortality.

4. *Implications for Immortality*

It is more difficult than it otherwise would be to make clear the unified oneness of the personality-body or the mind-body because we have no appropriate word by which to designate this fact. If we used the simple phrase *the man* few would realize that we were referring to the living unity of the mind-personality-body. "Consequently," as Professor Dewey says, "when we discuss the matter, when we talk of the relations between mind *and* body and endeavor to establish their unity in human conduct, we still speak of body *and* mind and thus unconsciously perpetuate the very division we are striving to deny."[92] We are still using the verbal, if not the mental, habits based and built up on the assumption that mind and body are two distinct things and that one of them, the mind, is somehow *inside* the other. These same verbal habits I am compelled to utilize, for lack of a better vocabulary, in this book and in this chapter. In order that there may be no misunderstanding I wish further to quote John Dewey, who sums up brilliantly what I have been trying to express.

"When we take the standpoint of action," he writes, "we may still treat some functions as primarily physical and others as primarily mental. Thus we think of, say, digestion, reproduction, and locomotion as conspicuously physical, while thinking, desiring, hoping, loving, fearing are distinctively mental. Yet if we are wise we shall not regard the difference as other than one of degree and emphasis. If we go beyond this and draw a sharp line between them, consigning one set to body exclusively and the other to mind exclusively we are at once confronted with undeniable facts. The being who eats and digests is also the one who at the same time is sorrowing and rejoicing; it is a commonplace that he eats and digests in one way to one effect when glad, and to another when he is sad.

"Eating is also a social act and the emotional temper of the festal board enters into the alleged merely physical function of digestion. Eating of bread and drinking of wine have indeed become so integrated with the mental attitudes of multitudes of persons that they have assumed a sacramental spiritual aspect. There is no need to pursue this line of thought to other functions which are sometimes termed exclusively physical. The case of taking and assimilating food is typical.

"It is an act in which means employed are physical, while the quality of the act determined by its consequences is also mental. The trouble is that instead of taking the act in its entirety we cite the multitude of relevant facts only as evidence of influence of mind on body and of body on mind, thus starting from and perpetuating the idea of their independence and separation even when dealing with their connection. What the facts testify to is not an influence exercised across and between two separate things, but to behavior so integrated that it is artificial to split it up into two things."[93]

Maybe the real difficulty lies in the necessity of expressing ourselves through abstractions. The terms *mind* and *personality* are abstractions which we use, like *digestion* and *respiration*, to designate certain activities of the human being. Unfortunately our language habits make it dangerously easy to separate such abstractions from the original functionings that gave rise to them and then to treat them as if they were somehow independent and self-subsistent. Mind, like digestion and respiration, is not a separate agent or thing-in-itself, but is a particular type of doing, of activity on the part of a human being. Thought always signifies thinking; reason is always reasoning.

It is so evident that digestion and respiration are functions, primarily, of the stomach and the lungs respectively that it would at once seem absurd to imagine them as operating without these organs. But since the complete functional dependence of personality and mind on the body and brain is less generally known and accepted, it does not offhand appear so unreasonable to talk of them as if they existed minus their indispensable physical base. Perhaps, however, if people were as anxious to have their digestion and respiration immortal as they are to have their personality and mind, they would forget with equal facility the original relationship of digestion and respiration to stomach and lungs.

With these warnings against possible misunderstandings of terminology, it is legitimate to state that the data I have reviewed unmistakably testify to the fact that man is a unified whole of mind-body or personality-body so closely and completely integrated that dividing him up into two separate and more or less independent parts becomes impermissible and unintelligible. In other words, modern science convincingly sustains the fundamental principle of the monistic psychology. Perhaps no one science alone proclaims this conclusion; but the sciences that deal with man, taken together and as a whole, most certainly do create an overwhelming presumption in its favor. Again and again their findings have inexorably led to the proposition that mind or personality is a function of the body; and that this function is, if we pay attention to William James's distinction, productive and not merely transmissive.

Now function means, in the first place, the characteristic activity of any distinguishable entity. But there is an additional meaning of the term which has come to be uniquely significant in the methodology of modern science. When one thing is so related to another that it varies in some determinate way along with that other thing, then either thing may be called a *function* of the other. As between the body and personality, the body seems to be the prior and more constant entity whether we consider the process of evolution, the development of a man from conception to maturity, or the daily round of human existence, during which the personality or mind is for considerable periods asleep or unconscious while the body is as alive and real as ever. Accordingly, it has been customary to regard the body as primary and to call the personality its function rather than the converse.

This functional relationship I have established in four main ways, by showing: first, that in the evolutionary process the power and versatility of living forms increase concomitantly with the development and complexity of their bodies in general and their central nervous systems in particular; second, that the genes or other factors from the germ cells of the parents determine the individual's inherent physical characteristics and inherent mental capacities; third, that during the existence of a human being from childhood to youth and from adulthood to old age, the mind and personality grow and change, always in conjunction with environmental influences, as the body grows and changes; and fourth, that specific alterations in the physical structure and condition of the body, especially in the brain and its cerebral cortex, bring about specific alterations in the mental and emotional life of a man, and conversely that specific alterations in his mental and emotional life result in specific alterations in his bodily condition. Thus, all in all, such a close and far-reaching functional relationship has been proven to exist between personality and body that we can hardly conceive of them as other than an inseparable unity. There can be no divorce between them; they stand in intimate and unbreakable wedlock, for better or for worse, till death them do part—by destroying both.

Another methodological tool of modern science that is of paramount importance for the question at issue is the *law of parsimony* or economy of hypothesis. This law requires that any scientific explanation be based on the fewest possible assumptions necessary for it to account adequately for all the facts involved. The basic principle was first formulated in the fourteenth century by the English philosopher, William of Occam, in the words: "Entities [of explanation] are not to be multiplied beyond need." This fundamental law of parsimony expresses negatively the scientific rule that every hypothesis must meet the requirements of affirmative empirical proof before being accepted. The principle of simplicity of hypothesis does not deny the truth that Nature often operates in a most complex manner; and under no circumstances can it override the observed facts of such complexity, as, for instance, in the organization and functioning of the human body. The law means only that we should not bring in hypotheses unnecessarily to explain a situation, whether it happens to be comparatively simple or comparatively complex.

For example, since Copernicus had no new facts with which to confirm his heliocentric hypothesis, the initial advantage of his theory, that the earth revolved around the sun, over the Ptolemaic theory, that the sun and other heavenly bodies moved around the earth, lay in the reduction of separate assumptions from seventy-nine to thirty-four. This was a sound use of the law of parsimony on the part of Copernicus. Later Newton made an immense improvement over him by accounting for the movements of the earth and heavenly bodies by *one* law of gravitation. Yet even today, with a great many more astronomical facts at our disposal, it would be possible to fit them into Ptolemy's scheme of a motionless earth as the center of the universe, *if* we added a sufficient number of new assumptions.

Another good instance of the meaning of the law of parsimony is provided by a controversy that Galileo had in regard to the mountains which he discovered on the moon. An opponent attempted to refute him by suggesting that the apparent valleys of the moon were filled with an invisible crystalline substance. Galileo answered by saying that if this were so, it was probable that the moon had on it mountains of this same invisible substance at least ten times as high as any he had observed! The reason why Galileo's reply is so effective is that it brings out the point that if we once start disregarding the law of parsimony, as his critic did, then we issue a general invitation to ridiculous hypotheses and impossible vagaries *ad infinitum.* *

Now the particular significance of the law of parsimony for the argument between the monistic and dualistic psychologies is that it makes the dualist theory distinctly superfluous. It rules out dualism by making it unnecessary. In conjunction with the monistic alternative it pushes the separate and independent supernatural soul into the limbo of unneeded and unwanted hypotheses. I have previously described in outline form the extraordinary complexity of the human body, its gradual evolution through hundreds of millions of years, and the infinite intricacy of the structure underlying the intellectual and emotional activities of human beings. In view of these facts it is surely not rash to claim that no supernatural soul is required to explain the great and varied achievements, powers and potentialities of man illustrated in every age and clime throughout the vast panorama of history. For the personality, which usually receives the credit for these things, is in truth hardly more remarkable than the body which is its base.

Yet it is this phenomenal and at the same time wholly natural body evolved through countless ages that the immortalists expect to be resurrected in the twinkling of an eye after total dissolution and decay; or to be adequately substituted for in the hereafter by some vague kind of spiritual or etheric body mysteri-

---

* For a twentieth-century example of such an hypothesis, let us consider the claim that flowers grow healthily because fairies secretly minister to them during the hours of darkness. This thesis is supported by Sir Arthur Conan Doyle, who became a Spiritualist in his later years. In his book *The Coming of the Fairies* (Hodder, Toronto, 1922), there are submitted alleged photographs of the fairy folk at work. I am of course an admirer of Sir Arthur's stories of Sherlock Holmes; and I believe that his account of the fairies also belongs purely in the realm of the imagination.

ously appearing out of the blue with no explanation and no history. Some of our theologians even have the audacity to call in science itself in support of these extravagant speculations. Professor John Baillie of Edinburgh University writes: "Do not the biochemists tell us that even in the present life there is an almost complete renovation of our bodily tissues within each seven-year period, so that there is no material but only a formal identity between the body I now have and the body I had seven years ago? The change to a heavenly embodiment would no doubt be of a still more radical kind."[94]

"Radical" in this connection is a mild word indeed. As if there were any valid comparison between the natural processes of continuity and gradualness that bring about changes in the human organism, and the supernatural operation needful, after the sharp and total break known as death, to produce from a decaying corpse a whole and healthy other-worldly body of unlimited powers! Dr. Baillie's little illustration from science is on a par with that other biological demonstration of immortality that relies on the example of caterpillars becoming butterflies, of which proof Voltaire remarked that it was not more weighty than the wings of the insects from which it was borrowed.

Applying now the law of parsimony to the particular function of thinking, we perceive that the complexity of the cerebral cortex, together with the intricate structure of the rest of the nervous system and the mechanism of speech, makes any explanation of thought and consciousness in other than naturalistic terms wholly unnecessary. If some kind of supernatural soul or spirit is doing our thinking for us, then why did there evolve through numberless aeons an organ so well adapted for this purpose as the human brain? If the brain, together with the rest of the body, is merely the instrument of an other-worldly soul, then this soul must be itself of immense complexity in order to direct the infinitely complex brain-body. But what could be more wasteful and contrary to the law of parsimony than to have the natural complexity of the brain-body duplicated on a supernatural plane?

There is no good reason for calling upon two separate and distinct entities to do a job performable by one. And if a God stood behind the scenes guiding the process of evolution, would he not have acted on this principle? For as the English philosopher, John Locke, shrewdly remarked, it is "not much more remote from our comprehension to conceive that God can, if he pleases, superadd to matter a *faculty of thinking*, than that he should superadd to it *another substance with the faculty of thinking*."[95] The extraordinary thing is that there should be thinking at all, not that a material body should be the medium of that thinking.

We must also ask: If the highly involved activity of thinking is not the function of the brain, then what *is* its function? And since the regular functioning of the brain, whether during concentrated thought or otherwise, demands and consumes physical energy, and even emits electrical charges, is it reasonable to suppose that something entirely other than the brain is doing all or most of the work? In pre-scientific days supernatural entities used to be assigned to all the forces of Nature in order to explain their activity; trees could not grow on their own account, nor streams flow, nor thunderstorms rumble. Souls, anima or individual gods were read into these purely natural phenomena as the moving principles behind their manifestations. In those times, too, metaphysical souls were attributed to the liver and the heart; while it was thought that diseases, especially insanity and hysteria, were caused by devils and demons entering into the human frame.

The more modern custom is to attach an other-worldly soul to the brain and to claim that this entity, coming like devils and demons from a mysterious realm beyond time and space, is the agent of thought. No one would dream of suggesting that a special stomach-soul is needed to explain the leading part that the stomach plays in digestion with its millions of cells displaying a cooperative wisdom that no council of chemists could equal; or that a special lung-soul or heart-soul is needed to explain the respective processes of breathing and blood circulation. And there seems to be very little more reason for postulating a brain-soul as well as a brain to explain the singular powers of thought native to human beings. It would indeed be surprising if while every other organ of the body performed its own inherent function without aid or support from any supernatural source, the brain, the most remarkable and complex organ of all, had to be activized by an extraneous spirit from a mysterious beyond.

If we turn to an examination of the laws of heredity and embryological growth, we reach similar conclusions. According to orthodox Christian doctrine God creates a human soul at the moment of or shortly after conception. This supernatural soul by some miraculous means then enters into the very essence of the embryo and itself acts, instead of the scientifically established genes, as the chief carrier and director of the characteristics of personality. But if this is so, then the generally accepted biological facts which I have cited simply do not make sense. For they seem to show convincingly that there is no need or opportunity for an other-worldly soul to take part anywhere in the proceedings. When, how and why does this enigmatic entity from another realm break into the never-halting sequence of natural cause and effect? Just as the finished human body is so infinitely complex that its development requires no explanation outside of itself and its surroundings, so the human embryo, intricately constructed and nurtured in a most sensitive and responsive environment, calls for no supernatural aid or interpretation. And to human parents, it seems, there belongs the full dignity and privilege of creating the whole of a child, soul or personality as well as body.

Let us suppose, however, to make a slight digression, that soon after conception a soul from on high enters the embryo, but that the embryo dies at the age of one month when in structure it closely resembles the embryo of any mammal. What kind of immortality can the soul of such an embryo be conceived to have? Yet how can it be conceived not to have immortality if souls are in general separable from bodies and if the souls of human beings in later stages of development are guaranteed a future life? Is it not illogical to attempt to draw a line anywhere in the life of a human being at which immortality, if there is any at all, shall be denied? St. Augustine and other noted churchmen have carefully considered this question.

Says Augustine, talking about abortions: "Who will dare to deny, though he may not dare to affirm, that at the resurrection every defect in the form shall be supplied, and that thus the perfection which time would have brought shall not be wanting?" And he goes on to explain that if a human being dies, "wheresoever death may overtake him, I cannot discover on what principle he can be denied an interest in the resurrection of the dead." He tells us, furthermore: "We are not justified in affirming even of monstrosities, which are born and live, however quickly they may die, that they shall not rise again, nor that they shall rise again in their deformity, and not rather with an amended and perfected body."[96] Clearly Augustine is not enthusiastic about the immortality of aborted embryos and of monstrosities; his common sense tells him that this cannot be. Yet he realizes that the logic of the Christian position demands that it shall be.

Indeed, in spite of a small group of immortalists who assert that only a chosen few shall attain a future life, the logic of Christianity demands that *every* human individual shall be immortal, whether living eighty days or eighty years after conception, whether monstrous or normal, whether sane or insane, whether a genius or a moron. And this logic applies, furthermore, not only to all the Christians, all the Mohammedans, all the Buddhists, all the atheists, all the Americans, Europeans, Chinese, Indians, Eskimos and others—approaching three billions *in toto*—who are alive on earth today; but likewise to all the millions and billions of men—Cro-Magnons, Neolithics and the rest—who have ever lived since *Homo sapiens* made his first appearance on this terrestrial globe thousands of centuries ago. But if this staggers the imagination, let us reflect that if all the countless generations and types of men are immortal, there is no legitimate basis on which to deny life eternal to the predecessors of *Homo sapiens*—to Neanderthal Man, to Homo Heidelbergensis and to Pithecanthropus Erectus—and to the super-apes that preceded them.

But the pageant of immortality cannot end here, for biology forces us to raise the same sort of question in regard to animals. If the living soul and body of man and sub-man are separable and the soul goes on after death, then must not this also be true in the animal kingdom, to which man, as evolution demonstrates, is so very closely related? Certain twentieth-century moderns, following the example of primitive peoples, are sufficiently invincible in their consistency to give an affirmative answer. If there is an after-life for an infant who dies at the end of ten days, then surely there ought to be one for good old Towser who was for ten years a well-loved, sociable and devoted member of the family. Many Spiritualists are confident of meeting animals and particularly dogs in the beyond. And if one visits the Hartsdale, New York,

Canine Cemetery, one finds that others, too, have borne witness to their faith in the survival of pet dogs, cats and canaries by the most touching and sentimental gravestone inscriptions.*

If, however, we grant immortality to the higher and more congenial forms of animals, such as dogs, cats, birds, horses and elephants, then on what logical basis can we deny it to rats, snakes, jelly-fish, house-flies and hornets? And since there is no hard and fast boundary between animal and vegetable life, how then can we rule out immortality for poison-ivy and pota-toes, for the beautiful flowers and the noble trees? Such conundrums are not gratuitous; they have to be answered. It is patently absurd to expect that all the myriad specimens of all the myriad species of life from the beginning of evolution are to go on existing forever in another world. Yet we are led into just such absurdities when we once start relying on the dualistic theory that man has an immortal soul or personality that can exist independently of the body.

* There follow a few characteristic inscriptions of this kind:

Grumpy: Our Loved one

His Sympathetic Love
And Understanding
Enriched Our Lives.
    He Waits for Us.

Rolls—My Darling, 1919-1926

List'ning from afar
Watching at the bar
Ready for his welcome
For me when I go home.

My adored Zowie

I do not cringe from death so much
Since you are gone my truest friend
Thy dear dumb soul will wait for mine
However long before the end.

Returning to the law of parsimony, we should further note that while it is of extreme importance in the establishment of individual facts, it is of equal importance in bringing such facts into an understandable and harmonious relationship with one another. Thus, "as between two theories each of which accounts for a certain group of facts, that one is to be accepted which accounts for them in such a way as to bring them into unity with as many other facts in other fields as possible, so that the mind may be able to embrace and control the largest mass of fact in terms of the fewest necessary assumptions."[97] Newton's law of gravitation, for example, as explaining the motions of the earth, sun and stars was the more acceptable because it also held for all other material bodies as well, in this manner linking together under one great principle things both terrestrial and astronomical. This extension of the law of parsimony, if applied to the monistic psychology, considerably strengthens it. For this particular psychology harmonizes beautifully with the other branches of science such as biology and medicine, physics and chemistry, where supernatural forces and occult entities have long since been banished.

Logically enough, the growing strength of the monistic view in modern times has been accompanied by a steady and increasing trend away from the dualistic psychology. This tendency has been reflected in a number of ways. In philosophy it has been apparent in the decline of the metaphysical Dualism that has usually gone hand in hand with psychological dualism; and in the rise of Hegelian Idealism, naturalistic Humanism and various versions of naturalism and materialism. All of these great systems cleave to a monistic psychology of one kind or another. And for this reason even the Idealists, sympathetic as they have been towards traditional religious viewpoints, have found it most difficult to make room for immortality. Indeed, there has been an internecine conflict in their camp over this very question. Of course, the other systems mentioned all definitely rule out the notion of a future life.

Throughout the entire history of philosophy the dualistic theory, regardless of the advance of science, has always caused extreme difficulty. It has meant the postulation of an agent soul or mind somehow attached to the body and somehow doing man's thinking for him. Thence it is an easy and common step to denominate this mind as the supernatural container and manipulator of all a man's ideas. Subjective ideas become the objects of the mind instead of objective things. There then develops an insoluble mystery as to how the ideas in one's mind can have any relationship to the outside world and how they can possibly be trustworthy as guides to action. Having started out with souls and ideas that belong to another realm, we are faced with the problem of how to bring them into an intelligible relationship with our this-earthly realm. So, led astray by an unworkable theory of knowledge, we find ourselves lost in the unending maze of modern epistemology, hopelessly pursuing the logic of a misbegotten argument through Locke, Hume, Berkeley, Kant, Hegel and the rest. And all this turns out in the end to be mainly the result of assuming at the beginning a dualistic psychology.

In religion as well as in philosophy the monistic implications of modern science have had very far-reaching effects. These implications have been influential in leading certain Protestant theologians to postulate all sorts of future-life bodies as vehicles for the immortal soul; and have encouraged special cults like the Spiritualists, the Swedenborgians and the Theosophists to make similar speculations. Spiritualism, especially, has made its bow to the monistic principle by offering abundant testimony purporting to show that spirits after death activize themselves through very real and very material bodies. The dear departed announce their presence by such physical feats of prowess as blowing tin trumpets, throwing about tambourines, beating drums, whistling, rapping on tables, moving furniture, kicking college professors in the stomach, pulling the hair of world-famous psychologists, taking over the vocal organs of mediums, leaving their thumb-prints in wax and having their photographs snapped by earthly cameras. It is no wonder, considering the unsubstantiality of the bodies which the Protestant Modernists promise and the strange whimsicality of the bodies which the Spiritualists bring forth, that the monistic findings of modern science have in some quarters strengthened the orthodox Christian belief in a resurrection of the natural body as the only safe, sound and sane route to the realm of immortality.

But this orthodox reliance on the resurrection is not really of very much assistance in making personal immortality seem plausible. For though formally and at first glance the resurrection concept, by promising a man that he will get back his former body, may appear to be consistent with a monistic psychology, in actuality it is not. This is because monism declares that it is the human personality and its *natural* body which are one and inseparable, and therefore implies that the *supernatural* body of the resurrection is not acceptable. Thus, while the resurrection theory comes a certain distance in the direction of the monistic principle by requiring *a* body—and one much more like the old one than any other theory allows—it seriously violates that principle by the *kind* of body it provides.

Furthermore, since the resurrection is yet to take place, some provision must be made for the long intermediate period between death and the rising of men from the grave. Here traditional Christianity has to resort to a psychology just as dualistic as that of Plato or the Protestant Modernists. And this is why one of the most acute thinkers of the early Renaissance, Pietro Pomponazzi, whose daring treatise, *On the Immortality of the Soul*,[98] was burned in Venice by the civil and religious authorities, expressed surprise that Thomas Aquinas and the Catholics did not declare for Platonic dualism outright instead of trying to be both dualists and monists at the same time.[99] In any case traditional Christianity is forced to bestow either explicitly or by implication some sort of body on the immortal soul during the intermediate state. Presumably this intermediate body must be somehow shuffled off or absorbed when the soul becomes united with the resurrection body.

Yet even should we overlook the mass of contradictions in the Catholic and Fundamentalist doctrine of the intermediate period and disregard the initial violation of the monistic psychology in the resurrection, who with any instinct for reality can possibly believe in this day and age in a literal resurrection of the discarded and decayed this-earthly body, dissolved into a myriad of particles of dust or ashes, or scattered in its component elements over the face of the earth or throughout the depths of the sea or become, by means of the economy of Nature, an integral part of the bodies of new living forms and persons? As for the alleged resurrection of Jesus Christ, there are any number of hypotheses based entirely on natural cause and effect that could account for the report. And it is to be remembered that the myth of the resurrection is just the kind of fable that might be expected to arise in a primitive, pre-scientific society like that of the ancient Hebrews.

If the resurrection doctrine is so weak a foundation on which to build an adequate immortality, what of the supposedly more intellectually respectable theories of etheric and spiritual bodies? Here again we find a concession to the monistic principle in the admission that some sort of body is essential, but again a violation of this principle in that the fate of the natural, this-earthly body is ignored. And when we consider the inexpressible complexity of the natural body and its brain, the age-long history and world-wide background of this organism in the processes of evolution, the complicated manner of its development from each conception to each maturity, and the delicate environmental balances necessary for its ordinary existence, then the substitute supernatural bodies offered by the Modernists, the Spiritualists and the others seem the most woefully inadequate of make-shifts and the most manifestly desperate of remedies.

If with any one of these proposed bodies we compare the promised resurrection body, taken in itself alone, in all soberness we must say that there is more likelihood of the latter coming into being and acting as a competent vehicle for the personality. Psychologically, moreover, the restoration of that very body with which we once walked the earth must always appeal more to our sense of imaginative reality than an unknown and unseen spiritual or etheric body. And also a literal resurrection seems more of a triumph over death: a man may die, but he does not *stay* dead. The promise that the grave shall open and the resurrected man emerge counteracts that forceful symbol of death constituted by burial beneath the ground. The Spiritualists, however, and the other modern immortalists really acknowledge the actuality of death; and all their guarantees of beautiful other-worldly bodies cannot offset that admission.

Since, then, immortality in the modern mode is even less acceptable than the old-time, outworn resurrection type, and since it is evident, too, that these and all other theories of personal survival violate the tenets of the monistic psychology and lead us into the most unreasonable extremes, we cannot do otherwise than give up entirely the idea of immortality. It now becomes clear that monism in psychology, insisting as it does on the intimate and indissoluble unity of body and personality, *ipso facto* rules out the possibility of a life beyond the grave. Though this psychology happens to be the prevailing one in scientific circles today, its adherents rarely mention its implications for immortality. Of course, from the standpoint of science, immortality remains outside the pale until it is affirmatively established beyond all reasonable doubt; the burden of proof is on the immortalist.

But I feel justified in advancing beyond the obvious and widely accepted proposition that survival after death is *un*proved. I would go considerably further than this and suggest that modern science, in establishing the monistic view on a firm basis, might even be said to *dis*prove the idea of immortality; just as in affirming the soundness of the evolutionary concept it disproves the theory of the separate divine creation of each species; and just as in showing insanity to be due to natural and ascertainable causes it disproves the notion that possession by devils accounts for this disorder.

In their book, *Religion and the Modern World*,[100] Dr. John H. Randall and Professor John H. Randall, Jr., write that "there is no room for an immortal spirit in man's frame that can leave its earthly habitation to dwell in any heavenly habitation beyond the limits of Space-Time. . . . It is not that any scientific faith could conceivably disprove such possibilities; it is rather that it makes them irrelevant. The man who thinks in terms of modern psychology simply does not entertain the notion of an immortal soul; it does not figure among his concepts." Now what we wish to emphasize is that when science and scientists treat the notion of an immortal soul in the way that the Randalls have accurately described, there is precious little difference between such an attitude and one which openly states: "We have disproved the notion of an immortal soul." If the idea of such a soul is as irrelevant in psychology as the idea of devils is in medicine, then to all intents and purposes immortality has been disproved just as much as possession by devils.

A defender of immortality says: "Nobody ever saw a dead soul; and till he sees the phenomenon, a physiologist ought in conscience to refrain from proclaiming the soul's mortality."[101] And still another immortalist tells us: "A negative presumption is not created by the absence of proof in cases, where, in the nature of things, proof is inaccessible."[102] If science proceeded on the basis of such statements, it would make little progress. Who ever saw a dead fairy, a dead devil, a dead centaur? Yet for lack of this seeing do most intelligent persons refrain from stating that such things exist only in the imaginations of men? And since Galileo's opponent was unable to obtain proof of invisible substances on the moon because in the nature of the case such proof was inaccessible, was Galileo called upon to let this hypothesis pass unchallenged? How indeed, then, can we be sure that invisible spirits, imperceptible to every sense, are not moving our hand when we write or that they are not the real cause of the match bursting into flame when we strike it against the box? There are literally millions of fantastic hypotheses, "where, in the nature of things, proof is inaccessible." And when we once cease to apply the law of parsimony, we fling open the door to all of them.

It is sometimes argued that since science, like religion, must make ultimate assumptions, we have no more right to rely on science in an analysis of the idea of immortality than on religion. Faith in the methods and findings of science, it is said, is just as much a faith as faith in the methods and findings of religion. In answer to this we can only say that the history of thought seems to show that reliance on science has been more fruitful in the progress and extension of the truth than reliance on religion. Furthermore, the assumptions of science conform with reason and are consistent both with one another and with the practical, everyday life of men. In accepting the assumptions of religion one has to adopt only too often the attitude of the eminent Church Father, Tertullian, who asserted: "It is certain because it is impossible."[103] And modern theologians, while gladly accepting the empirical results of science in the form of mechanical inventions and up-to-date medical techniques, inconsistently refuse to apply to their own field the scientific methods and assumptions that have brought about these advances. In any case we have no hesitation in stating that our approach to the question of immortality is primarily through science and through the enlightened common sense and logical analysis that go hand in hand with it. In short, our appeal is to the supreme court of human reason.

Now reason or intelligence at its best and most successful is essentially synonymous with modern scientific method. And there can be little doubt that modern science, supported and interpreted by the methodological instruments of functional analysis and the law of parsimony, and buttressed by the insistence of supernatural religion upon the need of some future-life body and by the implications from a dualism unmistakably in distress, renders a compelling verdict in favor of the monistic psychology as the only one in agreement with the evidence. Testifying always and everywhere to the union, one and inseparable, between the personality and the body, the monistic view stands today as one of the greatest achievements in the history of ideas.

Implicit in this monistic psychology is a denial, if not a disproof, of human immortality. This denial covers not only all those conceptions of the hereafter as a place ethically and hedonistically worth-while, but also notions, like those of the Old Testament Hebrews and the Homeric Greeks, which postulate an after-existence that is worse than useless. While, then, men cannot reasonably hope for any paradise or haven of blissful recompense beyond the grave, they cannot reasonably be fearful of any hell or bottomless pit of torment or of any gloomy Sheol. All in all, therefore, the findings of science, coupled with my earlier analysis of various immortality ideas, establish a very powerful case in support of our thesis that immortality is an illusion.

CHAPTER IV

THE ENVIRONMENT OF HEAVEN

1. *The Modern Dilemma*

IF VERY serious difficulties are inherent in the attempts of the immortalist to provide the personality with an adequate after-life body or vehicle of expression, equally serious ones are to be found in the endeavor to furnish the personality-body with a proper environment in the hereafter. That environment is, of course, a necessity; for the surviving personality must do something and it cannot be expected to function as a doer in a total vacuum. Moreover, what it does and the general background of its doings must be described sufficiently to seem worth-while and imaginable to the average man. For it is impossible to escape the fundamental consideration that survival must be of a certain *kind* if it is to be desirable, or even bearable. In ancient times, as we have seen, the repellent after-existence notions of peoples like the early Hebrews and the early Greeks taught this lesson well; in modern times there have been any number of persuasive legends and satires that repeat it.

The best of these is Jonathan Swift's account in *Gulliver's Travels* of the poor immortal Struldbrugs who form part of the population of Luggnagg. When these Struldbrugs "came to four-score years, which is reckoned the extremity of living in this country, they had not only all the follies and infirmities of other old men, but many more which arose from the dreadful prospects of never dying. They were not only opinionative, peevish, covetous, morose, vain, talkative, but uncapable of friendship, and dead to all natural affection. . . . Envy and impotent desires are their prevailing passions. . . . And whenever they see a funeral, they lament and repine that others are gone to a harbour of rest, to which they themselves never can hope to arrive. They have no remembrance of anything but what they learned and observed in their youth and middle age, and even that is very imperfect. . . . The least miserable among them appear to be those who turn to dotage, and entirely lose their memories."[104]

Now if the world were completely populated with beings like the Struldbrugs, we can be sure that a great religion would be built up around the hope of absolute death and a Messiah who would come to promise it. The moral of Swift's tale is repeated in the story of Ahasuerus, the undying and unhappy Wandering Jew, in Tennyson's poem "Tithonus," and in Hamlet's famous soliloquy on "To be, or not to be." It is a moral that no one who weighs the matter of immortality can ever afford to forget.

Let us cite a few examples of immortality descriptions that have served to convince believers that the world beyond is a real and concrete place worth going to. The ancient Egyptian abode of the dead reproduces with a wealth of detail the Egypt of this world. The everyday implements of life, the social customs, even the black fields and the broad River Nile are all duplicated beyond the grave. The Mohammedan paradise, lasting monument to the sensual imagination, is a realm filled with sparkling streams and shady groves, brilliant flowers and luscious fruits, soothing music and beauteous virgins clad in transparent robes. The Scandinavians of old immortalize their love of fighting in the halls and courts of Valhalla. There the warrior spirits take delight in battling one another all day long, while at night, with every wound healed, they banquet at a luxurious feast.

In China the custom long existed of burning paper replicas of horses, rickshas, boats, houses and other objects of daily existence, in order that the soul of the deceased should enjoy the other-worldly counterparts of his this-worldly needs. Recently even paper automobiles were sometimes included. This ceremony is a symbolic refinement on the primitive practice of "killing" useful things by breaking or burning them so that their "souls" will be released for the enjoyment of the deceased. In the well-known Happy Hunting Ground of certain American Indian tribes the emphasis is put on deer, buffalo, and fresh-water fish as ever-present accompaniments of the ever-successful chase. According to Burmese notions, the spirits of the dead build bungalows in the after-life country and devote themselves to the cultivation of rice. And among certain African tribes the resemblance between this world and the next is so complete that the latter is divided into countries, towns and villages corresponding to those on earth.

The Eskimos conceive of the hereafter as a place where the sun is never obscured by night and where reindeer, walrus and other Arctic animals abound forever. When missionaries tried to win certain of the Eskimos to belief in the Christian paradise, the latter made what must be considered the retort classic: "And the seals? You say nothing about seals. Have you any seals in your heaven?" "Seals? Certainly not. What would seals do up there? But we have angels and archangels, we have cherubim and seraphim, Dominions and Powers, the twelve Apostles, the four-and-twenty elders." "That's all very well, but what animals have you?" "Animals none. Yes, though, we have the Lamb, we have a lion, and eagle, a calf . . . but not your sea calf; we have—" "That's enough; your heaven has no seals, and a heaven without seals cannot suit us!"[105]

For Christianity in general we have only to refer

to the vivid and realistic portrayals of the life beyond in Dante's *Divine Comedy*, the broad schema of which still constitutes the core of Catholicism. And many other medieval artists, plastic as well as literary, gave almost equally sweeping and colorful representations of the hereafter. There was very little in the intellectual atmosphere of the Middle Ages to throw question on such portrayals. Indeed, such natural science as existed, especially the generally accepted Ptolemaic and Aristotelian astronomical views of the period, supported in literal fashion the artists' soaring imaginations. The ·common notions of the heavenly bodies enabled the faithful of that day to assign spatial locations to both heaven and hell as definite parts of the physical geography of a diminutive, bandbox universe. During the Middle Ages also, in accordance with good Greek precedents, the heavenly bodies were looked upon as unquestionably and infinitely superior to the lowly earth, whence the identification of *higher* with *better* which persists to this day. The spheres above knew no real change, since their life and motion were perfect and eternal. They therefore offered the most fitting possible home for all immortals.

The Copernican astronomy, degrading the heavens to the level of the earth and thus raising the earth to the level of the heavens, created a real problem for the immortalist. Later developments were equally disconcerting. The most distant stars or nebulae turned out to be governed by the same laws as the earth and the planets, to be composed of terrifically hot and flaming gases, and to be thousands of light-years away. Thus in all the vast reaches of the sky there appeared to exist no possible spot intrinsically superior, or even suitable, for a heaven. And even if there were, how, in the face of the law of gravitation, resurrected bodies or any other kind would get there, became a perverse mystery. In addition, the new science undermined the idea of locating hell beneath or inside of the earth, since it declared that the world was round and its interior far from hollow.

Ideas of time as well as of space contributed to a firm and easy faith in immortality on the part of the early and medieval Christians. The mythical biology and geology of pre-scientific days were very helpful here. When the longest length of time conceived was that of the supposed age of the earth and of the human species—widely accepted well into the nineteenth century as less than 6,000 years—eternity and immortality did not symbolize incomprehensibly and terrifyingly long time-spans. And when the end of the world was ever imminent, the prospect of the Last Judgment did not seem remote and tenuous. Although the idea of an earthly cataclysm close at hand had its greatest significance among the Christians of the first centuries A.D., even Dante gave creation but five hundred years beyond his day. "We have come," he said, "to the last age of the world."[106] But with the rise of modern science such notions, along with the old astronomy, went for educated men into the museum of outmoded theological antiques.

These brief references to the progress of thought since the flowering of Dante's genius bring out clearly the dilemma in which many modern immortalists find themselves. They can no longer describe the realm of immortality with the hearty and unquestioning naiveté of yore, if their descriptions are to retain intellectual respectability. It is true that twentieth-century Spiritualists do not hesitate to utilize the stellar regions as the homeland of the departed, and to map out a celestial geography overlooked in the reports of astronomers. These same Spiritualists reproduce earthly life in the hereafter with all the detail that characterized, for example, the old Egyptian accounts. But to an ever-increasing proportion of present-day immortalists such representations smack both of absurdity and a rather gross materialism. Their tendency is to refine the older and cruder conceptions of a future life to the greatest degree still consistent with belief in a worth-while survival of the personality after death. This means that they actually describe the hereafter as little as possible and that their meager descriptions lose, of course, the imaginative concreteness of former portrayals. In this policy they follow the example of the eighteenth-century German philosopher, Immanuel Kant, who concentrated on proving immortality as a postulate of the moral law and wasted scarcely a word in *describing* it.

These modern prophets of man's destiny would like to define immortality simply as "the survival of the human soul after death" or "the continuance of personality beyond the grave" without explaining exactly the meaning of "soul" and "personality" or the content of "survival" and "continuance." Warns one writer: "Even in skillful hands definitions may kill the subject they define. A dead faith is not of much service to you, and therefore, it is clear to me that he who must defend his faith in immortality must avoid killing it at the outset by chopping off its head."[107] Professor Pratt quotes a believer in personal immortality as follows: "To hold this faith without picturing the nature of the future life I find impossible, but I manage with ease and naturalness to keep those mental pictures in a flux, as it were, making them the poetry of my faith without giving them the definiteness which would challenge my own scientific criticism." No wonder that Professor Pratt comments: "This man's position is the wise one for most people who desire to keep their faith"; and "many people find that their belief in immortality is strongest when they think least about it."[108]

"As to the question of personal immortality I . . . do not worry over the details, but confidently leave the matter to God,"[109] says Professor Cornill. Dr. Harry Emerson Fosdick writes: "What lies across the sea, he [a man of faith] cannot tell; his special expectations all may be mistaken; but his insight into the clear meanings of present facts may persuade him beyond doubt that the sea has another shore."[110] "I believe," asserts Dr. Charles R. Brown, formerly Dean of the Yale Divinity School, "that personal consciousness survives the shock of that physical episode we call death. As to the conditions or employments of that future life, I have no conception whatever."[111] To support such statements certain passages from the Bible are frequently cited, such as St. John's, "It doth not yet appear what we shall be,"[112] and St. Paul's, "Eye hath not seen nor ear heard, neither have entered into the heart of man the things which God hath prepared for them that love Him."[113]

But our analysis has made plain that it is essential that at least *some* of the "details," "conditions," and "employments" of the future life should now appear and be with certainty foreseen; and that at least *some* of our "special expectations" should not be mistaken. That is why, however vague he may be on the particulars of the hereafter, Dr. Fosdick insists that immortality must mean more than mere everlastingness, that it must possess a certain high quality which transforms it from "bare immortality" to "eternal life." "Immortality is merely going on and on. Eternal life is having a kind of life so radiant in meaning that it is worth going on with. Immortality is mere continuance of existence. Eternal life is quality of experience."[114] That is why Dr. Henry P. Van Dusen asserts: "Concerning the nature of life after death we know practically nothing save one thing—and we want to know only one thing—that it is good."[115] It is why Dr. Lyman Abbott, after hazarding that the after-existence will be a "spiritual" place, writes: "For the rest, I neither know nor wish to know what the future life has for me. . . . I am sure that He whose mercies are new every morning and fresh every evening . . . has for me some future of glad surprise which I would not forecast if I could."[116]

A comparison of these statements with the after-life portrayals of ancient and medieval times sets for us in its most general terms the dilemma of the modern immortalist: How are descriptions of immortality to be sufficiently specific to make the hereafter imaginatively real and emotionally efficacious without at the same time becoming intellectually unacceptable and spiritually profane?

2. *Attempted Solutions*

It is enlightening to examine some of the formulae proposed by modern immortalists as a way out of the dilemma we have noted. Dr. William Adams Brown, for instance, recognizes the serious difficulties involved "when we seek to make real to ourselves the conditions of existence in the undiscovered country."[117] But he is more adventurous than Dr. Fosdick and Dr. Van Dusen and Dr. Abbott. For he goes on to say: "One conclusion certainly would seem to follow, that life then as now will be one of progress. There will still be new lessons to be learned, new battles to be fought, new experiences to be gained, new services to be rendered. It will not be a life of stagnation, but of activity, not of monotony, but of change." For children and backward souls "surely, the life hereafter must mean growth in knowledge and character." Indeed, "the crowning argument for immortality" is "that we need limitless time to satisfy the needs of the limitless spirit."

In the life to come, as here, "we shall have to do with conditions that are constantly altering. There too, as well as here, we shall be members of a society that is ever facing new problems, ever calling for new consecration. There too, as well as here, we may be sure, there will be lessons to be taught as well as learned, help to be given as well as received, experiences to be shared as well as enjoyed. . . . It is as true of the life to come as of the life that now is, that, if it is to be Christian, it must be a life of service. . . . Whatever qualities mark the character of Christ during His earthly life must reappear in our thought of our own future. Like His, our life must be one of filial trust. Like His, it must be one of brotherly service."

The attitude of Milo H. Gates, former Dean of the Cathedral of St. John the Divine, is also instructive. He admits that no one can describe heaven, but nonetheless expresses in the same sermon the opinion that "there are certain features of it perfectly evident. First, heaven is a place of harmony, its atmosphere is melody; second, it is a place of joy; third, it is a place of vision—we shall see as we are seen; next, it is a place of glorious reunion with those who have gone before—the great souls of all ages; lastly, it is a place of union with God and our Saviour."[118] Canon Streeter gives a similar kind of description when he sums up heaven as a place where there is Love, Work, Thought, Beauty, Humor and the Vision of God.[119] These smooth generalities of Dr. Brown, Dean Gates, and Canon Streeter concerning the hereafter are typical of what the modern immortalist says on the subject. And if Dr. Fosdick were called upon to define exactly the qualities which constitute "eternal life" and Dr. Van Dusen the content of "good" and Dr. Abbott the meaning of "glad surprise," they would be forced to make statements, if not identical with, at least as sweeping as those of Dr. Brown, Dean Gates and Canon Streeter. The latter have simply expounded the implications of what the former have said.

But what of the implications that follow from the assertions of this latter group of divines? Have not they, too, left much unsaid which is necessarily implied by what they have said? "Suppose," writes Dr. L. P. Jacks, considering this very matter of implications, "suppose we were credibly informed, by any means you choose to imagine, that a rose, a single flower fully formed, had been discovered on the planet Mars. How science would leap to her feet on receiving the information! From that single fact she could reconstruct the general characteristics of the flora of Mars, with the greatest ease and almost infallible certainty. A planet which can produce a rose must be able to produce ten thousand other things from the same conditions, and science could tell us in general what they are. Not the flora alone but the fauna would be involved. And beyond all that the fact would expand into a mine of information concerning the climate, the soil, the atmosphere, the seasons, and what not. We may say, with little exaggeration, that the whole planet would give itself away by letting out the single secret that it contained a rose. . . . A rose which survives in another world without a tree, without air, and without sun, is not a rose at all, but something else called by the same name; still less can it be the identical rose that grew in my garden yesterday."[120]

Let us apply Dr. Jack's method to the statements of Dr. Brown, Dean Gates, and Canon Streeter. An *active, fighting* and *working* personality-body surely implies an environment of resisting and cooperating forces. Activity does not go on in a vacuum; fighting does not go on without obstacles; working does not go on without materials. A "life of service" and "progress" with "new battles" and "new problems" in a "society" implies beings to be helped, causes to be espoused and ever-recurring difficulties to be faced. Indeed, such phrases definitely locate a certain amount of evil in the hereafter. "Growth in knowledge and character" implies natural continuity. There must be continuity not only within that unseen realm beyond but between it and this earthly plane of existence. Such continuity is basic to personality as we know it or can imagine it, because continuity is fundamental to the functioning of memory; and memory, as I have pointed out before, is essential to our awareness of self-identity through periods of time.

Change, growth and *progress* also imply successive stages in the career of an individual entity, animate or inanimate. Besides, therefore, connoting natural continuity, individuality and potentiality, these terms clearly imply natural durational time. The simplest definition of them entails the passage from one point in time to another, even if the change is confined to a succession of inward mental states. The most common synonym for immortality, namely, "the future life," points even more explicitly to clock-time. That life has a definite beginning—after death—though it has, to be sure, no definite ending. Plato, the Buddhists and the Hindus seek to avoid this entrapping of the soul in durational time by postulating a pre-existence with no beginning whatsoever. But this ingenious device is not convincing; for the very fact that the personality is born into the natural world, lives there, acts there, departs there at some specific moment, seems to entangle it inextricably with ordinary time. Nor is it possible, when the implications of descriptions point in the opposite direction, to escape durational time merely by fiat—by declaring dogmatically that the flow of experience in the future life occurs in a completely different kind of medium.

Professor Pringle-Pattison subtly analyzes the situation: "Duration," he insists, "is an essential element in any notion we can form of reality; and we must clothe the thought of immortality in the language of time, if the meaning is not to evaporate altogether. If we try to avoid this necessity by speaking of an 'eternal now,' a 'timeless present,' we must convey into that 'now' the feeling of 'that which was and is and ever shall be': otherwise it shrinks to the abstraction of a mathematical point. The attempt to discard the durational form becomes in the end an affectation, which betrays us into a negative position actually falser . . . than the popular crudities against which it is a protest."[121] Proceeding with our implications, it is easily seen that durational time itself necessitates a whole world-order. In recent scientific and philosophic thinking the old concept of an Absolute Time existing in and of itself has given way to the theory of a relative time which is an attribute of the unceasing event-series of the universe. Thus time becomes a quality of something more basic, the existence of which is therefore implied whenever time is present. Hence the bare existence of immortality as meaning life everlasting in a time sense, as meaning survival after death, implies a world-order very like that of our natural, this-earthly one, particularly in respect to including bodies in motion.

As to Dean Gates's assurance that the hereafter is a place "of glorious reunion with those who have gone before," this rather important detail has its own set of implications which we previously outlined and also illustrated with the Blake drawing. As we saw, if we are to recognize in the future life those who have gone before, they must be in forms definite and familiar. Indeed, all who go to the other world, we who come later as well as the earlier arrivals, must have the necessary equipment for recognition and reunion. This means not only visible and substantial forms, but the ability to see and hear, to speak and touch. And this means something very similar to sense organs. Finally, then, we come to realize that the body of this earth must be reproduced in all essential particulars. In this way the implications from two different directions meet and support each other: durational time implies bodies and space; active bodies attached to immortal personalities imply space and time. And bodies, whether animate or inanimate, will correspond to matter or to something very much like it.

Our whole study of the implications of immortality descriptions by modern churchmen can be summed up and brought to a head in the following statement of Professor Georgia Harkness: "Admitting frankly the impossibility of applying space imagery to a non-spatial world, we must stop trying to picture its nature *in any detail*. Some probable things about its nature we can derive from thought; such as continued personal identity with continuity of memory stretching over from this life, freedom from hampering physical limitations, the power to recognize and communicate with others, love and friendship, opportunities for growth, a chance to serve, and the conservation and increase of values attained in the earthly life. These possibilities are far more important than anything sense imagery could give us, and all of them follow from the nature of personality and the purpose of its preservation."[122] [*Italics mine*—C. L.] The fact that Professor Harkness evidently thinks that she has succeeded in not picturing the future life "in any detail" makes quite clear both the dilemma and the position of an important group of modern immortalists.

From such inferences as I have been drawing there is one suggested escape to which the modern immortalist frequently resorts. When he is pressed concerning the exact meaning or implications of his statements about the hereafter, he may say that his words must be taken in a "symbolic," not a "literal," sense. They must be understood "spiritually." For example, the term "body" should be thought of as "no more than a mere symbol" of our belief that, in some way at present inconceivable, spiritual values such as individuality, the power of mutual recognition, love and the capacity for ethical action will be preserved. Our immortalist goes on to say that he is attempting the difficult feat of portraying another world in inadequate this-worldly terms. At best, his descriptions must fall short of the reality, as when we find no language competent to describe the deeper feelings and experiences of our present life. It is the same stand as that of Socrates in the *Phaedo* when he stated: "A man of sense ought not to say, nor will I be very confident, that the description which I have given of the soul and her mansions is exactly true. But I do say that, inasmuch as the soul is shown to be immortal, he may venture to think, not improperly or unworthily, that something of the kind is true."[123]

This explanation of the immortalist is understandable; yet it often leads to confusion on the part of both himself and his audience. For both are liable to forget that if descriptions of the hereafter are to be taken symbolically, they are not at the same time to be taken literally. If "eyes" in the next world means "spiritual eyes" and "light" means a "spiritual light," a "mystic light," or a "light that never was on sea or land," then "eyes" and "light" do not mean at all what they do on this earth. These words cannot mean at the same moment *both* what they mean ordinarily and what they may be supposed to mean in a supernatural future. In relation to immortality, however, this difference in the meanings of the same words is not always kept clear; it is only too likely that "eyes" interpreted symbolically will retain much of the meaning of "eyes" as the most valuable sense equipment of mortal man.

Words are more than sounds, and are liable to carry with them the associations and atmosphere of their usual context. Furthermore, still another difficulty arises in interpreting immortality descriptions symbolically: the nature of that which is symbolized is totally unknown. Unlike ordinary symbols and metaphors, those of the immortalists do not and cannot refer to anything within our experience—unless, like Santayana, we take them as symbols of this-worldly values, needs and desires. Thus the temptation and tendency become even greater to fall back on the customary meanings of whatever words are employed.

To sum up, what the religious liberals or Modernists in effect do is to abstract certain values and activities from the natural world and transplant them to a supernatural one, setting them up there as self-existent and self-supporting. They leave behind the rich soil and complex conditions which buttress these goods in their original state, thus giving to them a "misplaced concreteness," to use Professor Alfred N. Whitehead's phrase. Even when conceding the need of the personality for a body, these modern immortalists tend to provide little or no environment for the surviving combination through fear of seeming absurd. They transform the immortal personality into a self-sufficient thing-in-itself, giving to it no home save a benign hope. And they present pale theories of immortality, using large words in order to escape from their quandary. Yet our accounting indicates that, in spite of considerable care, the Modernists actually imply in their descriptions much, and indeed most, of what they have discarded as naive and untenable in other portrayals.

3. Where Logic Leads

It might be better to do as the Catholics and the Fundamentalists, as the Spiritualists, the Swedenborgians and the Theosophists do—to give the personality unhesitatingly a body and the personality-body a complete environment. It might be preferable to acknowledge openly and finally the truth of Santayana's claim that "a future life is after all best represented by . . . frankly material ideals." For, "It would evidently have to go on in an environment closely analogous to earth; I could not, for instance, write in another world the epics which the necessity of earning my living may have stifled here, did that other world contain no time, no heroic struggles, or no metrical language. . . . If hereafter I am to be the same man improved I must find myself in the same world corrected."[124] Those groups which accept Santayana's suggestions are able to depict, in twentieth-century terminology, as varied and vivid a future life as could Dante in the images appropriate to medieval times. This means that their representations are bound to be superior in regard to emotional efficacy and imaginative reality. And these immortalists also have the advantage of clarity, since they know exactly what they mean and for the most part do not indulge in symbolic interpretations of immortality descriptions.

Consider for a moment the after-life of the Spiritualists, a place "like the earth with all its imperfections perfected and its beauties multiplied a thousand-fold."[125] Reveals Raymond, Sir Oliver Lodge's dead son, speaking from the Spiritualist beyond: "Everything that is necessary to man, everything that man in a sense makes his own, has an etheric duplicate. We see the etheric duplicate. . . . It may be that the chair you see at home, your material chair, and the chair that we see, which is your chair on our side, the etheric chair, are one and the same thing really. . . . You can mold an etheric body for a thing—a piano, a clock, a desk—by loving it and liking to have it with you."[126] This theory of etheric duplication enables the Spiritualists to look forward to a very up-to-date after-existence in which they can enjoy all the conveniences of modern technology and presumably even the wonders of atomic energy.

The Spiritualists, more than any other group, follow through with inspiring audacity the implications of personal survival after death. And one of the chief reasons for the hostility of the Christian Church towards them is that they discredit the idea of immortality by being so uncompromisingly literal and logical about it. The Spiritualists accept fully the saying that "if ghosts have clothes, then clothes must have ghosts." They grant immortality not only to personalities and their bodies and the garments that must clothe these bodies—for whoever heard of a nude spirit?—but to all the other good and necessary things of this earth as well. They supernaturalize and transform to another realm all the useful material objects of this-worldly existence, so that the etheric body of the immortal personality finds itself quite at home among all sorts of other bodies just as does the natural body in the mundane sphere. But even the Spiritualists are not altogether consistent. For instance, though there are sex distinctions in the after-life, the relationship between men and women there is to be purely intellectual and spiritual. And while there is marriage between true soul-mates, no children are ever born. Thus sex will exist, but without its usual emotions and consequences.

The question of sex in the after-existence has always been a perplexing problem for immortalists of every sect. The skeptical Sadducees, it will be remembered, confronted Jesus with this very problem. "There were with us," they said, "seven brethren: and the first, when he had married a wife, deceased, and, having no issue, left his wife unto his brother: Likewise the second also, and the third, unto the seventh. And last of all the woman died also. Therefore in the resurrection, whose wife shall she be of the seven? for they all had her. Jesus answered and said unto them . . . in the resurrection they neither marry nor are given in marriage, but are as the angels of God in heaven."[127]

Whatever Jesus may have meant by this reply, the orthodox Christian Church, like the Spiritualists, has not hesitated to perpetuate sex distinctions in the future life. And of course the resurrection of the former natural body makes this result inescapable. St. Thomas Aquinas and the Catholics are, however, careful to point out that just as there will be no eating, drinking and sleeping in the hereafter, so there will be no begetting. Although, then, the sexual members will be without use, they will not be "without purpose, since they will serve to restore the integrity of the human body."[128] That virtually no immortalists in the Christian West have ever made a place in the great beyond for the glories of full and unqualified sex love seems to be a sad commentary not only on their logic, but on their standards of what is good and beautiful.

Another question that almost all immortalists neglect, intentionally or unintentionally, is that of race and color in the hereafter. Will Negroes be black in heaven and Chinese yellow and the Indians of India brown? The general assumption in the Christian West seems to have been that the prevailing color in the after-life is white. But as that engaging play, *The Green Pastures*, indicates, there are those among the Negroes who believe there are black folk in heaven as well as on earth. And one can well understand why those who take pride in their race should deem it fitting and natural that its outstanding characteristics should have a place in the future life. How would white racists feel if they should awake in the beyond with the racial characteristics of peoples whom they have always considered inferior? Then, too, there is the matter of recognition. If the departed are to know one another in the next world, it will not do to have their skins too different in color from those they had on earth. And in general if there are to be in the realm of immortality bodies, solidity, motion and sound, no good reason is apparent why the quality of color should not exist there too.

These observations well bring out the fact that it is the constant practice of immortalists to make room in the hereafter for certain biological *goods* such as sex (without its sinfulness), flowers and the more congenial animals, but to ban the real and supposed biological *bads* which ordinarily seem to be necessary accompaniments. The outstanding example of this is the elimination of death, allegedly the greatest and worst of all biological evils. We must ask, however, whether death itself is not implied in the rather complete reproduction, either implicit or explicit, of earthly existence in most descriptions of immortality. Biologists, recalling the valuable role played by death in evolution, would have some especially salient remarks to make in this regard. But a sound philosophy of value may have something even more important to say, namely, that the values to be preserved in the realm beyond are values characteristic of *mortal* life.

Thus Professor C. J. Keyser in his most suggestive essay on "The Significance of Death" writes: "Temporal finitude of life is essential to its worth"; and "were it not for death, if life did not end, if it were a process of infinite duration, it would be devoid of the precious things that make us long for everlasting perpetuation. . . . All the sacred values that constitute life a priceless boon are subtly bred in the all-pervasive sense of temporal finitude. Death is not the tragedy of life; it is a limitation of life, essential to its beatitude; the tragedy is that, if it were not for death, life would be void of worth."[129] Santayana comments in his inimitable way: "The dark background which death supplies brings out the tender colors of life in all their purity."[130] Patently, then, the immortalist engages in the questionable procedure of transferring the values appropriate to mortal lives to a realm where all lives are immortal, and in the questionable expectation of their remaining the same values with the same significance.

That the implications of such immortality descriptions as those analyzed in the previous section should lead inevitably to reproductions of earthly life as complete as those of traditional Christianity and Spiritualism is not very helpful to Dr. Fosdick, Dr. Brown and like-minded clergymen. The revelation that many of the old-time theological crudities are implicit in their own portrayals of the hereafter places them in an embarrassing position. If they try to refine much further their conceptions of a future life, they will refine that future life out of existence entirely. As it is, the picture which they present of the immortal personality and its environment is so unsubstantial and thinly colored that it does not appeal to the masses of the people. On the other hand, these Modernists are not so lacking in education or a sense of humor as to fall back on the notions of orthodox Christianity and Spiritualism. It is no more possible for them to accept intellectually the resurrection, as it were, of practically the whole material world than the resurrection of the human material body.

There is one thing, however, that these Modernists in religion could do, although it would be a drastic step. They could follow through faithfully the logic of the situation and give up altogether the idea of a hereafter. For I submit that a careful analysis of the problem of a proper future-life environment, when conjoined with an analysis of the proposed future-life bodies and of the merits of the monistic psychology, makes belief in immortality today an intellectual anachronism.

CHAPTER V

THE FAILURE OF EVIDENCE
AND ARGUMENTS

1. *Concerning Spiritualists and Others*

IN THE face of such considerations as we have submitted in the last three chapters, what kind of reply can the partisans of immortality offer? They have two main lines of defense: first, the appeal to empirical evidence; second, the appeal to arguments. It was the alleged rising of Christ from the tomb and his ascension to heaven that provided the early Christians with what seemed to them incontrovertible testimony in favor of personal immortality. The resurrection of Christ was taken by the Church to be as definite and certain an historical fact as the crossing of the Rubicon by Caesar. It was the one outstanding and overwhelmingly convincing piece of supposed empirical evidence available for belief in immortality. And the orthodox faithful have treated it as such century after century and right up to the present day.

But as we have already noted, the growth of modern science, its manifold discoveries in the fields of biology, psychology and anthropology, and its general displacement of miracle by law, led many modern religious thinkers to question and surrender the idea of Christ's literal resurrection from the grave.* Possible

---

* Even granting the resurrection of Jesus, its significance for men in general has been questioned on the ground that Jesus was the Son of God and, in one sense, God himself; and that therefore what happened in his case carries little weight for ordinary humans.

explanations for the resurrection story readily come to mind. Jesus might have been taken from the cross and buried, apparently dead but actually in a state of suspended animation; his dead body might have been taken away from the tomb by his followers and deposited elsewhere; his disciples might have permitted their imaginations and desires to get the better of them in insisting that they saw him and talked with him subsequent to his death. After all, the appearance of ghostly apparitions among the living has been one of the most common, though always unverified, claims put forward by the credulous throughout the history of mankind.

The presumed historicity of Jesus' resurrection, like that of his virgin birth, is explainable, furthermore, as a natural although unjustified deduction from his magnificent character, from the love and devotion he awakened and from the way he so deeply moved all manner of men. The impact of such a great and appealing personality on a rather primitive culture established just the sort of psychological situation in which reports of miracles and superhuman accomplishments might be expected to take root. Myths of the kind which we find in the New Testament have, of course, by no means been confined to the career of Jesus. Plato, Alexander the Great, Roman emperors, Christian saints, Indian mystics and many others have shared like honors. The resurrection motif itself, with a sacrificial divine saviour slain for the redemption of the living and then mounting to heaven in triumph, was a frequent one among the pagan peoples of the ancient world. In any case David Hume's classic formula for the testing of miracles is decidedly applicable to the alleged rising of the dead Jesus: "No testimony is sufficient to establish a miracle, unless the testimony be of such a kind that its falsehood would be more miraculous than the fact which it endeavors to establish."[131]

No other "evidence" comparable in influence and effect has manifested itself to offset the widespread loss of faith in Christ's bodily resurrection. From time to time, self-anointed seers and mystics have aspired to the role of St. John the Divine in the Book of Revelation and have announced with due solemnity to the world the results of their private, first-hand glimpses of the glories of heaven and the terrors of hell. Emanuel Swedenborg, Swedish philosopher and mystic of the eighteenth century, may be taken as a typical case. According to Swedenborg, the Lord opened heaven to his direct view in the year 1710. Thenceforth, for thirty-five years, Swedenborg was able to converse with angels and spirits, to witness in vision the Last Judgment and the second advent of Christ, and to report in considerable detail on the nature of existence in the realm of immortality. Though the followers of Swedenborg founded a new religious sect, the New Church, with some influence in Europe and America, the doctrines of this cult have never captured the imagination of any important or numerically powerful group of the religious-minded.

Historically connected to some extent with the Swedenborgian movement, but offering what purports to be evidence of a future life far more weighty and empirical, are the divers varieties of Spiritualists and psychic researchers.* Their experiments have resulted in an imposing amount of what appear to be at least supernormal phenomena and have constituted real contributions to the field of abnormal psychology. But their findings have not carried a great deal of

* It should be noted that on the whole the Societies for Psychical Research are more scientific in their methods and more restrained in their conclusions than the Spiritualist groups. Among the psychic researchers are many who do not agree that the theory of personal survival is the best explanation of the strange and uncanny facts which they have uncovered; and others who do not think that *any* explanation so far offered is satisfactory.

conviction as proving the survival of the dead. The phenomena that occur are one thing, while the interpretation given to them as establishing immortality is another. Such phenomena are not characteristic simply of recent times, though only in recent times have they been recorded with any considerable degree of accuracy. As a matter of fact, ghosts, clairvoyancy, appearances at a distance, telepathy, conversing with apparitions, a sense of the presence of the dead and many other such occult occurrences have been variously reported as far back in history as the mind of man can reach. The hypothesis of existence beyond the grave has traditionally been a favorite explanation of these wonders. But today, as in the past, that suspiciously easy and sweeping hypothesis is subject to the very gravest doubts by all who have respect for scientific method and objective thinking.

No scientist worthy of the name considers an hypothesis proved until it is shown beyond all reasonable doubt to be the only possible explanation of the phenomena under examination. The Spiritualists, however, are very far from having demonstrated that the hypothesis of personal survival is the sole and certain explanation of the data they have gathered. In the first place it is generally admitted, even by leading Spiritualists themselves, that a very large proportion of the results obtained are contaminated by conscious or unconscious fraud on the part of the mediums or others participating. To the ordinary layman it will always seem suspicious that most of the Spiritualist experiments must be carried on in darkness or with very dim lighting and that the greater part of them have been repeated in broad daylight by professional magicians such as Harry Houdini[132] and Joseph Dunninger.

This is not to imply that all the performances of mediums can be reduced to the art of expert magicians or that some mediums do not possess the most extraordinary psychic powers. Undoubtedly, some of the things that mediums do are at present not wholly explicable according to any known scientific laws. But if a detective in a murder case is unable to find the murderer, he does not at once claim that a ghost must have committed the crime. And the Spiritualists are surely not justified in calling in supernatural spirits so promptly to explain even the most baffling phenomena. This is equivalent to the argument from ignorance, to saying that because we do not for the time being know the exact cause of a phenomenon, therefore it must be due to the influence of the dead.

There can be no doubt that much of what goes on during the séances of the Spiritualists can be understood in terms of purely naturalistic modern sciences such as abnormal psychology, religious psychology and psychiatry. For example, the common occurrence of a supposedly departed spirit taking control of a medium's mind or vocal apparatus and issuing thereby all sorts of statements seems to be closely akin to what happens in the case of dissociated or multiple personality. There is a temporary submergence or splitting off of the medium's normal personality and an arising from the psychic depths of a strangely unfamiliar and different personality. The process may be entirely unconscious; but the secondary personality speedily learns to play its role with singular skill, carries over from the normal state clews of knowledge suitable for its purposes and is quick to make the most of hints dropped by those present during its period of activity.

Studies of human dream-consciousness, of hypnotic trances, of hysteria, of epilepsy, of high-fever delirium and of the regular patients in mental hospitals suggest that the behavior and revelations of the ordinary medium have natural rather than supernatural causes. The additional fact that, for various reasons, close to four-fifths of the mediums or "Sensitives," as they are sometimes known, are members of the female sex is likewise not without significance. Two or three centuries ago such women were burnt as witches. And the witchcraft hypothesis is in a number of ways just as sensible as the Spiritualist interpretation.

Also, what is revealed through the medium is ordinarily so much a part of the regular furniture of the average mind that we hardly need resort for explanation to the talkative inhabitants of some other world. That communications from the beyond are, in general, so earth-bound and conventional is accounted for by the Spiritualists on the ground that it is very difficult for the departed to transmit complex and coherent messages about their new circumstances. But if immortal souls can dictate pages and pages of detailed description concerning the future life, showing how very similar it is to this one; if they can get across tedious two-volume dissertations on the higher philosophy and metaphysics; if they can produce, through the automatic writing of a medium, whole books of plays and poetry signed by spirits purporting to be Shakespeare, Shelley* and other great literary geniuses; if they can do all this, the excuse of the Spiritualists does not appear to be very substantial.

For if the best minds of the other world can deliver themselves of such lengthy remarks, often complicated though almost always commonplace, there

* Recently Mrs. Shirley Carson Jenney, who calls herself a Clairaudient Psychic, sent me an inscribed copy of her book, *The Fortune of Eternity* (1946), the contents of which Mrs. Jenney claims were dictated to her from "over there" by the spirit of Percy Bysshe Shelley. It is painful to report that the prose and poetry attributed to Shelley fall considerably below the quality of what he wrote when a struggling, earth-bound mortal in the early nineteenth century.

A few years ago a New York publisher was somewhat embarrassed to receive a manuscript entitled "The Autobiography of Jesus," allegedly dictated to the author from heaven by the spirit of Jesus.

seems to be no good reason why they should not be able to make real contributions to human knowledge and to the solution of earthly problems, especially since they are supposed to have grown in wisdom since their sojourn here below. And if spirits can, as claimed, locate lost jewelry and sundry knick-knacks for friends and relatives still on earth, then surely they should be able to clear up for the police at least a few unsolved murder cases in which their bodily counter-parts were the victims. Yet no criminals have as yet been apprehended in this manner. And desperadoes continue to operate successfully on the basis of the age-long assumption that dead men tell no tales.

But assuming for the sake of argument that the medium actually gets in touch with and transmits from a source that objectively and independently exists outside of her own conscious and subconscious mind, does this necessarily indicate that she has come into contact with an immortal soul? Considering how freakish and mischievous are many of the communica-tions and physical manifestations that occur at sé-ances, the hypothesis that impish and non-human demons or elfs are the cause is not without merit. The traditional belief of the Church in diabolical possession, still held in many quarters, is possibly more plausible than the theories of the Spiritualists. Or perhaps the medium is dipping into a great im-personal sea of consciousness or reservoir of memory that holds the psychic life of the past and of every deceased individual intact within it. It is also well known that human beings radiate energy and it has been suggested that somehow mediums sense and interpret the enduring traces of human vibrations which have left their mark on material objects and in familiar places. This might also account for the appearance of apparitions to persons of especial sensi-tiveness. But these apparitions would no more be conscious and organized personalities than are material reminders of dead persons in the form of photographs.

It is possible, too, that mediums might be in touch with faintly surviving personalities which go on for a time beyond death but gradually fade out completely. A temporary after-existence of this sort is hardly the same as the life everlasting of immortality. Or, as Mr. H. G. Wells suggests, perhaps there is survival of *fragments* of personal will and memory. "Suppose," he writes, "a medium to produce some trivial secret between myself and some departed intimate known to no one else; that no more proves that my friend is still mentally alive than a corrupting fragment of his face, with a characteristic scar, would prove his bodily survival."[133] Professor Broad, the English philosopher, proposes a similar theory. He believes that there may be a persistence after death of a "psychic factor" formerly an element in the living personality of the deceased. This "mindkin," as he calls it, "may become temporarily united with the organism of an entranced medium."[134]

In those rare instances where the medium reveals something concerning the life of the departed about which she apparently could not possibly have known, good guesswork and coincidence are, as in the case of other Spiritualist phenomena, much-neglected hypotheses. Then there is always to be considered the hypothesis of telepathy or mind-reading in relation to living persons who were acquainted with the deceased or had some knowledge of his career. And the theory of telepathy is adequate even if the medium comes forth with some verifiable intimate detail that could have been known only to the dead man himself. For previous to his demise, the fact in question could have been transmitted by means of unconscious telepathy either to the medium herself or to the mind of someone else from whom she could later take it. Telepathy is also a possible explanation of the often-reported

appearance of phantoms of the living, especially of
those who are going through some terrible experience
or who are on the point of dying. It is sometimes
argued that the existence of telepathy, which has by
no means been proved scientifically, would in and of
itself create a presumption in favor of personal survival on the ground that mind was transcending so
remarkably its ordinary powers. But this would seem
on a par with stating that the existence of wireless
telegraphy and radio communication creates a presumption in favor of the hypothesis of an interchange
of long-distance messages without proper and thoroughly material sending and receiving sets.

Other possible hypotheses that might account for
extraordinary psychic manifestations are those of
cryptesthesia (a hidden or sixth sense), clairvoyance
and extra-sensory perception. In the United States
since the early thirties investigations by Professor
Joseph B. Rhine at Duke University into extra-sensory
perception have given rise to something of a flurry in
academic and intellectual circles. Dr. Rhine claims to
have proved extra-sensory perception through experiments in which selected subjects identify, far more
frequently than the statistics of chance allow, different designs on the faces of cards in a pack of twenty-
five by looking at each card, with its face down, as it
lies on top of the deck.[135]

But many competent psychologists seriously question both Dr. Rhine's methods and his results. For
instance, he does not always use cards which are
beyond all doubt opaque, he eliminates subjects who
score low averages and he refuses to experiment with
cards on which, without the subject's previous knowledge, the symbols have been changed or replaced by
blanks, because he does not want to "deceive" his
friends. Moreover, other psychological laboratories in
America and Britain have not been able to confirm
the Duke experiments. We must conclude, therefore,

that whatever the implications of extra-sensory perception for ideas of immortality, it has not been scientifically demonstrated.[136]

Returning to the matter of telepathy, we may note that if an individual mind can produce effects on another mind over distance in terms of space, then it may well be able to do so over distance in terms of time. The observations of Professor J. B. S. Haldane in this connection are most pertinent. "Even," he says, "if we accepted the view of the Spiritualists that a medium can somehow get into communication with the mind of a dead man, what would this prove? If we accept Spiritualism we must certainly accept telepathy. Now, I can see little more difficulty in two minds communicating across time than across space. If I can transmit thoughts to a friend in Australia today, that does not prove that my mind is in Australia. If I give information to a medium in the year 1990, ten years after my death, that will not prove that my mind will still be in existence in 1990. To prove the survival of the mind or soul as something living and active we should need evidence that it is still developing, thinking and willing; Spiritualism does not give us this evidence."[137]

But even if the Spiritualist findings be taken as reliable testimony of an after-existence for the personality, the kind of future life indicated and the methods used to establish it are far from agreeable to the great majority of immortalists. The reasons for this are not difficult to discern. The whole atmosphere surrounding the Spiritualists' attempt to prove empirically a hereafter is likely to repel the sensitive and reverent immortalist. The common taint of fraud, the unpleasant odor of sensationalism, the inevitable association with morbid emotionalism, combine to create a general impression that this is not exactly a movement for the truly religious and high-minded. For not a few there is something inherently undignified in dear departed grandfather's indulging himself in table-rapping, playing weird tunes on cheap musical instruments or telling the secrets of his past to strange women mediums. For others, the whole business is deplorable because it gives over to public gossip the most intimate of private affairs.

As to the nature of the immortality promised by the Spiritualists, it was William James, long a most sympathetic student of psychic phenomena, who wrote: "The spirit-hypothesis exhibits a vacancy, triviality and incoherence of mind painful to think of as the state of the departed."[138] The great English scientist, Thomas H. Huxley, held a similar opinion. "Supposing the phenomena to be genuine," he declared, "they do not interest me. If anybody would endow me with the faculty of listening to the chatter of old women and curates in the nearest cathedral town, I should decline the privilege, having better things to do. . . . The only good that I can see in a demonstration of the truth of 'Spiritualism' is to furnish an additional argument against suicide. Better live a crossing-sweeper than die and be made to talk twaddle by a 'medium' hired at a guinea a séance."[139]

George Santayana makes the telling suggestion that the communications of mediums imply "that same ghostly, dismal, and helpless sort of survival which primitive men have always believed in. It is not so much another life as a prolonged death-rattle and delirium."[140] These reactions to the Spiritualist reports are typical of thoughtful people both within and outside the ranks of organized religion. The matter may best be summed up by saying that to the average immortalist the Spiritualist activities, methods, findings and descriptions of the hereafter seem distinctly gross and unspiritual; and that they make the Spiritualist immortality appear not in the highest sense worth-while.

Other evidence is sometimes adduced for immortality which can hardly be classed as more than semi-empirical, since it consists only of subjective personal experiences. For example, Dr. Minot Simons asserts: "Hosts of people experience a strange illumination which comes when they are brought personally close to the meaning of death in the loss of someone dear to them, whose vigor of life and whose strong, lovely and noble qualities of character have made a deep impression upon them. Before they had such an experience they may have been complacently skeptical about immortality, but now, to imagine the end of such vital and significant qualities is quite impossible. . . . The whole country had such a spiritual experience in the death of Lincoln. He was killed on a Good Friday evening. On the following Easter Sunday morning there was a mighty incoming tide of faith that such a personality could not have an end. . . . In the Great War the whole world had such an experience with death on a vast unprecedented scale."[141]

Dr. Clarence C. Little's statement is to be compared: "The death of my own parents within a day of one another completely wiped out pre-existing logical bases for immortality and replaced them with an utterly indescribable but completely convincing and satisfying realization that personal immortality exists."[142] Granting at once that, among the living, moving personal experiences follow death, the question again arises in regard to such testimony, what is the *meaning* of those experiences? Do they necessarily imply that there is immortality; or indeed anything else than that the loss, especially if sudden, of persons who are loved and admired comes as a tremendous shock to all the living who may be concerned?

Another approach to the matter of survival that is hard to classify is based on the claim that immortality must exist because there has been universal acceptance of the idea. In fact, while the belief in a worth-while hereafter has certainly been widespread during all periods of recorded history, there have been many individual dissenters and important culture groups, especially in recent centuries, that have taken no stock in the notion.* The argument is in any case a most feeble one, since universal belief in a proposition by no means proves it to be true. We have only to recall that there was once a fairly universal belief in the flatness of the earth and in the existence of magic.

The growing inability of modern minds to believe in the resurrection of Jesus Christ, the weakness and inappropriateness of the mystical and Spiritualist testimony in favor of a future life, and the inconclusive and indeed generally negative quality (as our chapter on science demonstrates) of the other empirical evidence which has a relation to the idea of immortality—all this makes it easy to comprehend why modern immortalists have laid such great stress on *arguments* rather than on proofs of an empirical nature. Instead of being able in the old-fashioned way to shout the doctrine of immortality from the housetops as an eternal truth, they have been forced to plead for it from their studies in subtle dissertations. Unlike Dante, who spent most of his time *describing* the realm of immortality, they have concentrated on attempting to persuade themselves and others that there *is* such a realm. In a sense these modern immortalists have returned to Plato, who, in spite of his genius, did not foresee either the resurrection of Christ or the advent of the Spiritualists and who submitted arguments, not empirical evidence, on behalf of a life beyond death.

Yet in another sense the modern defenders of immortality have deserted Plato, since their arguments are on the whole very different from the sort which he emphasized. Plato's case for immortality finds its

* I shall take up these points in some detail in my last chapter. See p. 253.

best and most complete expression in the *Phaedo*, where Socrates upholds the eternal life of the soul on a number of different grounds: the noblest kind of living is a kind of dying and the true philosopher is glad to have his soul released from his body through death; all opposites are generated out of each other and as life is always followed by death so death must be followed by life; knowledge comes from the recollection of ideas, showing that the soul had a pre-existence, and from this may be inferred an after-existence; the soul remains the same soul throughout life, while the body is constantly changing and renewed; the soul is not the function or harmony of the body and therefore unable to exist without it, for the soul controls the body whereas no existing harmony controls the instrument which produces it; the soul is in touch with absolute and eternal ideas and accordingly must itself be eternal; the soul is the life-giving power and can therefore never be subject to death, its very opposite; the soul, unlike the body, is a simple and uncompounded thing and is therefore indissoluble and imperishable.

These highly speculative and abstract lines of reasoning, scarcely even understandable by the common man, have never appealed except to a small group of the sophisticated. And by them they have been taken primarily as a form of poetry or as an intriguing bit of philosophical exercise. It is unlikely that the "proofs" of immortality in the *Phaedo*, many of which subtly assume their conclusions from the start, ever in themselves alone won anyone to a belief in an afterlife. The most influential of them, that centering about the complete simplicity of the soul, rests on an initial assumption almost as drastic and far-reaching as would be the assumption of immortality itself.

If modern psychology has shown anything at all, it has shown that to consider the soul or personality as a simple and unitary substance is as far removed from the actual fact as can be. Whatever else the human personality may be, it is certainly one of the most complex entities that exists. But even the pristine simplicity of the soul would not guarantee its imperishability; for what right have we to assume that a piece of psychic substance, no matter how simple, will endure forever? Furthermore, even if we allow that such a simple substance is by nature immortal, we have no certainty that its immortality will be worthwhile. On the contrary, if we recall the analysis of immortality concepts in Chapter II, we know that a desirable survival for a bare soul is self-contradictory and unimaginable. Finally, the argument from the simplicity of the soul as the royal road to immortality runs into all the difficulties of any attempt to escape the decree of death through the vagaries of a dualistic psychology.

2. *The Ethical Arguments*

The drawbacks of empirical evidence and the inefficacy and irrelevancy from a modern viewpoint of such arguments as we have cited from Plato have led present-day Christians outside the orthodox fold to rely primarily on the so-called ethical or value arguments for immortality. These arguments are phrased in various ways, but in the end they all come down to the same point, namely, that human personalities and their doings are intrinsically so valuable or so good, so important or so beautiful, that in all justice and reason they deserve, must have, and do receive immortality from the Powers-that-be in the universe. This proposition is not new. It is discoverable far back in the history of thought and, among other places, in the *Dialogues* of Plato. But it is only in the modern era that this argument has come to be so greatly emphasized and indeed to serve as the sole support of an increasing number of immortalists.

It was Immanuel Kant who gave the classic formulation of the ethical argument for the modern age. In his *Critique of Pure Reason* (1781), bearing down particularly hard on the argument from the soul's simplicity, he admits that no human intelligence can rationally understand how immortality is possible and that he has found it necessary to deny a *knowledge* of immortality "in order to find a place for faith."[143] In the *Critique of Practical Reason* (1788) he explains in detail what he means and sets up the immortality of the soul as "a postulate of pure practical reason."[144] Kant starts out by premising the inherent worth of human personality. "Man, and indeed every rational being as such, *exists* as an end in himself, *not merely as a means* to be made use of by this or that will."[145] Now the influence on man of the moral law, that is, "the disposition it produces in him to promote the highest good that can be practically realized by us, presupposes at the very least that the highest good is possible."[146] This highest good consists in "the union of virtue and happiness in the same person, that is, in happiness exactly proportioned to morality. . . . Happiness is the state of a rational being existing in the world who experiences through the whole of his life whatever he desires and wills."

But in this world "the most scrupulous adherence to the laws of morality cannot be expected to bring happiness into connection with virtue." For "the supreme condition of the highest good is the perfect harmony of the disposition with the moral law." This state is "holiness"; and it is attainable "only in an infinite progress towards harmony with the moral law." "Now, this infinite progress is possible only if we presuppose that the existence of a rational being is prolonged to infinity, and that he retains his personality for all time. This is what we mean by the immortality of the soul. The highest good is therefore practically possible, only if we presuppose the immortality of the soul. Thus immortality is inseparably bound up with the moral law."

Granting all this, however, how can we be sure that the controlling forces of the universe recognize this moral law and have both the ability and the will to grant the immortality necessary for its consummation? Kant has an answer. "If we suppose," he says, "for the sake of illustration, that there exists a rational Being who has all power, it cannot be in accordance with the whole will of such a Being, that his creatures should be unable to secure the happiness which their nature demands* and of which their obedience to the moral law makes them worthy." Our redoubtable philosopher then proceeds to turn his "illustration" into a dazzling *fait accompli*. "The moral law leads us to postulate not only the immortality of the soul, but the existence of God. . . . This second postulate of the existence of God rests upon the necessity of presupposing the existence of a cause adequate to the effect which has to be explained." In other words, only a rational and all-powerful God is a sufficient "cause" to guarantee the "effect" of a worth-while immortality; therefore such a God exists. What Kant's argument reduces itself to, then, is that men's moral aspirations are so excellent and noble that there *must* be an immortality which will allow their complete fulfilment.

If we compare Kant's position with that of traditional Christianity, we realize at once what a far-reaching change has taken place. From earliest Christian times the idea of immortality has had moral significance. A just and avenging God would mete out splendid rewards for the good in paradise and dire punishments for the wicked in hell. The ethical meaning of the hereafter was not customarily used, however, as an argument to win converts to a belief in a future life; it was rather announced as an integral part of that future life in the interests of moral control over men on this earth. The preacher said in effect: "There *is* a heaven

* Cf. p. 177.

and a hell. If you are good, you will go to heaven. If you are bad, you will go to hell. So be good." He did not say in the modern spirit, "Neither the good nor the bad receive their proper deserts in this world. *Therefore* there is a heaven and hell which you will please believe in." Orthodox Christian theologians argued for immortality, if they needed to at all, on the basis of Christ's resurrection or from the authority of the Church or the Bible. Like the ancient Hebrews after the repeated failure of the Messianic hope, they may well have been subconsciously influenced to believe in immortality because of the parlous state of earthly affairs; but that was not their conscious attitude or their explicit reason for faith in a hereafter. The parlous state of earthly affairs proved the inherent sinfulness of man and the vanity of this-worldly goods rather than the existence of an immortality.

Hence, Kant takes what had been an accepted and usually unquestioned part of the *description* of immortality, namely, its ethical content, and turns it, appending certain qualifications of his own, into an *argument* for immortality. Here we see an excellent example of how the reasons offered to make an idea acceptable are inextricably bound up in a constant interaction with the content of the idea itself. For Kant's argument, which democratically assumes that the moral law or "categorical imperative" is in some form present in every human heart, leads him to alter almost beyond recognition the moral significance commonly attributed to the after-existence. His heaven, if it can be properly called so, is whittled down to a vague "infinite progress" of a rational being "toward perfect harmony with the moral law." Furthermore, not only does the horrendous imagery habitually associated with hell drop out of the picture, but hell itself disappears. Kant talks about the attainment of perfect harmony between happiness and virtue in the beyond, but not about a perfect attunement between *un*happiness and sin. He apparently condemns no one to eternal torments, though he assigns everyone to a very long apprenticeship indeed for the attainment of the far-off goal of holiness and happiness. Thus immortality has moral significance a-plenty for Kant, but not on the basis of the old-time heaven-hell distinction.

It is revealing to examine some of the variations on Kant's ethical argument. For example, the argument from the infinity of the self maintains that complete justice can be done to every human spirit only if it has the opportunity to develop its infinite possibilities to their fullest extent. That is why we should have "limitless time to satisfy the needs of the limitless spirit."[147] Fichte was one of the first to stress this point, showing that the possibilities of the development of the self are literally boundless, that this infinite development can never be completed, and that this fact means for the self "the seal of its vocation for eternity."[148] Professor William Ernest Hocking writes: "The life of the unsatisfied self, whose importance the contemporary psychologist has discovered . . . is the best assurance that in the hidden arrangements of the universe this persistent flame, half choked and fitful in the present order, may continue its quest of breath and freedom in another."[149]

Stressing the growth of character, another immortalist avows that his own hope for a future life "is largely founded on what seems to me the obvious significance of the whole historic process, the training of character. For this the ordinary three-score years and ten do not appear to give anything like full scope. All sorts of powers and capacities lodged in us never get themselves expressed; life is too short or the environing pressure of circumstances too dense."[150] William James evidently had something of the same feeling when he wrote to a lady who had just lost her husband: "I can hardly express the sorrow I feel at your husband's being thus cut off almost before he had begun to show what was in him. . . . The whole thing is one of those incomprehensible, seemingly wasteful acts of Providence, which, without seeing, we can only hope may some day be proved to spring from a rational ground."[151]

Dr. Fosdick eloquently sums up in a similar vein: "The necessity of personal permanence to the reasonableness of human life may be, perhaps, most clearly seen when we consider the essentially limitless possibilities which inhere in knowledge and character. If death ends all, these possibilities are involved in man's very nature only that without excuse they may be brusquely and abruptly snatched away. . . . Death is a thief who breaks into the character and steals from it its essential nature of endless aspiration. . . . One generation of incomplete, aspiring persons is wiped off the earth, as a child erases unfinished problems from his slate, that another generation of incomplete, aspiring persons may be created—created and then annihilated."[152]

Though this reasoning clearly extends to those whom death calls after a long and happy life, it touches with special force the cases of those who die prematurely: in childhood, in youth or in the full vigor of middle age. War slays its tens of millions in the springtime or the prime of life; famine and disease take their scores of millions, so often preferring the tender young; accident overwhelms in sudden death the innocent, the strongest and the most promising. Even the *this*-worldly possibilities of these premature dead are stifled, let alone the potentialities which would have remained unfulfilled had they lived to a ripe old age. So runs the argument. As the inscription on the grave of a little girl in the burial ground of the Parish Church at Wrexham, Wales, so poignantly expresses it:

I wonder what I was begun for
Seeing I am so soon done for.

Closely related to the arguments stressing potentiality and progress is that based on the idea of evolution. "I believe in immortality," avows John Haynes Holmes, "as the logic of the evolutionary process. This process must be working to the achievement of some permanent and worthy end, if the world is sane. What can this be but the development of a soul which can outlive a cosmos doomed to a final cataclysm of ruin?"[153] In the same spirit Dr. Fosdick writes: "The manifest trend of the whole creative process is toward the building of personality." And, "If . . . a man believes that the universe means anything, he must, in the light of manifest facts, believe that it has been aiming at personality."[154]

The theory of evolution is also utilized to support what is called *conditional* immortality, which is said to stand in line "with the general method of evolution which has been selective throughout, with a gradual advance in the character of the survival-conditioning factor."[155] Conditional immortality in its simplest terms is the view that only those who are fit for or deserve eternal life will have it; the others will pass into oblivion. The "mutation" which is to raise one up into the immortal species is the possession of certain outstanding moral and religious qualities. "On the Conditional view all men are immortable—potentially immortal: whether that characteristic is developed and attained is a matter of a moral relationship to God."[156] "Man is a candidate for immortality. Life eternal is the lot of him who unites himself to God in faith. The immortalization of man is the aim of redemption."[157] Citing in addition to their own arguments an impressive number of supporting references from the Bible and the Apostolic Fathers, the adherents of conditionalism have won considerable support since the middle of the nineteenth century.

Another expression of Kant's ethical argument takes the form of reasoning from the inherent value of the human personality. "If death ends personality," says Dr. Fosdick, "the universe seems to be throwing away with utter heedlessness its most precious possessions." And speaking of Christ: "Does the world build a character like that, which has held now sixty generations in its spiritual mastership, and then throw it utterly away? Is God blowing soap-bubbles?"[158] In a similar spirit Dr. Dole writes about Christ's resurrection: "It is not necessary to believe that his risen body passed through closed doors and appeared to his disciples. The deeper fact is that his person seemed to those who knew him to be above the range of death."[159] As Emerson observes: "What is excellent, as God lives, is permanent."[160] Essentially, "we believe ourselves immortal because we believe ourselves *fit* for immortality."[161] Indeed, it may be said that the argument from the intrinsic worth of the personality is so old and so universal that it "has always been the real foundation of belief in immortality. Men have anticipated a life after death because life here seemed so worthful that they could not bring themselves to believe in its cessation. What is new in the modern statement of the argument is simply the frankness with which this fact is recognized."[162]

The value argument is the real heart of the case presented by Kant, who puts so much weight on the worth and moral dignity of the individual rational being that is man. But the contemporary immortalist, perhaps going farther than Kant would have sanctioned, extends the value argument way beyond the consideration of human personalities alone. "For," to cite Dr. Fosdick again, "the dominance of death means not simply the final end of individuals, but the final end of those spiritual values we have known here."[163] Immortality, then, is necessary for the conservation not only of priceless human personalities, but also of the great moral values such as love, goodness and justice. Denying that these values exist as eternal Platonic ideas either by themselves or in the mind of God, Dr. Fosdick concludes that they are "forms of personal activity that never would have existed without social life, and that have no meaning apart from relationships between persons. . . . What can altruism mean in a universe without separate personalities; or honor, or sincerity, or loyalty, or faithfulness? . . . The only hope of preserving the moral gains of humanity lies in the persistence of a community of human persons."[164]

The fact that a community of human persons may preserve these moral gains on this earth for, according to scientists, anywhere from two hundred million to a billion or even ten billion years is not enough for Fosdick and his confreres. The approaching end of a world supposedly now doomed by science as well as theology is a factor almost as important in their philosophy as in that of the early Christians. After the final chaos and cataclysm "not even the memory shall be left of any good that has been done under the sun, but with the death of the last man who falls in a world of graves, all the toil and sacrifice of the race come to their futile end. That is the world without immortality."[165] It is the age-long fear lest "the great globe itself, yea, all which it inherit, shall dissolve and . . . leave not a rack behind."[166] "Thus incomplete, unintelligible, and pathetic beyond expression, thus tragic and terrible, is life without immortality."[167]

For Professor A. E. Taylor, also, only immortality can save the situation. Otherwise "all human personal values" must perish. If there is no immortality, then "all the generations of mankind are fighting a forlorn hope . . . our life is blind, and our death is fruitless."[168] Dr. Falconer even goes so far as to say that on the supposition that death ends all, "the more value the race acquires, the more irrational the universe becomes."[169] For another immortalist, Mr. Louis De Launay, "the disastrous and annihilating thought is . . . the scientific conception of universal extinction: an extinction which engulfs sooner or later not only the family, but the nation, the race, humanity, all earthly achievements, the earth itself, the solar system, the universe. . . . If the men whom we serve must themselves also disappear in a few years; if very soon nothing will remain, neither country, science, art, nor humanity; if when our globe shall have accomplished a few more rapid revolutions in the heavens it must grow cold, become extinct and ultimately disappear into the infinite, without anything with which it has ever been occupied being transmitted elsewhere, then what is the use of it all?"[170]

What is the use of it all? That is the question. And the question arises from a certain sense of futility uppermost in the minds of these men when they envision a world without immortality. "I cannot help inferring," avers Professor Taylor, "that when all comes to the same thing in the end, no choice of mine between good and evil really matters much." Why should we continue to strive for the right or even for our own happiness "when the whole human struggle will be over and done with in a time which, in the history of the Universe, may be counted as a watch in the night?"[171] Without immortality life is meaningless, for in that case "physical force alone persists, the builder and destroyer of spirit and at last the sole survivor and victor over all."[172] It was in this frame of mind that Tennyson paced the Dover cliffs and shouted, "If there is no immortality, I shall hurl myself into the sea."[173]

The futility argument ends in the depths of despair. Since "the moral gains of the race are all social in their genesis and in their expression" and since, moreover, "spiritual quality is simply personality in action" and "in the very nature of the case cannot be detached from a man to be appropriated and preserved by God,"[174] the Deity is helpless to remedy the terrible situation implied by the absence of human immortality. Indeed the very existence of God may be, as I pointed out in the first chapter, involved in the question of immortality. To repeat Dr. Fosdick's conclusion, "If death ends all, there is no God of whom goodness, in any connotation imaginable to man, can be predicated."[175] And Dr. Gordon echoes this by claiming that unless men have immortality, the Power responsible for their existence is unreasonable and brutal. This practice of deducing the existence of God from the existence of immortality has as a precedent the argument of Kant. For if we examine his reasoning with any care, we see that he postulates God primarily to sustain the realm of immortality and to make possible there the fulfilment of the moral law.

The final variation of the ethical argument to be considered is what may be called the *instinct-fulfilment* argument. Assuming a more or less universal desire for immortality, this argument, in the words of the Reverend F. W. Farrar, former Dean of Canterbury, runs as follows: "Surely the instinctive sense which we all feel that we were not merely born to live for an insignificant span of time, and then to disappear forever, cannot be allowed to go for nothing. This belief exists among all men in every region of the world, and has nothing to do with flattering surmises of great thinkers. If it is a mere self-deception, then the light which leads us astray is light from heaven; a conclusion which, if we bear in mind what God is, we cannot possibly accept."[176]

As another immortalist puts it: "The rudest and the most polished, the simplest and the most learned, unite in the expectation and cling to it through everything. It is like the ruling presentiment implanted in those insects that are to undergo metamorphosis. This believing instinct, so deeply seated in our consciousness, natural, innocent, universal, whence came it, and why was it given? There is but one fair answer. God and nature deceive not."[177] To sum up this reasoning concisely, "He who has come to the inner certitude of the fatherly love, mercy and truthfulness of God is incapable of the thought that God could have implanted into our hearts a hope and longing which he did not intend to come to realization, so that he would in reality be playing a cruel game with us."[178]

These typical modern arguments on behalf of a future life throw not a little light on the increasing refinement of immortality descriptions. Those who take the bodily resurrection of Jesus Christ as the chief evidence for a hereafter not only assume that there will be a physical resurrection for all men but usually feel free to envision a full and detailed future-life environment. That kind of representation of the after-existence naturally goes with reliance on the resurrection. And the alleged empirical evidence of survival in which Spiritualists and kindred immortalists put their trust almost inevitably leads to remarkably complete portrayals of the great beyond. But very general arguments result in very general descriptions, though the implications of those descriptions may have any amount of specificity. Moreover, the ethical arguments undoubtedly have influenced to a large extent the type of general description given. It is noteworthy that most of the modern immortalists under consideration, including Kant, have omitted hell from the hereafter. Following a line of dissent from Christian orthodoxy that has always had at least a few adherents, they have been Universalists in spirit. That is, they have implicitly promised universal salvation for mankind, the eventual attainment of some sort of blessed immortality by every human soul.[179]

Let us consider how the ethical arguments naturally point in the direction of Universalism. Take the arguments based on the infinite possibilities of the self and on the concept of evolution. If the human self possesses infinite possibilities, wickedness as expressed on this earth is the actualization of only one of them. In the world beyond, other possibilities will have a chance to evolve into realities, particularly if there is unlimited time available. Hence no human soul can be judged as completely irredeemable; and hell becomes both superfluous and obnoxious. But these arguments also do something to heaven. Those who apply them are prone to drop altogether the term *heaven* with its association of attained perfection amid radiant light. If one tries to show that a future life is demanded in order that the training of character begun here below be properly continued, one obviously must not make existence in the hereafter too easy. What, for example, could be better for a still imperfect soul than work— not demoralizing drudgery such as has been the lot of nine-tenths of mankind in the past—but the ideal work of twentieth-century civilization, work that is meaningful, enjoyable and soul-strengthening? Paradise as a glorified Sunday rest-period has no place in such a conception.

Coming to the value argument, when an immortalist like Dr. Fosdick gives such great weight to the inherent preciousness of human personality as an argument for immortality, he is talking about *every* human personality. No character is devoid of worth for him, if only because it possesses the potentiality of becoming noble and good. Reliance on such reasoning all but forces Dr. Fosdick to abandon the heaven-hell classification; he could hardly argue from the value of personality as such if some personalities, even those, let us say, of the worst criminals, were of so little value that they could be forever condemned to the bottomless pits of hell. When Dr. Fosdick and other immortalists extend the value argument to a wider sphere, like results occur. They want to save the great social values such as altruism, love, justice, honor, goodness; but no hell is required for such a preservation. Indeed hell would only eternalize what they have no desire to see forever established: selfishness, hate, injustice, violence and evil. Such eternalization "is really impious, for it maintains the permanent and ineradicable character of evil in the constitution of the universe."[180]

The instinct-fulfilment argument also leads toward Universalism. Immortalists may be able to convince a man that God has implanted within him an "instinct" to live happily ever after death, but they would meet ridicule at once if they claimed that this "instinct" included a natural desire for the possibility of everlasting torments for either oneself or one's fellow-men. When the appeal to believe in immortality is made, either openly or in disguise, on the ground that there is some sort of profound desire for it and that this desire must be satisfied, the immortality described is bound to be of a fairly satisfactory kind. Otherwise the call to faith, at least when based on that foundation, is likely to fall on deaf ears. This observation extends to all the ethico-value arguments in so far as they are fundamentally akin to the instinct-fulfilment theory.

Of course, all this is not to claim that there have not been, besides the arguments employed, other factors in the last century or two making for a dampening of the eternal hell-fires. The trend towards democracy and collectivism has influenced immortality ideas by stressing the right of every individual to a happy life and the possibility of everyone reaching such a goal through the proper organization of science, the machine and the economic-political structure; humanitarianism and social awareness, displaying themselves in such tendencies as widespread charity and prison reform, have naturally balked at old-time descriptions of unending torment; and Romanticism, with its emphasis on love, the natural goodness of men and their universal educability, has run counter to the conception that any human soul can be essentially and hopelessly wicked.

In so far as God has been thought responsible for what goes on in the future life and in so far as the development of morals has refined and softened men's conception of him, a concomitant refinement has taken place in ideas of immortality. In addition, the increas- ing confusion in moral standards has helped to break down the old heaven-hell distinction. As long as it was possible to say definitely which were the sheep and which the goats, the Last Judgment with its final as- signment of all souls to everlasting heaven or everlast- ing hell seemed plausible and served as a means of ethical clarification for the theologians. But when final moral judgments have become much more difficult to make, then the clear-cut heaven-hell division becomes less acceptable and less useful.

The fact that immortality descriptions vary so widely and radically, not only according to the actual- ities and ideals of each culture concerned, but also according to the arguments put forward to prove the hereafter, is another indication, I believe, of the weak- ness of the whole case for a future life. For thousands of years the experts on an after-existence all over the world have been receiving private and direct revela- tions from the Almighty and other blessed spirits as to the state of the departed; they have been presenting to mankind annual, monthly and even daily reports as to what goes on in the realm beyond; and they have sub- mitted the greatest variety of evidence and argument that can be imagined to support their speculations.

At the same time these experts, all claiming access to the one and only truth about immortality, have bit- terly quarreled with and damned one another for the drastic disagreement and inconsistency amongst their respective accounts and arguments. Today disagree- ment and inconsistency among immortalists is as wide- spread and deep-lying as ever. It is true that there has been disagreement among scientists, too; but the scien- tists have, after all, made considerable progress and have revealed very large and unmistakable sectors of the truth. In the last two thousand years, however, the immortalists, so far as we can see, have not come one whit nearer to an intellectually acceptable account of the after-life or to intellectually acceptable evidence or arguments for its existence. The arguments in fashion at present are just as unsound and unconvincing as those offered in former times.

In view of all this, the remarks of the English novelist, Somerset Maugham, seem eminently sensible: "A very good test of the force of arguments on which you accept a belief is to ask yourself whether for reasons of equal weight you would embark on a practical operation of any importance. Would you for example buy a house on hearsay without having the title examined by a lawyer and the drains tested by a surveyor? The arguments for immortality, weak when you take them one by one, are no more cogent when you take them together. They are alluring, like a house-agent's advertisement in the daily paper, but to me at least no more convincing. For my part I cannot see how consciousness can persist when its physical basis has been destroyed, and I am too sure of the interconnection of my body and my mind to think that any survival of my consciousness apart from my body would be in any sense the survival of myself. Even if one could persuade oneself that there was any truth in the suggestion that the human consciousness survives in some general consciousness, there would be small comfort in it."[181]

3. *Turning Wishes into Proofs*

I have cited the instinct-fulfilment argument as one of the important variations of the general ethical argument for survival after death. What that argument in essence boils down to is the simple proposition that a deep and widespread desire for immortality proves the existence of immortality. Thus Ralph Waldo Emerson declares that the impulse to seek proof of immortality itself constitutes excellent affirmative testimony;[182] and "the blazing evidence of immortality is our dissatisfaction with any other solution."[183] Dr. Robert E. Speer repeats the thought: "I believe in conscious personal immortality because I want to and because I think so strong a want, so attested by the effects which flow from it in life, is its own warrant."[184] We could quote many other immortalists to the same effect. Here again Kant has given the hint.* His God is to guarantee immortality to men in order "to secure the happiness which their nature demands."[185] Now while Kant is plainly enough referring to men's moral nature, it is decidedly difficult to draw a line between men's moral demands and needs and their other demands and needs. And this troublesome consideration shows how thin is the distinction between Kant's line of thought and the instinct-fulfilment or desire argument as propounded by more recent immortalists.

The proposition that if we wish a thing strongly enough, therefore we can depend on its existing or coming to pass is, of course, the weakest of reeds upon which to lean. Were it a sound principle, the world would long ago have become a Utopia of universal happiness, and death itself would have been entirely abolished. But it is fairly clear that existence does not coincide with that grand old fairy tale where one puts on a magic wishing cap and then makes all one's dreams come true. To say with Emerson that our dissatisfaction with the idea of human mortality proves that there must be immortality completely overlooks the consideration that throughout all history the truth, both in big things and little, has frequently dissatisfied and made unhappy any number of people. And it is truly astonishing that either Emerson or any other responsible intellect has been able to take seriously such an argument on behalf of immortality.

If our desire to live a full three-score years and ten on this earth is no surety that we shall not die at thirty-five, what right have we to assume that a desire

* See p. 163.

to live forever proves that we shall not stay dead when we depart this mundane sphere? If human beings yearned to be as big as all space instead of as eternal as all time, their mere longing would not be thought a very dependable guarantee of its own fulfilment. They might deem it an outrage that they were not large enough to reach out and touch the stars just as children are genuinely disappointed at not being able to grasp the moon. But their chagrin would not be acceptable as proof that some day their gargantuan hope would be realized. Nor would a profound craving to have witnessed at first-hand the Battle of Thermopylae in 480 B.C. *ipso facto* establish the actuality of pre-existence. Yet the extraordinary logic of the Christian immortalists' argument for an eternal existence after death can be utilized with equal force by Buddhists and Hindus to support the idea of an eternal existence before birth.

As a matter of fact, while the positive desire for a life beyond is potential in every human being, there does not seem to be anything that can legitimately be called an instinct for immortality. There is a tendency towards self-preservation, but that is a different matter. This tendency, embodying itself in many different varieties of acts, is sometimes loosely referred to as an "instinct." It is common to the whole animal kingdom as well as to man and is as important as the sex urge for the continuance of life. Men sometimes more or less disregard it, but then they are either heroes or fools. Our inborn desire to keep on living is satisfied so long as our life endures; thus it is constantly being fulfilled in *this* world and is thereby nourished sufficiently to maintain it as a powerful factor in our thought and action.

It is very easy to mistake this will to live in the here-now for a will to live in some hereafter. It is very easy to forget that this "instinct," like any other, has been developed in relation to earthly existence and that presumably the locus of its gratification, like that of any other animal instinct, is in this life. The crowning objection, however, to the instinct-fulfilment argument resides in a consideration of the healthy fear of death in which the tendency towards self-preservation so often expresses itself. If our desire for immortality proves there is immortality, then, on the same principle that a powerful emotion implies the objectivity of that towards which it is directed, our fear of annihilation proves there is annihilation.

The ethical argument and its variations are closely akin to the instinct-fulfilment argument in the sense that they all turn wishes for a life beyond or motivations toward it into alleged proofs. They all assume that there *ought* to be an immortality and then convert this *ought* into a *must*. Now what moral men think ought to be is simply what as idealists they *wish* there to be. And it is no more reasonable to believe that the mere existence of a high and noble desire implies its necessary fulfilment than that the mere existence of a low and brute desire implies *its* fulfilment. To convert wishes and ideals into antecedent objects and powers has always been a common failing of human nature and is surely one of the most pathetic of fallacies. It involves a truly breath-taking leap in logic. Kant himself recognizes this point. For he is frank in stating the dependence of his argument on *faith* and his belief that the existence of immortality and also that of God are no more than postulates of man's moral sense. But it is noticeable that contemporary immortalists, whatever variation of the ethical argument they follow, usually try to create the impression that they are proving immortality through reliance on reason.

The exact method by which modern immortalists read their ideals into existence warrants careful study. What all of them do is to assume that what man considers supremely good or ethical or desirable should and does constitute one of the fundamental traits of existence as such. Thus they play the old game of anthropomorphism by giving a metaphysical or cosmological* standing to human wishes and ideals. For if the universe-as-a-whole is to be conceived as caring sufficiently for human personalities to make them immortal—if, as Dr. Fosdick insists, it is "friendly"—then it must be a universe at the very core of which exists a full appreciation of human standards. This means that goodness, justice, rationality, purpose, and so on must be among the ultimate metaphysical aspects of existence, characteristics of the cosmos at large instead of existent or potential attributes of Nature in some relative capacity.

In this wise the immortalists assign a metaphysical status to value in its inclusive and eulogistic sense of meaning everything that is good. And this implies for them above all a permanent status. For when we examine closely their declarations, especially their sense of futility in a world without immortality, we find that in their philosophy a true value is only one which is conserved forever in a durational sense. To be valuable, meaningful, non-futile, the achievements and efforts of man must count ultimately and absolutely. They must add something permanently; there must be no chance of that addition being crossed out in some cosmic collision. This conception of value follows naturally from its being given a metaphysical position. The metaphysical ultimates are all *per se* eternal. For they constitute the irreducible characteristics of the universe, of all existence, of being as such. So, by making value metaphysical, the immortalist makes permanency an inseparable and necessary accompaniment of value. Anything that is not permanent accordingly lacks value for him. Hence the futility argument for immortality.

* I am using the term *cosmological* as synonymous with both *metaphysical* and *ontological*.

This linkage of value with everlastingness is a very dubious kind of procedure. In the first place, it is similar to setting up mere bigness as the standard of worth in that it pushes into the background the qualitative aspects of value. "The length of things," flashes Santayana, "is vanity, only their height is joy."[186] And long ago Aristotle explained that good will not be "more good if it is eternal, since a white thing which lasts for a long time is not whiter than that which lasts a single day."[187] The glory that was Greece did not endure forever, but that did not make it less a glory. Heroism may bring death to a man, but that does not make him less a hero. Can anyone doubt that spiritually it is the quality rather than the duration of a life that counts when he considers the examples of a Shelley dying just short of thirty, a Jesus dying near the same age, a Keats dying at twenty-six and a Joan of Arc dying at nineteen?

Does anyone who has listened to a symphony of Beethoven seriously think that its intrinsic beauty and grandeur depend on the number of times it is played in the future? A great joy that has been felt remains a great joy that has been felt no matter how many worlds collapse. Neither immortality nor the lack of it can alter the fact that there was a great joy and that a human personality experienced it. While it is true that things must have some minimum duration in order to be experienced at all, neither the consummatory heights of experience nor small innocent pleasures wait on any assurance of life after death; they come without reference to the problem of immortality. The futility argument of the immortalist almost totally neglects these considerations; it throws into the discard the rich and unquestioning experience of every child, every artist, every lover, every partaker in the life of the spirit and the intellect.

In the second place, it is perfectly clear that the great values which the immortalists wish preserved

forever are the very values which human life has generated here and now in spite of its brevity, tragedy
and suffering. They themselves recognize this point
in granting that there are "values in living that inhere
in every day's experience and do not ask ultimate
questions about eternity."[188] Their argument itself
compels them to this admission. For if values existed
independently and eternally in another realm, as
suggested in Plato's *Dialogues*, then they would go on
existing whether or not human personalities survived
death. This is not the immortalists' view, however.
And so their argument forces them to say, in essence,
that the values produced in this life are not *really*
values and that the highest human accomplishments
are not *really* worth-while unless they are all set in a
framework of everlastingness.

To express the thought differently, the great immediacies of experience cannot be an end in themselves;
they have value only as a means to something else.
Happiness and good do not and cannot stand on their
own feet; they must have a justification in eternity.
Thus the defenders of immortality find themselves in
the awkward position of stating that it is futile and
meaningless that things of such immense value as
human personalities and human goods should endure
in their valuableness for so short a time.

This stand, if held to uncompromisingly, would
imply that were it by chance established that Plato
and Paul, Luther and Lincoln, and all the other great
and good figures of the past had not, as a matter of
fact, survived death as conscious personalities, their
lives, in spite of ennobling effects through long centuries, would now *become* futile. And human life today, were a future life in some way disproved, would
at once *become* worthless. The argument as stated
turns the assertion of immortality into the denial of
life's futility. But this denial can certainly be made
independently of any consideration of immortality.

The argument also twists around in a curious way the original case for a hereafter based on the inherent value of personality. It transforms the deduction, "personality is of priceless value (and non-futile), therefore it is immortal" into "personality is immortal, therefore it is of priceless value (and non-futile)." But plainly the immortalist cannot have it both ways; and he would appear to be on sounder ground if he trusted to the argument for a future life that assumes from start to finish that human personalities are worth too much to perish from the realm of being.

The futility argument has, to tell the truth, a strained and exaggerated air about it. It strikes a false note. These immortalists do protest too much, we think. Do they themselves really take seriously their fearful lamentations over a world where death is death? Or are they subconsciously exploiting current futilitarian moods to put across one last desperate argument to save the future life? Could it be that the standard of value based on eternal duration is simply an extension, a complex rationalization, of the strong desire for a durational span of life that will last forever? Or are these agonized immortalists bearing out the truth of Professor Sidney Hook's remark that "the romantic pessimism which mourns man's finitude is a vain lament that we are not gods"?[189]

Another possibility is that the immortalists, having eliminated hell from the hereafter, have to put it on earth in order to give heaven its full significance. For this-worldly existence in truth becomes a kind of hell if it actually is in itself futile, unintelligible, pathetic, tragic and terrible because of the grim and inexorable reapings of death. One of the basic premises, it is to be remembered, of Kant's original ethical argument is the impossibility of complete virtue and complete happiness ever being united in the same person here below. The stronger the possibility of such a union in this life, the weaker the Kantian position appears. Hence the better things become for mankind in the present world, the worse they become for the argument of Kant and his fellow-immortalists.

How the improvement of life on earth weakens the case for immortality is seen especially well in the infinite-possibilities argument. If one surveys the past, it is undeniable that the majority of mankind have had little access to the better things of life; have led narrow, frustrated and brief careers; and have gone down to their graves with many of their higher potentialities as human personalities unfulfilled. There is at least a possibility, however, that the social and economic systems of the future will provide everyone with opportunity and leisure for a free and full development of his capacities; that war and most other forms of violence will disappear into the records of history; and that the science of medicine and public hygiene will ensure long and healthy lives to all but a few incurables and the inevitable victims of accident.

If and when civilization ever reaches this level, most men will not feel that they have a legitimate complaint on the score that their possibilities have been stifled. No doubt the super-greedy will still claim that death unjustly prevents the fulfilment of their absolutely infinite potentialities. But no Utopia, whether of mortal or immortal life, can furnish the kind of infinite fulfilment which some immortalists talk about. For rational freedom in a world where time is real means the continuous and irreversible ruling out of some possibilities and the definite choosing of others. Every time we take one path, we dismiss into the limbo of unfulfilled possibilities what might have happened had we followed another. A man cannot do everything at once. And if he is wise, he will concentrate in one or a few fields where his aptitudes seem most promising. Liberty implies limitations. And no matter how many different realms the imperialists of personal experience are given to exploit, they will find this rule to hold.

The evolutionary argument for immortality, too, depends to a certain extent on the world's remaining static. For if the permanent and worthy end towards which the process of evolution has been working is the creation of immortal human souls, then it is implied that Nature has reached the peak of its development on this earth. When the huge Dinosaurs were the highest form of terrestrial life they might well, had they possessed the power of thought, have reflected as follows: "What big and splendid and remarkable creatures we are! The like of us has never been known on land or sea. We rule the earth. We are the climax of creation. Through millions and millions of years evolution has been working to produce us. There is, to be sure, that thing called death. But it is simply inconceivable that Nature should now proceed to scrap us. For if death is the end, then 'the universe seems to be throwing away with utter heedlessness its most precious possessions.' 'The manifest trend of the whole creative process is towards the building of'—Dinosaurs. And so we can be absolutely sure that our souls, at least, will live on forever in the realm of immortality."*

Now suppose that there evolve upon this planet—and this is a possibility—beings of a higher order, as far advanced beyond men as men are beyond the completely extinct Dinosaurs. Then the evolutionary argument for immortality comes to have about the same weight for man as for the Dinosaur. As a matter of fact, even granting that the animal, man, is the ultimate crown of creation, it would appear that the preservation of this species as distinct from every indi-

---

* The two quotations within the Dinosaur analogy are repeated from Dr. Fosdick's argument for *human* immortality. See pp. 167-168.

vidual in it is a worthy enough end for any evolutionary process.

As for the extension of the evolutionary concept to construct a theory of conditional immortality in which there is a survival of the spiritually fittest personalities, it is clearly illicit. The process of evolution works itself out in various ways in the sphere of the natural; there is no legitimacy in its application to the supernatural. And its use in the argument for conditional immortality is a pretty analogy and nothing more. The same kind of reasoning tries to find in the law of the conservation of energy a proof of personal immortality. Again, that law is applicable only to natural physical energy, and its extension to cover the case of immaterial and supernatural souls cannot be defended on any grounds known to science. The principle of the conservation of energy, like that of the indestructibility of matter, undeniably proves the immortality of the component physical elements of the human body; but beyond this it cannot go.

Proponents of the idea of immortality would be wiser if they did not attempt to win converts through such dubious citations of scientific laws. Not only do these demonstrations collapse when analyzed, but the laws in question can usually be turned with good effect against the immortalists. Thus it can be shown that organic evolution is far more concerned with the survival of the species than of the individual; and that the law of the conservation of energy includes in its operation an unceasing transformation of one form of energy into another, so that the basic energy, but none of its individual manifestations, is eternal.

The confusing of the natural and supernatural through specious analogies with scientific laws is further exemplified in the epithets which the immortalists so generously bestow on death. They brand poor death, for instance, as "insane," "unintelligible," "incomprehensible" and "wasteful." Now the eminently sane role of death in the course of evolution and in the economy of Nature is perfectly intelligible to a biologist. And death as the result of certain natural causes is perfectly comprehensible to a physician. If a man takes a stiff dose of potassium cyanide, or falls from a twentieth-story window and cracks his skull open on the sidewalk, or suffocates through submergence in deep water or receives a bullet through his heart, his death will hardly be called unintelligible or incomprehensible by the medical examiner. Only if a man did *not* die under such circumstances would it seem incomprehensible. Indeed, in such an eventuality something very like a panic might ensue, and with good reason.

The laws of Nature are so interconnected that the failure of one to operate is sure to imply that many others will also cease working in their accustomed way. If water cannot be depended on to suffocate a drowning man, neither can it be depended on to assuage his thirst or to fructify the crops. If a bullet through the heart cannot be counted on to kill a man, neither can it be counted on to kill a mad dog or a rattlesnake. If gravitation does not force to earth a man who slips off a high building, then the building itself is in jeopardy and all construction must cease. In the field of medicine proper, if certain causes cannot be absolutely relied on to bring disease or death, then no causes can be relied upon to defeat disease and death. And medicine as a science disappears.

If death, then, is intelligible to a biologist, a physician and even to the average bystander, why is it not so to the defenders of immortality? If death is one kind of natural event in a world of countless other natural events, why should it be singled out as any more incomprehensible than a change in the weather or the birth of a child? The answer implicit in the argument

of the immortalists is this: they are looking at death
not in terms of natural causation and the world that
is Nature, but from a supernatural point of view with
a supernatural criterion of what is intelligible and
comprehensible. Their reasoning thus assumes in the
wide sense a cosmology or metaphysics of Supernaturalism or Dualism. They wish Nature to grant an
exception to her laws in the case of human death and
thereby to show special concern for her men-creatures;
but they can guarantee this outcome only by making
Nature *super*natural.

For the immortalists not only is the event death
in its natural garb unintelligible, but it also reflects
back on life and makes that unintelligible as well. They
think that the extension of the personality's career
beyond the grave somehow *explains* what is for them
the mystery of life and of the fact that there should
even be such a thing as human consciousness. But a
pilgrim's progress lasting forever no more explains
why there should be human beings in the first place
than does a pilgrim's progress through an earthly span
of seventy or eighty years. Nor does postulating an
eternal pre-existence for the soul, as certain religions
do, fundamentally help matters. That the soul of man
should be given one world only to conquer is in itself
just as intelligible as if it were given a hundred or an
infinite number. And the attempt of the immortalists
to make everlastingness a principle of intelligibility
is no more acceptable than their effort to turn everlastingness into a principle of value.

There are other troubles connected with this matter of intelligibility. A cosmic order in which death
ends all is not, it is said, intelligible, rational or reasonable. "When one remembers," writes Dr. Fosdick,
setting things right, "that all science is based upon the
fundamental assumption that the universe is reasonable . . . it is clear that if personal permanence is necessary to the reasonableness of human life, which is the

most important part of the universe, we have proof of immortality."[190] Thus reasonableness is advanced to a metaphysical position as one of the ultimate traits of the universe. But reasonableness and *un*reasonableness are properly correlatives, taking their meaning and existence from each other; and it is therefore not possible logically to assign reasonableness a metaphysical status without doing the same for unreasonableness. Furthermore, it is plain that our modern immortalists are confused between reasonableness and susceptibility to reason, between rationality and understandability, between intelligence and intelligibility. Admission that the universe is intelligible, that is, open to intellectual analysis, carries no warrant for saying that it is intelligent; the fact that it or at least a considerable part of it, is understandable by the mind of man does not imply that it is itself rational; and the recognition that it is analyzable by reason working through the method of science does not mean that it possesses reasonableness.

When we take up the category of *good*, for which the immortalists so consistently claim a metaphysical position, we discover that it, too, has a correlative *bad*, calling out for equal rank in the administration of the universe. From this vexatious fact arises the so-called "problem of evil" in all philosophical or theological systems which attempt to set up the good alone as a cosmological ultimate. Solutions in the form of inventing a Devil as over-against God, Darkness as over-against Light, or Appearance as over-against Reality are disguised recognitions of the point concerned. Any system which promoted evil alone to a metaphysical status would run into the same issue under the guise of the problem of *good*. And since the ethical argument and its variations read good or value into the metaphysical core of the cosmos, they one and all become involved in the distressing dilemma described.

4. Can God Save the Situation?

The metaphysics of the immortalists will perhaps appear simpler if we realize that what it demands is nothing less than a good and intelligent and purposeful God. The existence of such a Being is not lightly to be assumed and in the modern world is subject to graver and more widespread doubts than ever before. We cannot in this book take up in detail the question of God's existence; that would entail a whole volume in itself. There are certain observations, however, that should be made. First, the same difficulties apply to the establishment of God as a metaphysical ultimate of the universe as apply to the elevation of good and rationality to that position. Second, the proof of God through the ethical argument for immortality and its variations, making the existence of the Almighty a corollary of that of the future life, is no stronger than the weak foundation upon which it rests. Those arguments all turn wishes for a hereafter into alleged proofs. But this procedure is just as illegitimate for demonstrating the reality of God as of anything else. Men may yearn for God, cry out that life is empty without him, lament that marriage and morals will collapse unless supported by his divine hand. Yet no amount of human anguish and desire will make actual a non-existent God.

Third, we should be on our guard against the theological tendency to establish the ideas of God and immortality through circular arguments. Thus it may be claimed, as in the ethical argument proper, that the moral nature of man demands immortality and a God to provide this immortality. Then, God's existence having been proved in this manner, it will be declared, as in some versions of the instinct-fulfilment argument, that there must be immortality, since it is inconceivable that God will not fulfil the expectations he has placed in man. In this way the actuality of a future life becomes alternately the ground and product of the existence of God. It is also a favorite device of the immortalists to argue for a hereafter on the basis of this world being so full of imperfection, tragedy and futility that there must be another to make up for it. Yet at the same time these reverend gentlemen, relying on the so-called argument from design, will insist that this world is constructed in such a wonderful and intricate manner, and is so clearly the best of all possible worlds, that a God must have been its architect.

Let us suppose, however, that God exists. Is man's immortality thereby insured? Not, we think, unless the question is begged by making "the guarantor of immortality" part of the very definition of God. The over-easy assumption that God will bestow immortal life on human personalities depends on the prior assumption that God considers these personalities important enough in the scheme of things to keep them going forever. This was a natural presupposition to make in the old days before the rise of modern science, when the earth was thought to be the center of the universe and the dimensions of time and space were worked out on a very diminutive scale. In the early centuries of the Christian faith, when the orthodox ideas of God and immortality were formulated, the end of the world was always considered just around the corner. In the Middle Ages this planet was supposed to be only a few thousand years old, and eminent figures like Dante gave it only a few hundred more years to last. This same opinion was widely prevalent well into the nineteenth century. And with such bases of judgment it did not seem unreasonable to conclude that man, as the highest of earth's creatures, was the darling of the universe, and that the main purpose of God in the whole creation was the salvation and perfection of individual human beings.

Modern science has completely and fundamentally

altered the primitive picture of things that encouraged this particular religious view. Our little planet revolves around a mighty sun more than a million times its size and nearly ninety-three million miles distant. And this sun is just an average-sized star and the solar system of nine planets which it rules, just a faint and microscopic blur upon the unimaginably vast canopy of the heavens. The nearest star beyond our solar system is 25,000,000,000,000 miles away or 4.27 light-years. A light-year (about six trillion miles) is the distance that light, speeding at the rate of 186,300 miles a second, travels in a year. The galactic system or Milky Way, the great star cluster to which the sun and its planets belong, contains some 100 billion stars and has an estimated diameter of 220,000 light-years.

During the twentieth century the astronomers have reduced the spatial significance of the earth even further by proving that the galactic system is only one out of millions and probably billions of similar galaxies or "island universes" scattered throughout the cosmos and each possessing its own thousands of millions of flaming stars. The nearest of these stellar clouds is about 160,000 light-years from the earth, while the distance of the farthest runs into *billions* of light-years. Dr. Edwin P. Hubble, of the Mount Wilson and Palomar Observatories in California, estimates that there may be in the neighborhood of 300,000,000,-000,000 nebulae in our "galacto-centric" universe. Sir James Jeans, the British astro-physicist, sums up the situation picturesquely: "At a moderate computation, the total number of stars in the universe must be something like the total number of specks of dust in London. Think of the sun as something less than a single speck of dust in a vast city, of the earth as less than a millionth part of such a speck of dust, and we have perhaps as vivid a picture as the mind can really grasp of the relation of our home in space to the rest of the universe."[191]

When we consider the time-spans of the cosmos we receive a similar impression of almost infinite vastness. Living forms of some kind have probably been in existence on this planet for as long as two or three billion years and the species man for over 500,000. Competent geologists estimate the age of the earth at around four billion years. Astronomers have not yet been able to reach agreement on precisely how the earth came into being and on its original relationship to the sun. The sun itself, like most other stars, is probably about five billion years old. Many have been the prophecies as to how long conditions on this earth will remain suitable for human life. Some scientists have set two or three hundred million years as the figure, others a thousand million and still others ten thousand million.

In the kind of stupendous cosmos that we have been describing, it may well be that God, operating with his infinite wisdom in an infinite environment, has other and far more magnificent plans afoot than the immortalization of an admittedly very imperfect and sinful race of men-creatures who have recently gained a foothold in one tiny corner of the universe. He may well reflect that these men-creatures are showing a very improper lack of humility in thinking that they are important and deserving enough to go on living forever either as individuals or as a species. It is quite apparent that God has plenty of time. If he has had the power and the patience to evolve on this earth through hundreds of millions of years animals as far advanced beyond the amoeba as are men, it would not seem at all surprising if in the next few hundred million years he evolved beings as much superior to men as the latter are to amoebas. On such beings God might deem it worth-while to bestow immortality. God's activities, however, are not confined to this earth. He has plenty of space as well as plenty of time. And it is not unreasonable to suppose that in other places in the vast cosmos there may exist beings of as high an order as men or even of a much higher order.*

Possibly God would not consider it his duty to give immortality to the individuals of *any* species, no matter how remarkable. Possibly he would feel that it was more important for the universe to flower eternally in myriad forms embodying beauty, nobility and other precious qualities, than that any one form should be eternal either in the realm of the natural or the supernatural. And perhaps William James, who laments with the futilitarian immortalists the transiency of earthly things, is more sensible than they when he writes: "A world with a God in it to say the last word, may indeed burn up or freeze, but we then think of him as still mindful of the old ideals and sure to bring them elsewhere to fruition; so that where he is, tragedy is only provisional and partial, and shipwreck and dissolution not the absolutely final things."[192]

If behind the long and devious processes of evolution the hand of God were governing the course of Nature, presumably he could have ruled out death as one of the instruments in the development of living species. That he did not do so would indicate that under the aspect of eternity, which is how God regards the happenings in our little world, death does not seem to be such a bad thing. But even if we grant that it is a bad thing, this does not imply that a God who is on the whole good must negate death for human beings by ensuring their continued existence in a future life. For obviously God does allow *some* evil to exist; and if *any* evil in the universe is consistent with the goodness of God, then it is impossible for us to determine the exact amount of evil that would be inconsistent with his goodness. Not only are we

* Cf. p. 264.

unable to look at the universe as a whole and see how all the multiplicity of events, things and ideas fit in with one another, but our own standard of good and evil and of their respective degrees may be very different from that of the Divine Mind.

I have been assuming all along that God had the *power* to guarantee human immortality if he so wished. What I want to point out now is that it may be impossible for a rational God to confer upon men the privilege of an after-life. If he obeys the rules, that is, the natural laws which he has himself established, he simply does not possess the power to extend the existence of conscious personalities beyond the grave. Professor William W. Fenn argues[193] that if you admit the existence of God, you admit the existence of a Mind not dependent on any physical structure; and that then it is easy to assume the possibility of men's immortality. But this does not follow. For even granting that God is a Mind dependent on no physical structure, he has obviously evolved human personalities in a very close relationship with physical structure and has in fact so intimately interconnected them with their bodies that their existence without those bodies is inconceivable. In short, the monistic relationship between personality or mind and body is an established psychological law. And in the face of this law God can bring about immortality only by becoming a miracle-worker in the old style, only by violating his own considered decrees and only by conjuring up out of nowhere resurrection bodies, etheric bodies and all the rest.

This is the only kind of God who can fulfil the heart's desire of the modern immortalist. And this is in fact the traditional Christian God. But Kant and his followers conceived themselves as being too sophisticated and modern to accept the crude God of orthodoxy. They reformed and refined their ideas of God just as they reformed and refined their ideas of immortality. Their conceptions of the future life implied much, if not most, of what they discarded as naive and untenable in other descriptions. Now we find that the modern immortalists' very up-to-date God, if he is to provide them with that after-life which plays such a central role in their philosophy, becomes by implication very much like the old-fashioned Almighty whom they thought they had left entirely behind. Not only must he be anthropomorphic in the sense of considering humankind as the very apple of his eye and each individual man as worthy of eternal existence, but he must also become a sleight-of-hand artist pulling immortality out of the hat through some capricious, preternatural trick. But if the hereafter is to depend on the existence of such a God, then indeed the immortalists are in a very bad way.

To sum up the purport of the chief arguments for immortality, it is my opinion that whatever part they assign to God, they signally fail to create a presumption in favor of a future life or to offset the strong evidence against it. And in some ways they tend to weaken rather than strengthen the case for immortality. For, since their major assumption is that existence must conform to the hedonistic or ideal desires of men, they give aid and comfort to the charge that ideas of immortality have been to a large extent merely wish-fulfilments or extensions of human vanity and egotism. These arguments appear to become, on analysis, rather feeble rationalizations of strong emotional forces in persons who are determined, no matter what, to maintain unshakable faith in a life beyond; the arguments bear out James Martineau's assertion that "we do not believe immortality because we have proved it, but we forever try to prove it because we believe it."[194] They make one suspect that the main reason why people still accept the resurrection of Christ as an unquestioned fact is their overwhelming urge to discover, at whatever intellectual cost, evidence for a hereafter. And the tenor of these arguments throws the same skeptical light on the easy acceptance by many persons today of the Spiritualist "proofs" regarding survival.

It might be more honest and even more convincing for the immortalists to take their stand with that heroic knight-errant of immortality, Don Miguel de Unamuno. In his remarkable book, *The Tragic Sense of Life*, Unamuno states that "faith in immortality is irrational" and that "all the labored arguments in support of our hunger of immortality, which pretend to be grounded on reason or logic, are merely advocacy and sophistry." Then he goes on to declare: "To believe in the immortality of the soul is to wish that the soul may be immortal, but to wish it with such force that this volition shall trample reason under foot and pass beyond it."[195] Here, as I see it, the issue is frankly and challengingly formulated. This chapter, and indeed this whole book, is intended precisely to show that to believe in immortality means to *trample reason under foot*.

Chapter VI

MOTIVATIONS AND SYMBOLISM

1. The "Desire" for Immortality

THAT IN practically all cultures, at least until recently, there is to be found *belief* in some sort of after-existence is not to be questioned. But to infer from this that there is an inherent and universal *desire* for a life beyond is a highly illegitimate procedure. As we have seen, many primitive peoples, including the Old Testament Hebrews and the Homeric Greeks, believed that there existed beyond the grave an unhappy and gloomy underworld where the feeble shades of the departed wandered about in unmitigated melancholy. Naturally enough, peoples with such a conception of the after-life had no burning enthusiasm to go to the abode of the dead. They viewed it as a far from attractive inevitability, frequently took an interest in it mainly for the sake of warding off the harm that the ghosts of the deceased might do the living, and sometimes simply regarded it with a bored indifference. It is quite possible, too, that at certain periods and among certain peoples the emergence of human individuality as such was not sufficiently pronounced to make a splendid immortality seem warranted for the average man.

As to the after-existence beliefs of Buddhism and Hinduism, there is considerable disagreement among scholars and even among the adherents of these religions themselves. One group claims that the ultimate goal of Nirvana means complete extinction or absorption of the individual personality; another that it is a state of conscious bliss comparable to the Christian's Beatific Vision of God. Whatever the correct interpretation, there can be no doubt that millions of Buddhists and Hindus look forward to their successive reincarnations after death with dread and despair, hoping for nothing so much as the total annihilation of their selves. And the beliefs and feelings of these Easterners should alone be sufficient to demonstrate that there is no innate and universal desire for immortality. For proof of this, however, we need not go outside of the Christian West. Even in the Middle Ages, the great centuries of faith, thoughts of the life beyond were likely to throw the majority of men into paroxysms of fear rather than ecstasies of joy; to arouse an attitude of melancholy resignation in face of the inevitable rather than one of overflowing gladness in anticipation of the glorious.

The supposed age-long, world-wide urge for immortality is a fine-sounding fiction that carries considerable plausibility because it does make some approach to the actual truth. For we do seem to find a universal law to the effect that every normal man, *if* the idea enters firmly enough into his consciousness and the counteracting forces of education and reason are not too potent, can be stimulated to desire a *worthwhile* immortality. And this means that the longing for an after-existence is a longing only *potentially* present in every human heart, since it does not become an actuality until the right kind of survival is offered in the right kind of way.

This constitutes no mystery, however, since as every modern advertiser knows, the same principle holds in regard to the exciting of desire for any object, real or imaginary. But because of various psychological and affectional factors that I shall take up later in detail, it is particularly easy to arouse the appetite for life everlasting; and when once set astir, this yearning can be developed through the appropriate techniques into such a powerful and seemingly permanent emotional pattern that it is readily mistaken for a human instinct. Presumably even in regions where the Hindu and Buddhist priesthoods hold out extinction as the final goal, the inhabitants, if exposed to the proper influences, could be taught deeply to desire immortality.

The early Greeks and the early Hebrews did not crave immortality mainly for the simple reason that they could not conceive of a desirable one, being unable to imagine a man as enjoying a decent existence when deprived of his earthly body. The religious revolution based on the life, passion and rising of Jesus Christ from the tomb supplied the necessary foundation for a satisfactory future life by promising the resurrection of the body. For a time there was a glad and glorious sense of complete victory over death; a psychological release of mind and soul perhaps unknown before that day. These feelings were buttressed by the belief that the world would shortly come to an end and that therefore the victory would soon become apparent and unmistakable to all. But the world stubbornly refused to enact this grand finale.

The Church Fathers proceeded to do their duty and to remind the faithful of original sin and the torments of hell. Their inventive minds, worried by what the soul should do between death and resurrection, seized upon the concept of purgatory and gave it a conspicuous place in the complex Christian theology. The holy Catholic Church then created the system of indulgences, providing for the remission of human souls' punishment in purgatory; and, incidentally, made the granting of these indulgences so much a matter of cash contributions to ecclesiastical coffers that the scandal of it occasioned Martin Luther's revolt that became the Reformation.

Hell and purgatory came to be so emphasized in

Catholic doctrine and practice that the masses of men could hardly be expected to look forward to immortality with a consuming eagerness. Apparently every effort was made to impress constantly on the minds of the people the dire penalties of retribution awaiting them as soon as they passed away. To aid in this, through the processes of association, death itself was represented in the most frightful manner possible. Revolting emblems of it everywhere met the eye: in the churches and the cloisters, on bridges and highways, in the carvings of tables and chairs, in the hangings of apartments, in rings and breviaries. Artists turned out series upon series of the gruesome "Dance of Death," depicting death as a ghastly skeleton leading his victims to an untimely end. He plays the fiddle at weddings; beats the drum in battle; shadows the scholar, the sculptor, the painter; stands leering beside the newborn baby in its cradle. The result was, as W. E. H. Lecky says, to make "the terrors of death for centuries the nightmare of the imagination."[196] St. Francis of Assisi was clearly out of step with the times when he referred mystically to "Brother Death."

Even Dante in his magnificent *Divine Comedy* devoted most of his space and his genius to the varied and exciting aspects of the next world's lower regions. But the more successful his vivid portrayals of hell and purgatory as art, the more effective they were in filling the minds of his readers with grim forebodings of the life beyond. Dante's heaven was far less convincing than his other conceptions and constituted a distinct anti-climax. The saintly Thomas Aquinas would not permit hell to be forgotten even in paradise, declaring that "in order that nothing may be wanting to the happiness of the blessed in Heaven, a perfect view is granted them of the tortures of the damned."[197] This statement was based on the general principle that an awareness of the opposite misery always increases the relish of any pleasure.

The priests and highpriests of the Church no doubt sincerely believed for the most part that their terrifying doctrines were morally necessary and entirely true, but it was altogether natural for the plain man to recoil in dismay from their dread prophecies. With what cruel and awful literalness these doctrines could be taken is well shown by the remark of "Bloody Mary," Catholic Queen of England in the sixteenth century, to the effect that: "As the souls of heretics are hereafter to be eternally burning in hell, there can be nothing more proper than for me to imitate the Divine vengeance by burning them on earth."[198]

The leaders of the new Protestant Church, while they eliminated purgatory, did not make the future state look any more attractive on the whole. Calvin, with his ruthless insistence on the very small number of God's predestined elect, frightened the multitude into piety. Fire and brimstone sermons became the order of the day. In England the great preacher, Jeremy Taylor, predicted: "Husbands shall see their wives, parents shall see their children tormented before their eyes. The bodies of the damned shall be crowded together in hell like grapes in a wine press, which shall press one another till they burst."[199] In America the stern voice of Jonathan Edwards, the noted Puritan theologian, rang out in warning to sinners: "The God that holds you over the pit of hell, much as one holds a spider, or some loathsome insect, over the fire, abhors you, and is dreadfully provoked: his wrath towards you burns like fire. . . . You are ten thousand times more abominable in his eyes than the most hateful venomous serpent is in ours. . . . It would be dreadful to suffer this fierceness and wrath of Almighty God one moment; but you must suffer it to all eternity. There will be no end to this exquisite horrible misery."[200]

The heads of the wicked, Edwards prophesies, "their eyes, their tongues, their hands, their feet, their loins, and their vitals shall forever be full of a glowing, melting fire, fierce enough to melt the very rocks and elements; and, also, they shall eternally be full of the most quick and lively sense to feel the torment . . . not for one minute, nor for one day, nor for one year, nor for one age, nor for two ages, nor for an hundred ages, nor for ten thousand or million ages, one after another, but for ever and ever, without any end at all, and never, never be delivered!"[201] These are but brief samples of the vast quantity of dire exhortations that came forth from Protestant pulpits century after century. The average believer, feeling that there was more than an even chance that he and his would meet a most unwelcome fate, was inclined to shudder when he thought of the world to come. No assurance that his enemies and other malefactors would boil in hell could free him from the apprehension that he, too, might share the same destiny. No talk about the pearly gates and golden streets of heaven could counteract the creeping fear within his heart.

There were, of course, important exceptions to this state of mind, particularly among the cultured minority and the professional philosophers. Like their prototypes in all ages, they tended to rise above the more vulgar religious superstitions. It is true that the philosophers, ever intellectual imperialists *par excellence*, were always looking for another world to conquer and reared great systems demonstrating that mere death could never stop the invincible spirit of man. But on the whole they were lacking that queer quirk of the imagination which envisages hell-fires and other devilish torments for the vast majority of mankind as a victory over the tomb. Some went so far as to deny altogether personal survival after death, the greatest of these being Benedict Spinoza in the seventeenth century.

At about the time that the advanced ideas of the French Enlightenment were spreading farthest

throughout Europe, an important change regarding
the nature of immortality began to become manifest
in the Church itself. Certain Protestant preachers,
tired and disgusted with the doctrine of eternal punishment, reintroduced the old heresy of Universalism
and taught that all human souls would eventually be
saved. For various reasons this theory of Universalism grew stronger and stronger during the nineteenth
century. A distinct trend set in towards slackening
and indeed extinguishing, the everlasting flames of
divine retribution. Today hell, even among religious
groups which still formally include it in their theology,
is decidedly out of fashion. At the same time there has
developed among Christians, and among non-Chris-
tians, too, more and more of an active, positive desire
for immortality. This modern longing for a future
life is directly connected with the modern tendency
to make that realm beyond the grave seem more
worth-while and less forbidding. And there are undoubtedly other influential factors behind this phenomenon, such as the added emphasis on the individual ego which accompanied the rise of capitalism
in the modern world.

On the terms now so frequently offered, with hell
abolished and happiness guaranteed, few normal persons would choose to turn down the gift of immortality. For surely well-nigh all men would be glad
to continue living in another world which promises to
prolong an enjoyment already present or to bring an
enjoyment so far absent; to have a chance to do and
experience all those things for which there was not
time or opportunity in this life; to go to a place where
Ponce de Leon's romantic quest for the elixir of youth
has been answered once and for all by the assurance
that everyone shall possess eternally the health and
vigor of the prime of life. It is begging the question
to say, "An eternity of life, of happiness, of this same
old self? How monotonous, how boring it would be!"

For if there really is unceasing joy and bliss awaiting us on the other side of death, then boredom, monotony and other ills are excluded by definition.

Those comparatively few Westerners who insist that they want oblivion are motivated, I think, by several considerations. In the first place, they may be recoiling in horror and disgust from the orthodox and traditional Christian view of immortality that puts so much emphasis on eternal punishment. In the second place, they may be afflicted with the idea of endlessness. "Is it never to end?" protests one individual. "The thought appals. I, little I, to live a million years —and another million—and another! My tiny light to burn forever!"[202] Another writes: "I feel time lasting indefinitely, space lengthening without end, something like a never-stopping crescendo. It seems to me that my being gradually swells, substitutes itself to everything, grows by absorbing worlds and centuries, then bursts, and everything ceases, and I am left with an atrocious pain in the head and in the stomach. It is eternity which is frightful."[203]

Declares a third: "It is the aimlessness of the process which afflicts the mind; for it is a progress which leads nowhere, which has no goal, seeing that, after ages of forward movement, you are precisely as distant from the imagined end as when you started."[204] Comparatively few believers in the Christian West have thought through the full meaning of durational eternity; have ever asked themselves the simple question: Do I, who know so well the length of one earthly life, really believe that this conscious self of mine is to go on existing for 500 million years and then 500 hundred million more and so on *ad infinitum?* If persons who have faith in immortality asked themselves this question, they would perhaps pass into a temporary state of intellectual vertigo.

In the third place, the wooers of extinction may be genuinely tired of or dissatisfied with life on earth and be simply unable to imagine that the completely happy after-existence promised by the modern immortalists can possibly come true. And in this judgment they are certainly displaying considerable common sense. But the fact remains that granting the reality of the paradise which the more optimistic immortalists portray, the average citizen would hardly decline the opportunity of going there. Sophisticated unbelievers will claim that interest in immortality is vulgar and that only Philistines could want a life beyond the grave; but their protestations smack of the grapes that have soured. It is only honest for those who do not feel able to take stock in a worth-while immortality to admit that such a continuation of existence has often been at least a pleasant dream.

Professor James H. Leuba finds that a considerable number of those who do not believe would take great satisfaction in the assurance of a future life.[205] Analyzing the other unbelievers, he goes on to say: "With the normally constituted individual, the realization of the absence of ground for a belief usually abates and even removes the desire for it. . . . The reasonable man tries to suppress desire for the unattainable and sometimes succeeds."[206] The unbeliever may therefore be sincere in asserting that he does not desire immortality, but he is liable to forget that he might like to have it very much if he thought it within the bounds of possibility.

2. Specific Motivations

I have stated that there are various psychological and affectional factors in human nature which make the desire for immortality easy to arouse. These same factors, of course, make the belief in immortality easy to inculcate. We shall now consider them. And we can begin no more appropriately than by examining that inborn tendency, already mentioned, of human beings to preserve and protect their lives amid the vicissitudes of fortune. This tendency includes an indefinite number of specific reactions to specific and often unique situations. Only in a very vague and summary way is the tendency classifiable as an instinct. It is by no means all-powerful, since human reason and emotion bent on other objectives can overrule it.

Men commit suicide by premeditation and knowingly risk their lives in all kinds of adventurous exploits below, upon and above the earth. Divers and submarine crews disappear beneath the waters never to be seen again; explorers go forth defiantly to die along the frozen wastes of the poles, and mountain climbers upon the icy precipices of unscaled peaks. Aviators daily live dangerously. Throughout history men have sacrificed themselves for the ideals they found compelling, as they did by the millions in the Second World War. Yet during all these most hazardous forms of activity men cling to life to the very last. Indeed, if the tendency towards self-preservation did not on the whole prevail, neither the human individual nor the human species would long endure. And if this tendency had not been a predominating force throughout the long course of evolution, there would have been no intense and competitive struggle for existence, no survival of the fittest, and therefore no man to meditate on the meaning of such things.

Such observations in the end amount to little more than the truism that life is life and will continue to be a forward-pushing and active enterprise as long as it is life at all. This is true of all forms of life, from the humblest to the highest; the lowliest plant will do battle for its place in the sun. The vital urge in any species or any individual is prior to the dawn of mind. It is not something rational or based on experience; it is innate and spontaneous. New-born babes, hovering uncomprehending between life and death, will fight desperately for their niche in the world; octo-

genarians, fatally ill and lapsed into total unconsciousness, will struggle to the end to maintain the faintest
foothold on existence.

But when mortality and its meaning once become
clear, the native tendency towards self-preservation
takes on the additional form of *conscious* fear of death
and love of life. These two states of minds are different expressions of the same fundamental behavior
pattern and they alternate in human beings according
to circumstance. It is readily seen how natural it is
for men to interpret this fear of death and love of life
as a positive wish for a hereafter; how natural it is
for them to ease the fear and indulge the love by
persuading themselves that there actually is a transcendental existence beyond the grave. Thus they express their simple desire for the continuation of present
life in this world as a profound desire for a future life
in another world.

The wholly natural desire of living forms to keep
on living does not, in the main, noticeably abate
among the aged of the human species. In fact, many
old people cling to existence more determinedly than
at any other time in their lives. At the age of eighty-
eight, a few days before his death, Charles Renouvier
stated: "When a man is old, very old, and accustomed
to life, it is very difficult to die. I think that young men
accept the idea of dying more easily, perhaps more
willingly than old men. When one is more than
eighty years old, one is cowardly and shrinks from
death. And when one knows and can no longer doubt
that death is coming near, deep bitterness falls on the
soul."[207] This last thought of Renouvier is especially
important. Though today the greater proportion of
mankind still die in youth and middle age, almost all
individuals in these age periods expect to go on living for a considerable time to come. But the elderly
know for certain that death is waiting for them just
around the corner and that before long they must

meet the fate of all mortals. They may begin to feel
something like the condemned prisoner awaiting execution on a set day. And they are bound to lose the
relative unconcern of younger people for whom death
is a matter of the vague and far-off future.

Another point worth noting is that those who have
survived middle age can with some accuracy take the
measure of their lives, judge just how far their achievements have fallen short of their aims, and see, also,
that now it is too late to retrieve their weaknesses,
their mistakes and their plain bad luck. In youth, no
matter what missteps we make, there is always the
prospect of a long future in which to correct or counteract them. So long as we are not beyond our fifties,
it is never too late to mend; but in the sixties, the
seventies and the eighties this proverb is far less applicable. Men in these latter stages of maturity are
inclined to dream more insistently of a second life
where they will have a second chance, where circumstances will be more propitious and where they will
really be able to do justice to themselves. Rare indeed
is the man who towards the close of life does not feel
that he has been, in one respect or another, something
of a failure and who does not wish that he might
have an opportunity to remold his career.

Ilya Metchnikoff, the celebrated Russian biologist,
found that "the desire to live, instead of diminishing
tends, on the contrary, to increase with age."[208] This
opinion is the more convincing because Metchnikoff
himself was an ardent advocate of developing what he
called the "instinct for death," that is, a positive desire
to die on the part of old persons comparable to the
wish to sleep when tired. He believed that almost all
human deaths are premature and caused by some kind
of simple violence or by that more complex form
of violence known as disease, and that therefore this
potential instinct has been prevented from expressing
itself. His ideal was "orthobiosis," which is "the de-

velopment of human life so that it passes through a long period of old age in active and vigorous health leading to the final period in which there shall be present a sense of satiety of life and a wish for death."[209]

Walter Savage Landor, on his seventy-fourth birthday, wrote four lines which give consummate expression to what Metchnikoff had in mind:

> *I strove with none, for none was worth my strife.*
> *Nature I loved and, next to Nature, Art:*
> *I warmed both hands before the fire of life;*
> *It sinks, and I am ready to depart.*[210]

In all his widespread and careful researches on the subject Metchnikoff discovered only two cases of old people in whom the instinct for death was sufficiently well advanced to accord with his theory. And it is doubtful whether his ideal of a universal instinct for death among human beings will ever be fulfilled. For besides meaning universal old age it would entail a perfect timing for the arrival of death that could be rarely expected. So long as there is a physiological energy in the body that serves to keep life going, there will usually be as its counterpart a psychological desire to keep life going. If death came only when the physical strength of the body was entirely exhausted, then we might well accept it with the same readiness as sleep. The trouble is that most people die when the physiological vitality of many parts of the organism is still strong and when, therefore, the psychological urge for life is also strong. For death is ordinarily due to a breakdown in one section of the organism which has fatal results for the body as a whole.

All this is not to overlook the fact that a number of the aged who are miserable, weak and losing the use of their faculties one by one, may devoutly wish for a speedy and painless end. But this is a wish likely to arise in intelligent people of any age who are afflicted with incurable illness and suffering. And in some cases the conscious will to have life terminate may overcome, through an act of suicide, all the factors, subconscious as well as conscious, that make for the continuance of life no matter how distasteful it may be. Yet in practically all cases of suicide or would-be suicide it is to be remembered that the person desires to die because this life no longer seems *worth-while* and not because he craves non-existence. However unbearable his condition, he would normally accept with alacrity the offer of a rejuvenated life beyond the tomb where he would enjoy everlasting health and happiness. Thus, the positive desire or definite decision to depart this world by no means implies a predilection for oblivion.

The idea of extinction is so repulsive, according to Plutarch, that we may "almost say that all men and women would readily submit themselves to the teeth of Cerberus, and to the punishment of carrying water in a sieve, if only they might remain in existence and escape the doom of annihilation."[211] The poet Heine cries out: "How our soul struggles against the thought of the cessation of our personality, of eternal annihilation! The *horror vacui* which we ascribe to nature is really inborn in the human heart."[212] Unamuno takes the position of being a defiant conscientious objector against personal extinction: "If it is nothingness that awaits us, let us make an injustice of it; let us fight against destiny, even though without hope of victory; let us fight against it quixotically."[213] Dylan Thomas protests:

Do not go gentle into that good night.
Rage, rage against the dying of the light.[214]

Even Thomas Huxley, a very tough-minded scientist who had no faith in immortality and who died in 1895, writes near the close of his life: "It is a curious thing that I find my dislike to the thought of extinction increasing as I get older and nearer the goal. It flashes across me at all sorts of times and with a sort of horror that in 1900 I shall probably know no more of what is going on than I did in 1800. I had sooner be in hell a good deal—at any rate in one of the upper circles where the climate and company are not too trying."[215]

In a questionnaire conducted by Professor F. C. S. Schiller 22 per cent of those who answered asserted that they preferred any sort of a future life to annihilation.[216] Thus it is apparent that for some men the prospect of the most gloomy and hateful variety of after-existence can serve as a kind of psychological buffer against the stern and stark idea of annihilation. And this is understandable. For to try to realize that when once we close our eyes in death, we shall never, never open them again on any happy or absorbing scene, that this pleasant earth will roll on and on for ages with ourselves no more sensible of what transpires than a dull clod, that this brief and flickering and bitter-sweet life is our only glimpse, our only taste, of existence throughout the billion infinities of unending time—to try to realize this, even to phrase such thoughts, can occasion a black, sinking spell along the pathways of sensation.

To the profound aversion towards non-existence we can to a large degree attribute, among those unable to believe in personal survival, the interest in various substitute or vicarious types of immortality that I summarized in the first chapter.* The most important of these are ideal immortality, the attainment of a certain high and noble quality in life and intellect; biological immortality in the ongoing generations of one's children and descendants; and social immortality through the continuing impact of one's personality,

* See pp. 23-24.

work, fame or even impersonal achievements on successive societies of the future. The strength of the bent towards fame is seen in the characteristic efforts to preserve one's name and memory among the living by means of countless different devices. And it is evidenced in the general preference among males for sons, who will carry on the family name.

In Plato's *Symposium*, Diotima says to Socrates: "Think only of the ambition of men, and you will wonder at the senselessness of their ways, unless you consider how they are stirred by the love of an immortality of fame. They are ready to run all risks greater far than they would have run for their children, and to spend money and undergo any sort of toil, and even to die, for the sake of leaving behind them a name which shall be eternal."[217] The economic and social effects of this sentiment, operating through the distribution and expenditure of wealth, have been and are immense and incalculable. But even for the greatest men we can think of today, what will the immortality of fame amount to, one wonders, a million years from now?

The universal shrinking from death is often augmented by the fear of dying, that is, fear of the process, gradual or sudden, that brings to a final conclusion our stay upon this earth. This process, particularly if in the form of long-drawn-out illness may indeed entail much physical pain and mental anguish. Even when it is short it may involve terrible suffering, as when people meet death in some frightful automobile or airplane accident. Yet only a comparatively few men perish in this manner; and there can be no doubt that on the whole the terrors of dying have been greatly exaggerated. There is much good evidence to the effect that the last moments of life are for the vast majority far from an ordeal.

The eminent English physician, Sir Arbuthnot Lane, tells us: "In the course of my life I must have

seen scores of people die. Some of them were people
who in life had been horribly afraid of death. Yet I
don't think I can remember a single instance where,
when their time came, this fear did not leave them, to
be replaced by a wonderful state of peace and calm. I
have never known anybody really resent death when
their last moment has come. They have clung desperately to life so long as they could; and may have
regretted bitterly the parting with their friends and
all that they held dear, but not one who was conscious
to the end ever seemed to regard death as a horrible
climax to life. In all such cases it came as a perfectly
natural and undisturbed happening."[218]

Sir William Osler, the noted surgeon, gives testimony of the same nature. "I have careful records," he
writes, "of about five hundred death-beds, studied
particularly with reference to the modes of death and
the sensations of the dying. . . . Ninety suffered bodily
pain or distress of one sort or another, eleven showed
mental apprehension, two positive terror, one expressed spiritual exaltation, one bitter remorse. The
great majority gave no sign one way or the other; like
their birth, their death was a sleep and a forgetting."[219] Whatever the facts, however, men have long
been accustomed to attach to death the blame for all
the afflictions, actual and reputed, of the process of
dying. Thus, they have placed on innocent death a
guilt which properly belongs to life itself; and this
miscarriage of justice has been of considerable influence on the philosophical and religious attitudes of
mankind.

Much of the dismal and oppressive atmosphere
that usually surrounds the disposal of the dead is also
transferred, through the processes of association, to
death. No matter how skilful the embalmer's art, no
matter how calm and reposed the appearance of the
body, no matter how beautiful the floral decorations,
it is at best not a pleasant thing to view the cold and

unresponsive corpse of a beloved intimate, so appallingly like yet unlike the living person. That last intense look at the dead body lying in the coffin may haunt for years the inner recesses of the mind. Funeral services, however short and simple, however unaccompanied by crêpe and tears, do not result in happy memories. And the final procession to the cemetery, behind a sable hearse, and the final lowering of the coffined body into the grave are experiences that leave grim and indelible traces on the souls of the living.

The fact that we have been accustomed to associate the personality of the departed with his body may lead us to half-imagine that the man himself is in the coffin and in the ground, as common idioms, such as "he would turn in his grave," well illustrate. So we may conceive of the deceased as perhaps overwhelmed by the absolute solitude, stillness and darkness. Thoughts of the inevitable decay and dissolution of his body may also come to plague us; and we may meditate, Hamlet-like, concerning the unflattering destiny that overtakes what was once a man. These painful reflections we may even carry forward to that day when our own familiar body may be interred. These are indeed morbid thoughts, but they are thoughts that not infrequently arise in conjunction with ordinary burial customs and the well-known fate of corpses.

Closely connected with the natural interest in immortality that results from the general tendency to seek life and avoid death is the fact that the very structure and functioning of the human personality encourage confidence in continued existence. "I not only postulate a morrow when I prepare for it, but ingenuously and heartily believe that the morrow will come. . . . Every moment of life accordingly trusts that life will continue; and this prophetic interpretation of action, so long as action lasts, amounts to continual faith in futurity."[220] By far the greater part of rational deliberation directly or indirectly concerns our future and confidently assumes that that future will occur.

William Hazlitt has a marvelous passage on the initial incredibility of extinction: "To see the golden sun and the azure sky, the outstretched ocean, to walk upon the green earth, and to be lord of a thousand creatures, to look down the giddy precipices or over the distant flowery vales, to see the world spread out under one's finger in a map, to bring the stars near, to view the smallest insects in a microscope, to read history, and witness the revolutions of empire and the succession of generations, to hear of the glory of Sidon and Tyre, of Babylon and Susa, as of a faded pageant, and to say all these were, and are now nothing, to think that we exist in such a point of time, and in such a corner of space, to be at once spectators and a part of the moving scene, to watch the return of the seasons of spring and autumn, to hear

The stockdove plain amid the forest deep,
That drowsy rustles to the sighing gale

—to traverse desert wilderness, to listen to the midnight choir, to visit lighted halls, or plunge into the dungeon's gloom, or sit in crowded theatres and see life itself mocked, to feel heat and cold, pleasure and pain, right and wrong, truth and falsehood, to study the works of art and refine the sense of beauty to agony, to worship fame and to dream of immortality, to have read Shakespeare and belong to the same species as Sir Isaac Newton; to be and do all this, and then in a moment to be nothing, to have it all snatched from one like a juggler's ball or a phantasmagoria; there is something revolting and incredible to sense in the transition, and no wonder, that, aided by youth and warm blood and the flush of enthusiasm, the mind contrives for a long time to reject it with disdain and loathing as a monstrous and improbable fiction."[221]

But we must supplement Hazlitt to remark how very difficult, if not impossible, it is concretely to envision ourselves as non-existent. We may see with the mind's eye our own death-bed, view upon it our own rigid and lifeless corpse, witness our own funeral service, but we ourselves are always there as living observers. Whether we shift our imagination two thousand years back to the assassination of Julius Caesar or indefinitely forward to the first air flight for man's colonization of Mars—indeed no matter how many thousands of years our minds pry into the future or into the past or however far afield into space—*we* are at the scene of action busily playing the reporter's role. And in this sense we are truly egocentric.*

Freud characteristically comments upon the matter: "Our own death is indeed unimaginable, and whenever we make the attempt to imagine it we can perceive that we really survive as spectators. Hence the psychoanalytic school could venture on the assertion that at bottom no one believes in his own death; or to put the same thing in another way, in the unconscious every one of us is convinced of his own immortality. . . . What we call our 'unconscious' (the deepest strata of our minds, made up of instinctual impulses) knows nothing whatever of negatives or denials—contradictions coincide in it—and so it knows nothing whatever of our own death, for to that we can give only a negative purport."[222] Thus, as Edward Young writes in his famous poem, *Night Thoughts*, "All men think all men mortal but themselves."

Yet, while the *limitations* of the imagination help

* One of America's most acute philosophers, Professor F. J. E. Woodbridge of Columbia, thought that the impossibility of men's imagining themselves non-existent was the most powerful motive of all towards belief in personal immortality.

in some ways to make acceptable the belief in immortality, at the same time its very power and scope can have a like effect. One does not have to belong to any religious cult to have the experience of remembering a dead person so vividly on occasion that it seems as if he himself must still exist. We are habitually and normally able to recall images of departed personalities that have far more reality-tone than memories of places which we know for certain to be objectively existent. When someone close to us dies, especially if suddenly, the sheer momentum of our mental habits often makes us feel, "Why this is impossible. He *can't* be gone." It takes time for us to overcome a curious feeling of unreality and to readjust our minds to the new situation. Such mental states lead easily to the claim that one has a sure and dependable sense of the objective though invisible presence of the dead. In dreams we may see, talk with and even touch the dead. And in view of these well-known facts it does not seem surprising that the living should report in good faith that even during waking hours they carry on social intercourse with the souls of the deceased. Men will probably keep on "seeing" various species of ghosts and apparitions to the end of time. For those who will not let reason discipline their imaginations, such visions will always seem a reliable indication that there is another life.

A kindred motivation behind belief in immortality is the commonplace distinction, much stressed in our earlier chapters, between body and personality or soul. Among many peoples the phenomena of dreams, trances and the ordinary human shadow have encouraged credence in the soul as an entity able to exist separately and independently of the body. A more inclusive and modern position is that of Dr. Holmes: "I believe," he avers, "in immortality because not otherwise can we explain the discrepancy between soul and body. Early in life these two begin to pull apart—the body to fail and the soul to grow stronger and ever stronger. Physically we begin to die when spiritually we are most ready to live."[223] Dr. Fosdick expresses much the same thought when he says that "the assertion of our immortality involves the faith that we are invisible, spiritual personalities."[224]

These and many other similar statements by immortalists seem to be in essence far more proclamations of the soul-body distinction and of the value of the soul than convincing arguments for immortality; they indicate that the immortalists think the very existence of the soul or personality to be in jeopardy unless it is eternal. The discerning Professor Woodbridge aptly phrases our point when he writes that proofs of immortality "illustrate the radical difference between body and soul and turn the illustrations into evidence."[225] A comparable situation arises when men, utilizing familiar religious terminology, fight for the more individualistic values under the banner of the immortality of the soul.[226]

The strongest single motivation, however, supporting belief in a future life is in my opinion the effect on the living of the death of friends, relatives and even entire strangers. Unutterable grief over the loss of a beloved child or parent and intense desire to be with him again are natural and universal human feelings. And they lead, as there is abundant evidence to show, quite directly to hope or conviction of a hereafter. I have already cited in another connection Dr. Little's statement that the almost simultaneous death of his parents completely satisfied him that personal immortality exists. The great biologist, Henri Pasteur, writes: "My philosophy is of the heart and not of the mind, and I give myself up, for instance, to those feelings about eternity which come naturally at the bedside of a cherished child drawing its last breath."[227] A young man of thirty-one says: "My belief in a future life and in recognition after death have been strengthened by the death of my little boy." Another confides: "The death of a near friend a year ago has profoundly affected my life; it seems as if a part of myself is gone and that I shall never recover my wholeness until I am with him again."[228]

Friedrich Schleiermacher leaves us a letter from a close friend who has just lost her husband: "Schleier, by all that is dear to God and sacred, give me, if you can, the certain assurance of finding and knowing him again. Tell me your inmost faith on this, dear Schleier; Oh! if it fails, I am undone. It is for this that I live, for this that I submissively and quietly endure: this is the only outlook that sheds a light on my dark life,—to find him again, to live for him again. O God! he cannot be destroyed!"[229] There are numerous cases on record of people killing themselves to preclude being parted from the beloved dead.* Paralleling these profound reactions on the part of the bereaved are the strong hopes of those who are dying or whose time is short to meet again the loved ones they are leaving behind, or at least to watch their development. It is not difficult to understand why people should have such intense feelings in the face of death or why they should interpret these feelings as valid reasons for belief in a future life. Probably the greater proportion of believers in the world today would agree with William James that "the surest warrant for immortality is the yearning of our bowels for our dear ones."[230] There can be no doubt that the idea of immortality will continue to exercise an appeal "as long as love kisses the lips of death,"[231] in the words of Robert Ingersoll.

But it is not only *love* for the departed that leads to hope for their immortality. The attachment to them may be negative and in the form of secret dislike or hatred. In most families there exists a certain amount of antagonism among the different members; and in

* See p. 16.

some, bitter quarrels are the rule rather than the exception. When one member of a family passes on, the others, no matter how innocent of being remiss, are likely to reproach themselves for neglect and harsh words. They may have a distinct sense of guilt and be anxious for an opportunity to show more affectionate feelings toward the relative who has died.[232] By their devotion to his memory and their hymns of praise to his good qualities they will try to prove to him that, after all, they loved him deeply. But unless he still exists somewhere as a conscious person, their efforts are in vain. Hence they cherish the thought that at least temporarily he has survived death and is able to appreciate their attitude.

Attesting to the far-reaching effects of the loss of dear ones is the fresh and absorbing interest which the matter of immortality often takes on for the sorrowing survivors. A widow or a grieving parent will order a whole shelf of books on the future life, will suddenly become devoutly religious or will go in for Spiritualism with a vengeance. Then as time passes and the hurt grows less, as the bereaved gradually becomes more and more adjusted to the new situation, his preoccupation with the hereafter diminishes. Thus Dr. Lawton finds that the normal Spiritualist attends services for only a relatively short period, usually not more than one or two years.[233] A merely temporary credence in survival, then, may function as a psychological shock-absorber or therapeutic. And in general what many people really want is *belief* in immortality rather than immortality itself.

It should be noted here that the orthodox Spiritualist, Catholic and other religious practices in relation to the dead by no means always have a curative effect. By encouraging the bereaved to keep on constantly and indefinitely thinking about the departed, saying masses for his soul, or trying to converse with him through mediums, these practices sometimes keep open and raw the painful wound of death. They may prompt the mourners to withdraw from the world and its fruitful activities and to center their thoughts upon the memory of the beloved dead. Especially is this a danger in Spiritualism with its continual and morbid emphasis on actual discourse with the personalities of the departed, its ghoulish spirit photographs and its experiments, following out the tradition of the Witch of Endor and other historical celebrities, in raising phantoms from the depths of nowhere. Nor is it exactly healthy to have constantly that eerie feeling that the dead are always present and perhaps watching your every move. Thus the natural concern with the theory of survival that results from the death of the near and dear may be abnormally stimulated.

When some great and well-loved public figure dies, members of the community may be moved to reflect upon a hereafter whether or not they knew the man personally. The passing of a president, a king, a leading statesman or, in some countries, a motion picture star, will cause millions to speculate on the meaning of death. A similar result may follow the large-scale loss of human life in some terrible catastrophe, such as a mine disaster, the sinking of a ship at sea, a calamitous flood, fire or earthquake. During the First World War, when millions and millions of men were dying on the battlefields of Europe, concern over a life beyond registered a noticeable increase. "Not for a century," claims an observer, "has interest in the great themes of death, immortality and the life everlasting been so widespread and so profound. The war has made a new heaven; let us trust that it may aid in making a new earth."[234] One writer, Winifred Kirkland, impressed with how the war filled whole populations with the spirit of what she calls "the New Death," makes the astonishing statement: "If even for a few generations we act on our conjecture of immortality, the larger vision, the profounder basis of purpose, will so advance human existence *as to make this war worth its price.*"[235] [Italics mine—C. L.]* And many a Christian clergyman rejoiced over the effect of the First World War in bringing a revival, through suffering, of belief in immortality and other religious doctrines.[236]

While reactions to the death of others differ considerably according to the individual temperament, it is not to be doubted that frequently the most bitter heart-ache occurs when persons are cut off prematurely or when their demise is sudden and totally unexpected. Often these two conditions of dying suddenly and long before one's time coincide. When we read in our morning newspaper of nine young and healthy college students being abruptly snuffed out by carbon monoxide gas as they lay sleeping during the night,[237] we are deeply shocked both at the swift horror of the accident and at the measureless unfulfilled potentialities that came to an end with the death of these youths. We sense, too, the unspeakable anguish of the families concerned, proud of these fine sons and brothers, devoted to them over long years, and bringing them up with loving and sacrificial care only to have them snatched away as they were about to step out into the world and show their mettle. Added to all this is the frustrated feeling of these families at having no chance to say good-bye, no opportunity to speak a last affectionate word or to make some gesture of endearment. On the other hand, to take a very different sort of case, when an old man full of years and honor passes peacefully away during the natural decline of senescence, we are not likely to feel that death is a cruel and awful thing. In fact, we may feel that it has carried out a function both proper and beneficial.

Hence we must classify the widespread reaction

* Cf. p. 261.

to *premature* death as one of the major motivations toward belief in immortality. It is appalling to realize that the First World War claimed some 10,000,000 lives, combatants and non-combatants. The comparable figure for the Second World War totaled 50,000,000. A majority of the victims of course were in their youth or middle age. In the United States accidents alone account for more than 100,000 deaths a year, while more than 20,000 commit suicide. Each year more than 250,000 children perish before reaching fifteen. No less than half of all deaths in America occur during youth or middle age, that is, before the age of sixty-five.

Now since the U. S. record as regards the death-rate and longevity is one of the best in the world, the situation in most other countries is measurably worse. In India, for example, the average expectation of life is approximately thirty-two years, according to latest estimates of the United Nations. These various figures show clearly why there is a common feeling that death cheats our friends, our families and all mankind out of a large portion of experience that is rightfully theirs. If every human being, both in the United States and elsewhere, lived to be seventy or eighty years old, one of the most potent factors leading to credence in immortality would disappear.

Mortals seek many different kinds of compensations in immortality besides those already mentioned. One man may primarily want another existence because he was unsuccessful in love, another because he never received proper recognition from the socially elite, another because his yearning for knowledge remains unsatisfied. This last motivation has often been strong among persons of high intelligence and scientific ability; it was, for instance, undoubtedly an important factor in Plato's interest in immortality. Among religious people the desire to attain a clearer vision of God and to be with Christ has of course been a sincere and powerful element in the hope for life eternal.

Sometimes the thirst for knowledge after death takes the form of sheer curiosity as to what is going to happen on earth; and many an immortalist has had the quaint notion that from the other world, as from a ringside seat, he will look down upon this globe and behold the varying progress of men and nations, of friends and favorite causes.

There are additional motivations that might in general be called philosophical. Thus the English Hegelian, Bernard Bosanquet, is of the opinion that "the longing for continuance is at bottom the longing for the satisfactory whole. . . . What we really care about is not simple prolongation of our 'personal' existence, but, whether accompanying prolongation or in the direct form of liberation, some affirmation of our main interests, or some refuge from the perpetual failure of satisfaction."[238] Closely akin to this is the notion that only if there is immortality does life have "meaning." This is merely another way of saying that without immortality life is futile or irrational. And as I have already pointed out in the previous chapter, very far-reaching metaphysical and ethical assumptions are involved in such statements. They clearly depend on a whole philosophy of value which is of dubious validity, and which is little more than a rationalization of the all too human tendency to insist on a cosmic standing for human desires and ideals.

To borrow the phraseology of John Dewey, the immortalists have a craving for the sure, the fixed, the stable as over-against the uncertain, the changing, the precarious.[239] Or, in Dr. Horace Kallen's language, they want perfect freedom, that is, "the smooth and uninterrupted flow of behavior; the flow of desire into fulfilment, of thought into deed, of act into fact" in a realm where "danger, evil and frustration are non-existent."[240] So it becomes apparent that, in general, frustration of any human impulse, ambition or ideal may be influential in leading to belief in a beyond.

Especially is this true of the more egoistic and self-assertive activities, though concern with a hereafter does not necessarily imply selfishness.

Just as bad health is one of the chief props of the modern religion known as Christian Science, so it can become one of the prime incentives towards belief in immortality. In heaven the sick, the halt and the blind will have glorious and perfect bodies no longer subject to the shortcomings of earthly development and the strains of medical experimentation. The chronic invalid will rise every morning with the vigor of a young athlete about to run a race; the nervous wreck will feel and exude nothing but strength, self-confidence and calm; the bent, ill old man, slow in mind and dull in sense, will step forth as in the prime of life, erect, handsome and alert. Such is the promise of paradise. And it extends not only to those who are definitely ill, but to all who were born with or acquired any sort of deformity. There will be no hunchbacks in the great beyond; and if a man loses a leg here, he can be sure that God will give him back a much better one in heaven. Even those who are rather plain of countenance can expect some improvement in the realm of immortality.

Most of the motivations behind belief in a future existence which I have been citing might become compelling for any human being regardless of his station in life or his share of this world's goods. But it is of the very highest importance to remember that the great masses of men since the beginning of history have been moved, in addition, to hope for a hereafter because of the sheer economic and social misery in which they have for the most part lived. Poverty-stricken, lacking the very necessities of life, crushed by grinding toil, they have had ample reason to flee for refuge and recompense to visions of a world beyond. Shut out from the rich empires of art and culture, denied access to education and opportunity, ever the most numerous victims of the bloody wars that have perpetually plagued mankind, these masses have easily and naturally fallen prey to hallucinations of a blessed hereafter where everything will be set aright. And they have listened with eager ears to the teachings of kings, priests and other henchmen of the *status quo* to the effect that if they remain resigned and humble on this earth, they will have a marvelous reward in heaven. Karl Marx makes a trenchant comment: "The mortgage held by the peasants on the heavenly estates guarantees the mortgage held by the bourgeoisie on the peasant estates."[241]

While no doubt a number of upper-class religious propagandists have had their tongues in their cheeks, especially in modern times, there is no reason to think that most of them have not been devoutly sincere. Indeed, their very sincerity has enabled them to take with good conscience the position that since the well-deserving among the oppressed and suffering masses will in any case receive their proper recompense in paradise, it is not worth while to try to do much about their condition here. An ingenious variation of this attitude is the theory that since character-building is the purpose of existence, the trying and unhappy experiences of this life are simply God's inimitable way of developing and strengthening the soul.

Along with everything else the common people have swallowed religion's bogey-man story about the terrible punishments in the after-life for those who do not conform to established standards of conduct and who are too presumptuous in challenging the settled habits of exploitation. Fear of retribution after death, however, does not imply a weakening of the belief in immortality; and, on the contrary, by deeply involving the emotions, may serve to strengthen it. As I have already pointed out, for long periods of history the prevailing sentiment towards a future life was one of fear rather than of hope and joy. Since the precepts of the Church have always constituted for a large proportion of the workers and peasants their chief education, they have accepted whatever emphasis—whether on heaven or hell—that the Church has chosen to make. In general, the brute weight of authority and tradition has been one of the prime causes of belief in immortality.

A drastic change in the economic and social system, making the world a safer and saner place to live in, would have far-reaching effects on the extent and strength of belief in a hereafter. A more rational social order would, in my judgment, quickly result in a sweeping decline in the influence of immortality ideas. And we have here an excellent supporting illustration for the economic interpretation of history in which economic forces and relationships have a decisive influence on such important elements of the cultural superstructure as religion. This is not to say that in some species of economic Utopia the wish to believe and the belief in such a significant religious idea as that of immortality would automatically and completely disappear. There still would exist those motivations towards belief inherent in the biological and psychological structure of human beings. There still would exist personal frustration, due to such causes as unsatisfied ambition and unrequited love. There still would be premature death from accidents and disease.

But the frustrations would take place on a level unconnected with the maladjustments that come from strain and worry over the basic necessities of a decent existence. Mental and emotional security would increase with economic security, while devotion to the great objectives of the new society would drive personal troubles and Freudian complexes into the background. There can be no doubt that the emphasis in contemporary civilization on individualism and the expansion of the ego has tended to encourage psychological traits that foster the urge for self-perpetuation. The tendency, however, in a more cooperative commonwealth stressing collective effort would be to develop the altruistic rather than the egoistic impulses of men. Everyone would be taught the ideal of fulfilling himself in socially useful activities rather than in those with merely personal significance. In this much improved society of the future the increased freedom from disease, war and violence in general would bring about a corresponding decrease in premature death. All in all, in such a social order many of the most potent factors of the past and present that have led men to seek supernatural consolation in an after-life would be reduced to a minimum.

The remaining factors, such as the drive towards self-preservation and the difficulty of imagining oneself non-existent, would be relatively unaffected by the new social and economic conditions and would have to be specifically dealt with by education and science. Some people desire immortality, moreover, not because they are downtrodden and miserable on this earth, but because they are having such a fine time here that they want to go on with it in another life. In this connection Professor Taylor testifies that in his experience it is just "when we feel most alive and vigorous in soul and body"[242] that we are surest and most desirous of a life beyond. And it is possible that in a cooperative and peaceful world society, where a greater proportion of the people than ever before would presumably be enjoying full and happy lives, some might cast eyes of longing in the direction of an after-existence because of their very feeling of vitality. In such cases the idea of immortality would be compensatory in the sense of counteracting the sense of unhappiness that results from the reflection that a present happiness must end.

The converse of the proposition that a higher and happier form of society will weaken the belief in immortality is that a prior weakening in this belief will help to bring about a better society. If they fully realized that this life is all, men would be less prone to accept without the stiffest sort of resistance the rank injustices and irrationalities of present existence. Those who seem condemned by circumstance to poverty and misery would put up a much stronger fight to better their lot. It would not be so simple to persuade millions of men to sacrifice their lives in frightful wars if they recognized that death was the absolute end. Increasing lack of faith in a hereafter would also react against the general conservative influence of supernatural religion. The very fact that disbelief in immortality can be an important factor in stirring the masses of the people to militant action makes many sophisticated members of the upper classes reluctant to have the truth about death too widely broadcast.

It is, of course, grossly inaccurate to say, as some careless critics do, that all immortality ideas are merely compensatory or wish-fulfilling. This neglects the fact that among primitive tribes these ideas have been pseudo-scientific principles of explanation designed to make intelligible such phenomena as dreams, trances and apparitions in which the dead appear to play a part. More important still, it overlooks the dread with which large numbers of mankind have regarded existence beyond the grave. Where fear of an after-life is the prevailing sentiment and desire for it weak or non-existent, it is difficult to understand how the idea of immortality can be classed as a wish-fulfilment. This does not mean, however, that the inclusion of hell in the hereafter in itself deprives the future life of its quite common character of wish-fulfilment. It all depends on the emphasis given to hell and the extent to which men feel that they are likely to go there rather than to heaven.

The simple idea of hell has often functioned as a necessary complement of heaven in an all-embracing moral or hedonistic wish-fulfilment. Men may devoutly desire hell—for other people. And the assumption that the Powers-that-be in the universe, in the role of cosmic police officers, will deal severely with whatever man considers evil is no less a reading of wishes and ideals into existence than the assumption that they are supporting everything he deems good. In fact it is the same anthropomorphic assumption expressed differently. The concept of hell is compensatory in so far as it serves to provide a vicarious victory over the evils that so frequently win the day in this-earthly life. Like the idea of heaven it is only too likely to cut the nerve of effective action against the ills of this world. One of the most impassioned of the early Church Fathers, Tertullian, gives us a most instructive paean of transcendental triumph: "How shall I admire, how laugh, how exult when I behold so many proud monarchs groaning in the lower abyss of darkness, so many magistrates liquefying in fiercer flames than they ever kindled against the Christians; so many sage philosophers blushing in red-hot fires with their deluded pupils."[243]

Now if a Christian really believes, with Tertullian, not only that his virtuousness will bring him eternal reward in paradise, but also that the wickedness of his enemies and oppressors will be revenged and punished in hell, he can afford to take a very serene view of the woes of this life. If he himself happens to be a member of the ruling class instead of one of the underdogs, his pangs of conscience regarding some of the more brutal and nefarious practices of the governing authorities can easily be assuaged by his inner assurance that the guilty will receive their proper deserts in the next world. If God can be depended upon to wreak stern justice in the hereafter on the heads of tyrants and malefactors, then why should anyone bother too much about them in the here-now? And where hell is taken seriously, this logic applies

just as much in the modern world as in the ancient and
medieval.

Even ideas of hell can, then, to a certain extent
be rightly designated as wish-fulfilments. When we
turn to the idea of heaven, "the land of pure delight,"
we find that the wish-fulfilment interpretation is fully
justified. Analyses of the motivations behind belief in
a blessed immortality, of the arguments supporting it
and of the descriptions that are part of it all point to
this conclusion. In the last chapter we saw how the
so-called ethical arguments stressed in modern times
involved little more than turning human wishes into
proofs. And if we call to mind any characteristic portrayals of paradise, we see at once that they conform
to the familiar earthly life, needs and desires of the
particular people concerned.

In the realm beyond, the Egyptians must have
their River Nile, the Mohammedans their alluring
young females, the Scandinavians their warlike Valhalla, the American Indians their Happy Hunting
Ground, the Christians their saints and angels. The
Book of Revelation promises that the righteous in
heaven "shall hunger no more, neither thirst any
more; neither shall the sun light on them, nor any
heat."[244] No vast penetration is required to realize
that this passage was written by someone who thought
that the climate in Palestine was more than a trifle
too hot. On the other hand, when missionaries told
the Eskimos about the excessive warmth of hell, these
inhabitants of the frozen north, evidently rather tired
of so much ice and snow, responded by asking eagerly
the way to the infernal regions.[245]

Naturally enough the ethical distinctions in heaven
vary with the standards and ideals of this-worldly
cultures. In one culture the brave will be awarded
the choicest places in the next life, in another the
humble; in one culture the strenuously active, in
another the devoutly contemplative. In Christianity

itself there have been shifts of emphasis according to time and place. In former ages, for example, paradise, reflecting common this-earthly attitudes, was conceived of as a state of inactive bliss, as an eternal rest-home where the weary righteous could cease from their labors and bask forever in easeful ecstasy. Today, however, when joyous and rewarding work is comparatively more widespread and at least held out to everyone as an ideal, there is a tendency to picture heaven as a place where fruitful activity will continue and souls will press on to unending development and improvement.

A motivation akin to simple wish-fulfilment in lending support to dreams of immortality is the human predilection for the dramatic. An after-existence where you can be reunited with your friends and family is plainly a more exciting prospect than death as the absolute end. Then there are all the other imagined delights, beauties and adventures of the hereafter, including the chance to meet the many great and glamorous figures of the past. Add a purgatory and hell as colorfully described as in the *Divine Comedy*, and the panorama of immortality becomes an absorbing drama with enormous theatrical appeal, particularly for those whose lives are on the humdrum side.

That there should be such a large element of wish-fulfilment in immortality ideas does not in itself disestablish them. To desire a thing greatly no more *dis*proves than proves its existence. But if we deeply wish something to be true, we must be doubly on guard to prevent our emotions from influencing our judgment on the question. And in the case of immortality, with such a wide and powerful range of motivations encouraging belief in the idea, there is reason to regard an affirmative answer with considerable suspicion. Especially does this hold true today when there is so much emphasis on the pleasant aspects of the future life, and hell is considered so out-of-date. For

these various reasons I believe that for the modern
mind one of the most appropriate and penetrating
comments that can be made on the points at issue
is to be found in Rupert Brooke's satire entitled
"Heaven."[246] I give this poem in full:

> Fish (fly-replete in depth of June,
> Dawdling away their wat'ry noon)
> Ponder deep wisdom, dark or clear,
> Each secret fishy hope or fear.
> Fish say, they have their Stream and Pond;
> But is there anything Beyond?
> This life cannot be All, they swear,
> For how unpleasant, if it were!
> One may not doubt that somehow, Good
> Shall come of Water and of Mud;
> And, sure, the reverent eye must see
> A Purpose in Liquidity.
> We darkly know, by Faith we cry,
> The future is not Wholly Dry.
> Mud unto mud!—Death eddies near—
> Not here the appointed End, not here!
> But somewhere, beyond Space and Time
> Is wetter water, slimier slime!
> And there (they trust) there swimmeth One
> Who swam ere rivers were begun,
> Immense, of fishy form and mind,
> Squamous, omnipotent, and kind;
> And under that Almighty Fin,
> The littlest fish may enter in.
> Oh! never fly conceals a hook
> Fish say, in the Eternal Brook,
> But more than mundane weeds are there,
> And mud, celestially fair;
> Fat caterpillars drift around,
> And Paradisal grubs are found;
> Unfading moths, immortal flies,
> And the worm that never dies.

And in that Heaven of all their wish
There shall be no more land, say fish!

3. Symbolic Interpretations

Symbolism as a term, when applied to ideas of immortality, may have a two-fold significance. It may mean an interpretation of immortality concepts as approximations to an unknown supernatural. Or it may mean, as in this chapter, the taking of immortality descriptions and arguments as illustrative of certain events, experiences and ideals in the life of man on this earth. It regards representations of the future life as a kind of poetry, even though the immortalists creating this poetry intend it as literal prose. For the creation of symbols, like the enjoyment of them, is often carried on unconsciously or semi-consciously, especially in the field of religion where words and ideas have such rich emotional overtones. In this sphere it is neither easy nor always possible to draw a definite line between what the faithful take and intend as literal and what as symbolic. In a broad sense immortality ideas have symbolized all the motivations which have led men to believe in a life beyond the grave. Thus, they have often constituted poignant expressions of the hate and fear of death, of grief and love, of frustration and egoism, of the thirst for knowledge and the lust for sensuality. And in their function of wish-fulfilments they have symbolized whatever was considered enjoyable, good or ideal in the earthly environment of the describer or desirer.

All portrayals of the future life that have moral significance constitute ethical judgments on this world, although at the same time attempted delineations of the next. The preacher has immortalized in heaven whatever he deems the true, the good and the beautiful; and by emphasizing the indestructibility of the human personality he has made plain what he judges the supreme value of all. Taking his descriptions as a whole, it may be said that the immortalist, following Plato, has laid up a pattern of the perfect city "which he who desires may behold, and beholding, may set his own house in order."[247] Paradise in this sense becomes a synonym for Utopia. And according to the psychologist, G. Stanley Hall, the idea of immortality has made man "much more anxious to prolong and enlarge his mundane life. The great and good things he expected beyond he now strives to attain here. He wants more, not less, as of old in this life, because he expected so much in the other."[248] Similarly, stories of the soul's pre-existence in a blessed state, as in Plato's myth in the *Phaedrus,* may be equated with accounts of those Golden Ages of the past in which man was supposed to have reached the zenith of his career.

It is possible to construe some of the main synonyms for immortality in a like manner. The noblest this-worldly philosophies are ever aiming at "a future life," "a hereafter," "another world" in which the great social ideals will find a more complete embodiment. In this sense all reform and radical movements are following out the Lord's prayer by trying to bring heaven to pass on this earth. Thus William Blake sings:

> *I will not cease from mental fight,*
> *Nor shall my sword sleep in my hand,*
> *Till we have built Jerusalem*
> *In England's green and pleasant land.*[249]

But it is always to be remembered that the future states pictured by humanistic idealists are utopias of this-worldly reconstruction, not of other-worldly escape, like those of the immortalists.

Descriptions of hell and purgatory also illustrate the familiar process of projecting earthly circumstances into the beyond. The presence of these two departments in the hereafter ensures the doing of perfect justice and symbolizes the ethical and other evils that afflict the human race. "To be in Hell," says Professor Irwin Edman, "has been to experience eternal torment, and there have been, as there are still, human pains which, though they last but a brief period, are eternal in their character and bitterness."[250] In addition, the idea of the Last Judgment, in which we are forever damned or blessed on our earthly records alone, may well symbolize the undoubted truth that our fellow-men render a last and final estimate of us according to the quality of our lives here in this world.

Once we have lived, it is true forever that we have lived; true forever that we fought for the right or surrendered to the wrong. Death rounds off our lives and sets them in a frame, so that our fellow-men can see and judge and pass eternal sentence on us. Death, the great leveler, the universal democratizer, makes no exceptions. All stand equal before it, unable, no matter what their worldly circumstances, to escape a solemn and final reckoning. In this respect the traditional Christian idea of immortality is far sounder than the one current among modern churchmen, which promises that everyone shall ultimately be saved. The latter view robs death of its momentousness and the Last Judgment of all meaning. It sugar-coats the stern finality of death and tells a tale that the strong-souled Puritan Fathers would have laughed to scorn.

The discerning student, by examining the immortality concepts of a people or period in the light of interpretative symbolism, should be able to learn a great deal about the culture in question. For instance, the fact that among a number of primitive tribes only the chiefs and other persons of rank went on after death to immortality, while the common people perished, reveals important knowledge about existing

this-earthly social conditions. With the Leeward Is-
landers none but the wealthier members of society
were able to go to the heaven of "sweet-scented
Rohutu"; "for only they could afford to pay the heavy
charges which the priests exacted for a passport to
paradise,"[251] a custom reminiscent of certain practices
in the Catholic Church. In ancient Peru the royal Incas
and a select group of nobles were supposed to go at
death to the mansions of the Sun, while the masses of
the people went to an inferior after-world of their own.
In ancient Egypt, too, kindred conceptions of immortality based on class prevailed during several dynas-
ties. A most significant study of immortality descriptions could be made showing how they symbolize, in
ways varying from the crude to the subtle, the shifting
class relations of this world.

Turning to some of the more outstanding docu-
ments, we find excellent examples of how, in general,
immortality ideas function symbolically. In the Old
Testament the development of after-life notions clearly
represents recurring and special crises in the history
of the Hebrew people. It will be recalled that the Old
Testament writers and prophets for the most part
envisaged the future existence as a sad and dreary
place, and that they were far more vitally concerned
with the future fate of the tribe or nation on this
earth. They thought of rewards and punishments
chiefly in this-worldly terms. It was only after the repeated failure of the Messianic hope with its promise
of this-worldly justice that the stern and exact Israelites, who had traditionally demanded an eye for
an eye and a tooth for a tooth, looked to other-worldly
justice to provide the proper sanctions for conduct.
And it is interesting to note that at first and for some
time subsequently they conceived a blessed immortality for the righteous as applying to Jews only.

The kind of reflection which the Exile and other
such catastrophes stimulated in reference to the nation

had already been anticipated by Job in reference to the individual. It was inevitable that Job, accepting the doctrine of a retributive judgment enforced in this existence, should address protests and queries to God when he discovered that, as a matter of fact, the wicked prospered and the righteous, including himself, suffered bitter misfortunes. The eventual shift of retribution from life this side of the grave to life the other side was the logical outcome. It was especially understandable in view of the gradual evolution in Israel, starting with Jeremiah and Ezekiel, of a theory of ethical individualism which upset the old standards of corporate responsibility and retribution.

This new conception of individual responsibility undermined the idea of God's punishing the iniquity of the fathers by afflicting the children or rewarding the goodness of the fathers by blessing the children. And since obviously neither the fathers nor the children of any generation received their just deserts on this earth, the moral dilemma could only be solved by postulating a realm of compensation beyond. Perfect justice in a future life for both the nation and the individual was, as we know, the final result which emerged in Israel. In view of these considerations, we can state without hesitation that the development in Hebraic notions of immortality symbolized important moral situations and crises germane to this world.

By universal acknowledgment, however, the symbolic function and status of immortality descriptions have received their finest and most complete exemplification in the *Divine Comedy* of Dante. In his incomparable epic this foremost poet of Christianity sums up and celebrates his own ideals and those of his time, including many which belong to every great age of human endeavor. Dante, living at the height of an outstanding epoch in human history, offers in his treatment of immortality something of a contrast to the shifting conceptions of the Old Testament. For his detailed representations of the other world illustrate and interpret a rounded and finished set of ethical standards. Each important moral good the poet enshrines on an altar of its own in the realm beyond; each bad he degrades to a little hell. He gives his last judgment on *this* world by telling a marvelous story about the *other*. Here is no dull textbook on ethics; no platitudinous, tiresome sermon. Yet here is the best moralizing and perhaps the most effective teaching in the history of Christianity.

A complete account of the symbolism in Dante's famous work would have to be well-nigh as long and detailed as the poem itself. It is sufficient for us to call attention to a few conspicuous examples. To begin with, that the poet was not without a this-worldly moral chart in his plotting of the after-life is clearly shown by his constant reliance on the Church doctrines of the time and on the whole medieval store of antique culture, particularly Virgil's *Aeneid* and Aristotle's *Ethics*. Turning explicitly to Dante's hell and purgatory, we find significant his judgments as between the lesser and the greater sinners. For instance, in Limbo, the first circle of hell, nearest to the sunlight, he places the spirits of those who lived virtuously but without faith in Christ: ancient poets such as Homer and Horace and wise philosophers such as Socrates and Plato—all the noble characters of antiquity. Next to this distinguished group, in the second circle of hell, where punishments are comparatively lenient, we come upon unlawful lovers; while we meet the gluttons just below in the third, where Santayana remarks with acumen, drunkards would have been lodged by a Northern mind. The less intemperate lovers and gluttons we discover in corresponding positions in purgatory. Evidently Dante agrees with Aristotle that the various offenses of incontinence are the most excusable.

The great sins are of a different nature. That is the reason Dante puts most of the heretics in the sixth circle, far down into hell, where the punishments are excruciating; and why he dooms an arch-heretic and schismatic such as Mohammed to one of the lowest pits of the eighth circle, in the very depths. Those guilty of ordinary pride, which is only too likely to lead to heresy, find themselves in the bottom-most round of purgatory. In the lowest ring of Inferno, frozen deep in the ice of Cocytus, lies Lucifer, the supreme example of pride's revolting against the will of God. With him are the arch-traitors Judas, Brutus and Cassius; while lesser traitors occupy slightly higher rings of this ninth and lowest circle. In this fashion Dante mirrors in the next world not only the uncompromising and belligerent attitude of the Church towards pride and heresy, but also the social condemnation of treachery, the most heinous offense possible in a feudal society based on mutual performance of obligations.

Equally revealing is the situation in paradise. There we meet in the seventh heaven, far above men of mere learning and wisdom like Thomas Aquinas, those blessed souls who spent their earthly lives in ascetic retirement and devout contemplation. Except for certain saints they are the nearest of all to that pure and boundless Empyrean where dwell the angels and Almighty God. Here again the this-worldly ideals of his age give the key to the underlying principle of Dante's careful discriminations in the realm of immortality. It is to be noted also that a certain meagerness in the acceptable hedonistic ideals of the time is reflected in the poet's descriptions of heaven. As Dr. Randall puts it: "Even the most imaginative visions of a Dante could find no colors in which to paint a satisfying eternity. The furniture of Hell lay only too ready at hand in the world of men, but in Paradise the poet could discern only a play of radiant light, and wisely filled that part of his journey with the doctrines of holy faith."[252]*

The fact that immortality ideas again and again have symbolized moral ideals indicates why moral ideals have again and again become inseparably tied up with immortality ideas in the minds of men. An analysis of early survival conceptions, such as those of the ancient Hebrews and Greeks, shows that at first there were no ethical distinctions made in the after-existence. Human morality was not originally, then, dependent in any way on a belief in immortality. As soon, however, as immortality descriptions start to take on ethical significance and to include the good-bad distinctions of this earth, moral standards once self-supporting may become inextricably interwoven with conventional dogmas concerning the hereafter.

The heaven-hell classifications of the next world, originally the effects of corresponding differentiations in this, soon begin to shine with a light of their own, fierce or pleasant, especially when embodied in magnificent poetry and stirring ritual. They may gradually come to be considered as the primordial patterns. They then enter upon their career of enforcing and encouraging moral conduct in this mundane sphere. Indeed, ethical standards once new may become in the minds of succeeding generations so closely bound up with descriptions of immortality that the standards seem to depend fundamentally on those descriptions,

* In a personal letter to the author, George Santayana makes a comment most relevant to this point: "Orthodox heavens are peaceful: souls are not supposed to change and pass through new risks and adventures: they merely possess, as in Dante, the truth of their earthly careers and of their religious attainment. In other words, souls in heaven are mythical impersonations of the truth or totality of those persons' earthly life." (*The Letters of George Santayana,* edited by Daniel Cory. Scribner's, 1955, pp. 294-5.)

and to stand or fall with them. Sometimes symbolization works too well.

There can be little doubt that if symbolic interpretations are applicable to ancient and medieval immortality ideas, they are also pertinent to modern ones. If we turn back to the descriptions and arguments of modern immortalists, we shall at once see that this is so. In almost all the descriptions we find, for example, emphasis on progress and potentiality as underlying motifs. This is expressed in a variety of ways ranging from talk about work and new problems to talk about growth and change or the evolution of character and knowledge. It is in the modern ethical arguments, however, that symbolism is best revealed. There, it will be recollected, immortality was declared necessary in order to conserve the great values such as goodness, justice, rationality and human personality itself. Now whether there is or is not immortality, whether a future life is or is not essential for the maintenance of these values, it is clear that our modern eschatologists have been promulgating a definite set of ethical standards. They have been saying at the least that whether or not the great values have a status in eternity, they are great values nonetheless; and that of all the things knowable by the mind of man these values most deserve to be everlasting.

In recent times, moreover, there has been an increasing tendency consciously to interpret immortality as symbolizing experiences admittedly confined to this world and human life. As Schleiermacher expresses it: "Not immortality outside of time and behind it, or rather in time but only after the present; but the immortality which we can have immediately and now in this temporal life, and which is a problem in whose solution we are always engaged. In the midst of the temporal to be one with the everlasting, and to be eternal every moment, this is the immortality of religion."[253] Human experience, it may be said, gives many intimations of this kind of immortality. Mystics, artists, lovers, thinkers—all know those intense and all-absorbing immediacies, those ecstatic flashes, which seem beyond and above time, when the sense of duration is lost and a feeling of pure infinity comes over the soul.

In the modern world Spinoza was the philosopher who set the fashion for this so-called ideal immortality: Though "the mind can imagine nothing, nor can it recollect anything that is past, except while the body exists," yet "in God, nevertheless there necessarily exists an idea which expresses the essence of this or that human body under the form of eternity." Therefore "the human mind cannot be absolutely destroyed with the body, but something of it remains which is eternal. . . . Eternity cannot be defined by time, or have any relationship to it. Nevertheless, we feel and know by experience that we are eternal. For the mind is no less sensible of those things which it conceives through intelligence than of those which it remembers. . . . We feel that our mind, in so far as it involves the essence of the body under the form of eternity, is eternal, and that this existence of the mind cannot be limited by time nor manifested through duration."[254] "If we look at the common opinion of men, we shall see that they are indeed conscious of the eternity of their minds, but they confound it with duration, and attribute it to imagination or memory, which they believe remain after death."[255]

This sort of immortality, which is decidedly not equivalent to personal survival, comes to every man, whether good or bad, stupid or intelligent. But one man may make more of his mind eternal than another by coming to a greater degree into contact with eternal things, by pursuing more intently "the intellectual love of God," and by living more constantly among those ideas which make possible the understanding of things "under the aspect of eternity." In this manner, Spinoza transforms immortality "from something temporal and problematic, an endlessly continued existence, into something timeless and intrinsic, a quality of life."[256] There are eternal and deathless things, namely ideas, deathless because they have never, in the first place, entered the vale of life. Living things, such as human beings, may attain deathlessness or eternity in so far as they come into contact with deathless things. But such eternity is not to be defined in terms of prolonged life; for it is a realm where there is neither death *nor* life. It is a realm of immortality in the original sense of that word; a realm, therefore, of not-death or deathlessness. *Deathless, eternal, timeless* and *immortal* become synonyms for one another.

While this theory of immortality has received its greatest emphasis in the modern age, it is old in origin and is, in fact, sometimes called Platonic because it was suggested in the *Dialogues* of Plato. Perhaps the most explicit statement appears in the *Timaeus:* "He who has been earnest in the love of knowledge and of true wisdom, and has exercised his intellect more than any other part of him, must have thoughts immortal and divine, if he attain truth, and in so far as human nature is capable of sharing in immortality, he must altogether be immortal."[257] In this sense the true philosopher, whose "magnificence of mind" makes him "the spectator of all time and all existence,"[258] attains immortality here and now.

We may well ask, however, whether the doctrine of ideal immortality is not just as much Aristotelian as Platonic. Aristotle asserts that while there is no personal immortality, "the active intellect" is immortal and eternal.[259] And in line with this he writes that "a man, as far as in him lies, should seek immortality and do all that is in his power to live in accordance with the highest part of his nature, as, although that part is insignificant in size, yet in power and honor it is far superior to all the rest."[260] Also, so far as we know, the actual experiencing of ideal immortality has never occurred except on an Aristotelian or monistic basis, that is, with mind and soul cooperating with the natural body.

Returning to the field of religion, we find that many immortalists combine the concept of ideal immortality with a belief in the literal *post-mortem* survival of the personality. To quote Dr. Lyman Abbott: "Living forever is not immortality. Immortality is living the life that cannot die, because it is the life of the spirit. If we wish to believe in such life as a life hereafter, we must believe in it as the life worth living here; if we wish to possess it hereafter we must wish to possess it here. . . . If we live here and now the immortal life, then, if we are mistaken and there is no life after the grave, still we shall have been immortal. It were better to live an immortal life and be robbed of the immortality hereafter by some supernal power than to live the mortal, fleshly, animal life, and live it endlessly."[261] Dr. Fosdick is also typical: "Note the meaning of that phrase 'life eternal.' It does not primarily denote something after death. It primarily denotes a kind of life which we may live now. 'This is life eternal, that they might know thee, the only true God, and Jesus Christ, whom thou hast sent.' But to know God and Christ is something that a man can begin now. Eternal life is not simply *post-mortem*: it is also a present possession. Always distinguish, therefore, between immortality and eternal life."[262]

This doctrine of eternal life or ideal immortality receives considerable support in the Bible itself. It can be argued that to an extent the New Testament sustains it; in the Gospel of St. John the expression "eternal life" occurs some seventeen times and in the Epistles of John six times. The key passage among many pertinent ones is that which Dr. Fosdick himself has quoted: "This is life eternal, that they might know thee, the only true God, and Jesus Christ, whom thou hast sent."[263] Another strong support is: "Neither shall they say, Lo here! or lo there! for behold, the kingdom of God is within you";[264] and "I am come that they might have life, and that they might have it more abundantly."[265] Likewise the verses in Matthew: "If any man will come after me, let him deny himself, and take up the cross, and follow me. For whosoever will save his life shall lose it: and whosoever will lose his life for my sake shall find it. For what is a man profited, if he shall gain the whole world, and lose his own soul?"[266] None of these crucial statements of Jesus implies in itself survival of the personality after death.

Close in spirit to the notion of ideal immortality is the symbolic interpretation of the concept of the resurrection. Here again, in modern times, Spinoza leads the way. "I conclude," he writes, "that the resurrection of Christ from the dead was in truth spiritual, revealed only to the faithful, and to them after their capacity; consisting in this, that Christ was gifted with eternity and rose from the dead (the dead, I mean, in that sense in which Christ said: let the dead bury their dead), in that by his life and death he gave a singular example of holiness; and he raises his disciples from the dead in so much as they follow the example of his life and death."[267] "I take the passion, death and burial of Christ literally, but his resurrection I take allegorically."[268] Spinoza means, as I understand it, that Christ's resurrection and ascension took place in the moral realm; that physical death cannot touch anyone essentially who is spiritually risen *now;* that men's lives possess a significance that no ending in time can extinguish. *Death* itself he uses partly in a symbolic sense, just as does St. Augustine when he describes the "death" of the soul through sin and through God's consequent abandonment of it.

A symbolic meaning for both death *and* birth is a usual accompaniment of the symbolic understanding of the resurrection. So, we hear about the "birth" of the new self, the "rebirth" of the soul, and "twice-born" men. This is accurate language as expressing the sudden awakening of an individual to some great new insight or to the desirability of an entirely fresh way of life. We can agree that "one certain thing in a man's life of any worth is that he dies many deaths."[269] In this sense the death of the old Paul and the birth or resurrection of the new took place on the road to Damascus. And later Paul himself frequently used the same kind of symbolism we have been discussing. Thus he states: "To be carnally minded *is* death, but to be spiritually minded *is* life and peace."[270] According to the above usage, then, birth, life and death all signify spiritual instead of biological states.

Still another meaning is given to the concept of resurrection by certain of our modern literati. D. H. Lawrence, for instance, in a poem entitled "The New Word,"[271] writes:

> *Shall I tell you again the new word*
> *the new word of the unborn day?*
> *It is Resurrection.*
> *The resurrection of the flesh.*
> *For our flesh is dead*
> *only egoistically we assert ourselves.*

Lawrence's idea of resurrection, emphasizing salvation through sex, would very likely have been called "death" by St. Paul. But though Lawrence's view of what is "spiritual" may be very different from that of the other interpreters I have mentioned, he is at least akin to them in thinking of "resurrection" as a present spiritual state rather than a future miraculous phenomenon occurring after death.

Applying some of these ideas to the race as well as to the individual, Dr. Albert E. Ribourg declares: "We are always dying and being born again, into better and larger spheres, always failing that we may succeed, always submitting that we may conquer. Every living life is a continuous resurrection. The power of resurrection is not only seen in the individual life, but also in the life of the human race. The progress of the race is not a continuous ascent, but a decay and a resurrection. The history of the last nineteen centuries has been a history of successive eras of resurrections. Dead nations have awakened, new things have come out of the graves of the old, and it is more so than ever."[272]

In a similar vein Rabbi Stephen S. Wise says: "The crucifixion and resurrection are not single or singular events which befell one Jew 1,900 years ago. They are symbols of the life and hope of the human race in its upward march forever."[273] Dr. G. Stanley Hall, turning to the wider social meanings of the resurrection, becomes enthusiastic: "It left as its far more precious and perennial result a futuristic attitude of soul inspired by hope for both the individual and the race."[274] The resurrection "is truer than fact because, set free from specific date and place and given the world-wide scope that belongs to it, it is the most precious and pregnant symbolization of the eternal and inevitable resurgence of the good and true after their opposites have done their worst."[275]

These allegorical renderings of the resurrection fit in well with modern theories of the origin of the resurrection idea. "The Christian Christmas and Easter," we are told, "are built on ancient agricultural rites celebrating the death and rebirth of the vital forces of Nature. . . . The Christian mystery of the incarnation and the resurrection is an ancient myth found in many peoples; it seems to have crystallized out of the immemorial rituals for appeasing the gen-

250 The Illusion of Immortality

erative forces of Nature and sharing their phallic power. . . . For an agricultural society, the rebirth of vegetation in the spring is of momentous concern. . . . Winter kills, and spring revives."[276] Men, in sympathetic affinity, must also die and undergo renewal. But this process can occur without the death of the body, through the mystic death of the old self and the mystic birth of the new. Here was the core of the ancient mystery religions. Those who were initiated were born anew, resurrected, immortalized. Thus, far back in history there appears to be factual support for a symbolic interpretation of the resurrection.

There are other and less obvious possibilities of symbolism in immortality ideas. For instance, Professor Dewey has suggested that the Christian conception of immortality, by putting us on probation in this world, symbolizes the metaphysical category of contingency and its ethical counterpart that our future depends on our present action and foresight.[277] Also it can be argued that those who believe in the immortality of personality are correct in a way not immediately apparent. Since Nature undeniably has the capacity to produce what it has produced, and since it has produced intellectual and moral beings once, and since it has infinite and everlasting time before it, it may well produce such beings again. Thus the creation of personality seems to be one of the eternal potentialities of Nature, and in this sense personality may be immortal.

This review of the more important and influential ways of interpreting immortality symbolically confirms the conclusions of the last section in casting doubt on the idea of personal survival. It shows how tempting it is for men to seek solutions of this-earthly moral difficulties by setting up in their imaginations a realm beyond the tomb. It indicates how easy it is for men to mistake the moral principles that may be embodied in immortality ideas for promises of a literal after-existence; to misread the poetry of heaven and hell as the science of a very real other world. And our study also throws light on why even rather sophisticated people, who are totally unable to believe in an actual future life, feel that there is a great deal of valuable moral truth expressed in immortality ideas, why they dislike having these ideas analyzed too carefully, and why they are reluctant to give up the use of at least the *word*, "immortality."

My own position is that while symbolic interpretation brings out the only truth that immortality ideas have ever had, this whole procedure is fraught with grave dangers. For those who indulge in it are only too likely, either intentionally or unintentionally, to fail to make clear that they no longer consider acceptable the traditional meaning of immortality as signifying a life after death. And in any case their abstruse redefinitions of immortality and the resurrection cannot be expected to have much emotional efficacy or religious value. They will appeal here and there to certain esoteric religious, philosophic and esthetic groups, but for the great masses of men they will have little significance.

It would be cold comfort indeed to tell a grieving parent that his deceased son was really immortal because he had attained a grasp of the higher mathematics during his lifetime. And this indicates why the ordinary citizen, even if he were able to achieve the aristocratic ideal immortality, would not be much interested. He would regard it as a rather wretched substitute for the good substantial after-existence he had once been guaranteed. And he might well ask, if ideal immortality means having a vision of eternal things, then why would it not be far better to keep on having such visions forever in a durational sense? How very much more desirable would it be if ideal immortality were combined with personal survival! And Dr. Fosdick and practically all Christian priests or ministers, of whatever sect, would echo him.

These reflections make it evident, in my opinion, that in the future as in the past the idea of immortality will have its greatest and most widespread influence under the aspect of its primary meaning of existence beyond the grave. This influence, no doubt, will for some time be considerable, but I believe that it will continue steadily to wane. Yet so deep-seated and complex are the emotions that sway people towards faith in immortality that probably there will always remain among the sons of men some who give credence to this age-long and beloved illusion.

Chapter VII

LIFE WITHOUT IMMORTALITY

1. *An Affirmative Philosophy*

Assuming that immortality is an illusion, what then? What effect does or ought this knowledge have on the living of our lives? It was no less a person than Ralph Waldo Emerson who said: "No sooner do we try to get rid of the idea of immortality than pessimism raises its head. . . . Human griefs seem little worth assuaging; human happiness too paltry (at the best) to be worth increasing. The whole moral world is reduced to a point. Good and evil, right and wrong, become infinitesimal, ephemeral matters. The affections die away—die of their own conscious feebleness and uselessness. A moral paralysis creeps over us."[278] In an Easter Day address, to take a typical contemporary statement, Bishop Manning warned that loss of faith in the life to come robs men "of their hope and vision and joy in life here and now" and "makes this life inexplicable and futile and unmeaning to them."[279] Now all of us know plenty of persons living today who, rejecting belief in or skeptical of immortality, show no signs of moral paralysis, decay of the affections, loss of happiness, or feelings of futility. Indeed, perhaps the best way to answer such assertions as the above is not to argue, but simply to point.

First of all, I would point to that considerable number of the great and the good of the past who, disbelieving in personal survival, yet led most fruitful and vital careers. Among the ancient Greeks are the famous philosophers, Democritus, Aristotle and Epicurus; and the two notable physicians, Galen and Hippocrates. Among the ancient Romans are Lucretius and Marcus Aurelius, Julius Caesar and Pliny the Elder, Ovid and Horace. The foremost Arabian philosopher, Averröes, one of the outstanding intellects of the Middle Ages, denies the immortality of the individual human personality, as does his school in general. Passing to modern philosophy, we find upholding this same conclusion such illustrious minds as Benedict Spinoza, David Hume, Baron d'Holbach, Ludwig Feuerbach, Auguste Comte, Karl Marx, Friedrich Nietzsche, Ernst Haeckel, Herbert Spencer and Bernard Bosanquet. Men of action with such varying backgrounds and careers as Vladimir I. Lenin, Jawaharlal Nehru, Sun Yat-sen, Vilhjalmur Stefansson, Robert Ingersoll and Clarence Darrow unite in treating the idea of a future life as a total illusion. The American inventor, Thomas A. Edison; the botanist, Luther Burbank; the biologist and Nobel Prize winner, Hermann J. Muller; the chemist and Nobel Prize winner, Linus Pauling; the psychologist, G. Stanley Hall; and the founder of psychoanalysis, Sigmund Freud, agree that there is no after-existence.

The three most eminent of twentieth-century American philosophers, Morris R. Cohen, John Dewey and George Santayana, are convinced that this life is all. Following suit are outstanding Humanists or naturalists such as Professors Abraham Edel of the College of the City of New York, Sidney Hook of New York University, Horace M. Kallen of the New School, Roy Wood Sellars, formerly of the University of Michigan; and Joseph L. Blau, John H. Randall, Jr., and Herbert W. Schneider of Columbia University. Benedetto Croce and Giovanni Gentile, the leading philosophers of modern Italy, reject the idea of a future life. In England Bertrand Russell, Julian Huxley and Sir Arthur Keith, Bernard Shaw, H.G. Wells and Harold

J. Laski, have taken the same stand. And Albert Einstein asserts that he cannot believe "the individual survives the death of his body, although feeble souls harbor such thoughts through fear or ridiculous egotism."[280] This roll of distinguished disbelievers in personal immortality—and there are many others—in and of itself refutes such statements as those of Emerson and Manning.

Other figures of great note can be listed as regarding the idea of immortality with varying degrees of doubt. The Chinese sage, Confucius, would only say: "While you do not know life, what can you know about death?"[281] Buddha, founder of one of the world's leading religions, leaves undetermined whether the goal of Nirvana implies extinction or consciousness for the personality.[282] Other agnostics on the question of immortality have been Cicero, the Roman orator; John Stuart Mill, the English utilitarian; G. F. Hegel,* the German idealist; William James, the American pragmatist; Thomas H. Huxley, the well-known biologist; Charles W. Eliot, renowned President of Harvard University; and Robert Louis Stevenson, the author, who talks about "this fairy tale of an eternal tea party."[283] Of course, skeptics concerning immortality, even if they do not reach the stage of downright denial of an after-life, do not use the idea of survival as an inspiration to action or as a motive for morality. Hence our roll of doubters, like that of the definite disbelievers, makes the dire lamentations of the immortalists seem more than a trifle extravagant.

In 1914, Professor Leuba conducted a statistical inquiry among distinguished American scientists that supports these considerations. He found that a large proportion of them either disbelieved in or doubted the existence of a future life.[284] Out of one thousand

* There is some doubt as to Hegel's position and there are those who classify him as an unhesitating disbeliever in immortality.

scientists responding to the questionnaire only 50.6 per cent, a fraction over half, expressed belief in immortality. Among the more eminent of these men the percentage of believers was 36.9 per cent while among the less eminent it was 59.3 per cent, thus showing that the greater the scientist, the greater the likelihood of lack of faith in immortality. Further inquiry brought out that the highest proportion of skeptics and disbelievers were among the biologists, sociologists and psychologists, the last-named group taking the lead here with a figure of 81.2 per cent. Professor Leuba explains this fact on the ground that these classes of scientists more than any others recognize the ruling presence of law in organic and psychical life. This harmonizes with our own opinion that biology, psychology and their associated sciences provide the most convincing evidence against the idea of personal survival. Professor Leuba repeated his study in 1933 and reported that a considerably higher proportion of scientists disbelieved in or doubted immortality than in 1914.[285]

There are illustrious peoples as well as individuals who have gotten along very well without belief in immortality. The Old Testament Hebrews had a highly developed moral code that depended not in the slightest on the belief in gloomy and ethically neutral Sheol. The same statement holds true in regard to the Homeric Greeks and their dismal Hades. The Athenian Greeks at the very height of their civilization in the fifth century B.C., one of the greatest creative periods in the history of man, were not influenced to a decisive extent by the notion of a life beyond the grave. While the Athenians frequently discussed the theme of immortality, their general attitude is reflected in the great Funeral Oration of Pericles as reported by the historian Thucydides.

In this address there is no suggestion of personal continuance after death or of preoccupation with the idea. Pericles is clear that the lustre the Athenian dead have achieved is a this-worldly, humanistic one. They sacrificed themselves "to the commonwealth and received, each for his own memory, praise that will never die, and with it the grandest of all sepulchres, not that in which their mortal bones are laid, but a home in the minds of men, where their glory remains fresh to stir to speech or action as the occasion comes by. For the whole earth is the sepulchre of famous men, and their story is not graven only on stone over their native earth, but lives far away, without visible symbol, woven into the stuff of other men's lives."[286]

In later centuries, during the decline of Greece, the Epicureans, who commanded the allegiance of a great many intelligent men, made the denial of an after-existence a cardinal doctrine of their philosophy. And though there was some disagreement on the matter among the Stoics, they formulated and followed their sublime and heroic way of life with little or no reference to the conception of a hereafter. Throughout the history of Europe, especially during the Renaissance and modern times, large numbers of persons have not included faith in a beyond as a part of their philosophies, as the Church itself has indicated in many a resounding blast. And of course in India, so far as this-worldly conduct is connected with belief in an after-existence, it is in the main with a conception far removed from the Christian doctrine of a worth-while personal survival.

In the world at present, we find in Soviet Russia the leaders of the nation and a majority of the people possessed of a positive disbelief not only in immortality, but in God as well. Yet in the Soviet Union we have witnessed since the Communist Revolution of 1917 an impressive outpouring of constructive labor and energy during both war and peace. Other peoples may dislike the ethical standards which the Russians have established and the goals for which they are striving, but it is irrefutable that these Russians have had the strength and initiative to build a new form of society which constitutes a challenge to the rest of mankind in such important fields as economics, education, health and science. Likewise other countries where the Communists have won control, such as Czechoslovakia, Yugoslavia, and China with its close to 1,000,000,000 inhabitants, are now actively following a Marxist philosophy which specifically repudiates any idea of a hereafter and at the same time encourages vigorous effort and hard work.

Only, then, by shutting one's eyes to much of the past and much of the present can one possibly maintain that belief in immortality is necessary for the good life, the spiritual life, the intellectual life, the happy life, the strenuous life or the useful life. "It may indeed be said that no man of any depth of soul has made his prolonged existence the touchstone of his enthusiasms. . . . What a despicable creature must a man be, and how sunk below the level of the most barbaric virtue, if he cannot bear to live for his children, for his art, or for country!"[287] Or for humanity as a whole, I may add. What Pomponazzi stated back in the sixteenth century, when discussing the matter of recompense in heaven, always has been and always will be true, namely, that it is more virtuous to act ethically without hope of reward than with such hope.

In effect, the immortalists build up their case for the moral need of a future life by belittling the intelligence and decency of ordinary men, in short, by libeling the human race, including themselves. For there are precious few of them who, if they were deprived of their faith in immortality, would thereupon give up the moral habits of a lifetime and cease to be good citizens, kind fathers and devoted shepherds of their flocks. And it is positively indecent to claim that men will act decently only if they are guaranteed the *pourboire,* as Schopenhauer called it, of *post-mortem* existence. Nor is it possible to believe that the great religious heroes of the immortalists, from Jesus to Phillips Brooks, would have been small and selfish men had they been convinced that death meant the end.

It was not a religious leader, however, but a noted agnostic, Thomas Huxley, who gave the classic expression of protest against the shallow philosophy of the professional immortalists. In a famous letter to the author, Charles Kingsley, Huxley writes concerning his son's funeral: "As I stood beside the coffin of my little son the other day, with my mind bent on anything but disputation, the officiating minister read, as a part of his duty, the words, 'If the dead rise not again, let us eat and drink, for tomorrow we die.' I cannot tell you how inexpressibly they shocked me. . . . I could have laughed with scorn. What! because I am face to face with irreparable loss, because I have given back to the source from whence it came the cause of a great happiness, still retaining through all my life the blessings which have sprung and will spring from that cause, I am to renounce my manhood, and, howling, grovel in bestiality? Why, the very apes know better, and if you shoot their young, the poor brutes grieve their grief out and do not immediately seek distraction in a gorge."[288]

It is my conviction that the frank recognition of human mortality, far from undermining morals and stopping progress, will, other things being equal, do exactly the opposite. People will then realize that here and now, if ever, they must develop their possibilities, win happiness for themselves and others, take their stand and do their part in the enterprises that seem highest. They will understand as never before the reality of quickly-passing time and the serious duty of making the most of it. It will be an excellent thing for everyone to know that there is no heaven of angelic alchemy that can transmute a copper life to gold. The compensatory aspects of belief in immortality will no longer dull the nerve of effort. Furthermore, to confront with simple and unfailing courage the stern fact that death means death is in itself an ethical achievement of deep significance and one that strongly sustains the moral obligation of men to seek and accept the truth wherever it may lead.

The Reverend Kirsopp Lake, for many years Professor of Ecclesiastical History at Harvard University, has unequivocally asserted that the growing disbelief in personal survival is a social gain, having "raised rather than lowered the standard of life. The pursuit of individual Immortality consumed a lamentable amount of energy in past generations. To attain salvation was thought to be the object of existence. . . . Men went on year after year thinking of nothing so much as how to save their own souls. . . . In general there was produced a type of selfishness all the more repulsive because it was sanctified. In place of a quest for Immortality there is today among the most active and virile of our contemporaries a new attitude towards life; for they have almost suddenly ceased thinking about their own Immortality and regard their work as more important than their own souls. . . . The object of their work is in their minds the improvement of the world in which our children are to live. It is an unselfish object, and the pursuit of a better world for another generation to inherit has become the surrogate for the hope of a better world above for ourselves to enjoy."[289]

In striving for that better world upon this earth, would not men fight harder, for example, against war and the menace of war, if they were convinced that the millions who die in international conflict forever lose their right to live? We see the other side of the coin when the belief in immortality is utilized as an apology for war. Thus *The New York Times* of September 11, 1950, at the height of the Korean War, reported as follows on a Sunday sermon by Monsignor William T. Greene of the Catholic Church:

"Sorrowing parents whose sons have been drafted for combat duty were told yesterday in St. Patrick's Cathedral that death in battle was part of God's plan for populating the 'kingdom of heaven.'" And in England in 1954 the Archbishop of Canterbury, the highest church dignitary in the land, expressed the opinion that "the hydrogen bomb is not the greatest danger of our time. After all, the most it could do would be to transfer vast numbers of human beings from this world to another and more vital one into which they would some day go anyhow."[290] Such statements made in all seriousness demonstrate how religious faith in an after-life may weaken the struggle for world peace.*

Expressing the military viewpoint is the comment on an earlier edition of this book by a former captain in the United States Army and a graduate of West Point. He wrote me that if a commander in the armed forces looks upon death as "a mere episode in an individual's life, about as important as graduation from grade-school, then whatever natural gift of sangfroid he may have is given an immense reinforcement. . . . It means that, without in any way needing to steel himself to a hard, pitiless inhumanity that will both warp him and insensibly vitiate his purpose, he can yet view the carnage incidental to battle and not be perturbed at it in any way, knowing that, whatever it looks like, even so far as the precious individuals themselves are concerned, it is hardly more important than if his men had nose-bleeds, or thumbs sawed off while guiding logs through a gang-saw."**

As I pointed out in Chapter V, it is possible to give up entirely belief in immortality and still retain

* Cf. pp. 222-223.
** Cf. Plato's opinion, p. 37.

faith in some kind of God. In modern times, especially, many thoughtful persons, of diverse philosophical and religious allegiances, have taken this position. All this, however, is not to say that for those who have been taught for long years to rely on the assurance of a beyond, sudden loss of that illusion may not constitute a great shock and for some even lead to spiritual disintegration. The crumbling of a cornerstone in one's philosophy is a serious matter. But such crumblings do not usually occur abruptly; the process is gradual, giving time for a new and different principle of action to take the place of the old. No single idea, such as that of immortality, is in my opinion all-important; what is of supreme importance is an inclusive and integrated philosophy of life, one that places the individual in a definite relationship to both society and Nature. This is what men need; this is what Christianity at its best has provided. It is what other ways of life—Stoicism, Epicureanism, Confucianism, Buddhism—have given. Today in the modern world we have available purely secular philosophies more appropriate for the modern scene. And these make no point of relying on the promise of immortality, or specifically deny that promise altogether.

What these modern ways of life have in common is a devotion to the this-worldly welfare of men. The most enlightened of them, such as Humanism,[291] Materialism[292] and Naturalism,[293] set up the happiness, freedom and progress of all humanity as the supreme goal. This ultimate loyalty to the ultimate interests of all mankind, including one's own finest possibilities, is, I would suggest, a thing high enough and broad enough for any man to integrate his life around. As an incentive to the good life it is far more effective and noble than reliance on individual immortality and the philosophy that goes with it. Philosophies and religions of egoism and wish-fulfilment are pardonable and perhaps necessary in the childhood of the race; but mankind is growing up at last and can well afford to leave behind the attachments and symbols of immaturity. We would do well to heed the counsel of the poet Don Marquis:

> *Give up the dream that Love may trick the fates*
> *To live again somewhere beyond the gleam*
> *Of dying stars, or shatter the strong gates*
> *Some god has builded high: give up the dream.*
> *Flame were not flame unless it met the dark—*
> *The beauty of our doomed, bewildered loves*
> *Dwells in the transcience of the moving spark*
> *Which pricks oblivion's blackness as it moves;*
> *A few more heartbeats and our hearts shall lie*
> *Dusty and done with raptures and with rhyme:*
> *Let us not babble of eternity*
> *Who stand upon this little edge of time!*
> *Even old godheads sink in space and drown,*
> *Their arks like foundered galleons sucked down.*[294]

No matter how important or irreplaceable a man may seem to himself or others, the world will get along without him, as it did before his birth. And it might help to instil a proper humility and sense of proportion if everyone would reflect that when he dies, there will remain on earth at least over 5,000,000,000 human beings to carry on. That the descendants of our present three and one-third billion inhabitants may at the end of two hundred million or a billion or a trillion years find this earth unlivable, owing to the sun's becoming too hot or too cold,* should not greatly agitate us. Even the absolute certainty of that eventuality a trifling million years from now would not seem very terrible. In his some 500,000 years of ex-

---

* Professor Harlow Shapley, former Director of the Harvard Observatory, estimates that the sun will continue to radiate sufficient heat to maintain human life on this planet for at least ten billion years.

istence the species man has made a considerable number of notable achievements, none of which would be less notable if the world one day ended.

The most significant of these achievements have come to pass only in the last few thousand years, since the invention of what is known as science, which, in its modern and most successful form, has been on the scene for only a few hundred years. So in a million more years man's accomplishments might well exceed the most sanguine expectations and the most ambitious dreams. In that time he might discover, for instance, how to bring about the mutation which would result in a new species, Superman. It is conceivable that either man or Superman might, through science and particularly through nuclear power, gain such control over the mechanisms of this whirling planet, the solar system and the sources of energy and heat that extinction of life on this earth could be postponed indefinitely.

Today, especially since the successful launching of earth satellites, we can envision the possibility of human migration by means of atomic-propelled rocket ships to some other planet in our solar system, or beyond, where life could flourish. It seems likely that in this universe of infinite space and time many other planetary systems have come into being. In his book *Of Stars and Men*, Professor Shapley offers the opinion that scattered throughout the unending array of galaxies with their more than 100 quintillion stars, there are certainly 100 million planetary systems, and probably far more, in which some degree of organic evolution has taken place.[295] If this is true, then without much doubt living forms at least as highly developed as man already exist in other parts of the cosmos.

As I noted earlier,* it is quite conceivable that science should some day be able to preserve indefi-

* See p. 73.

nitely the vitality of human organisms and thereby bring about a species of immortality for human personalities. Of course, no matter what strides are made in medicine and its associated sciences, human beings will always be subject to fatal accidents. But with this qualification it is conceivable that men might ultimately learn how not to die. Romantic and attractive, however, as this possibility may seem at first glance, it would not be without its drawbacks. If practically nobody departed this earth through death, there would arise a population problem far more critical than any with which the world has ever been confronted. And even as things are, the spectacle of old and stubborn men in high places has caused wits to suggest the motto, "While there's death, there's hope!"

Santayana adds another most relevant consideration when he observes: "Not a single man or woman has ever existed whom I should wish to engage to play forever, rather than fill my theater from age to age with fresh faces, and new accents of nature. Continual perfection would be my ideal, not individual perpetuity."[296] Thus, while it may well be desirable, and some day possible, to extend the normal span of human life to a hundred years or more, the preservation of individual lives interminably would be of doubtful value.*

The progressive lengthening of the life-span through the elimination of the causes of premature death is a rational and humane idea. If 90 per cent of the people in every country lived to a good old age, the larger part of the unhappiness caused by death would disappear. The way to meet the challenge of premature death is not to promise men consolation in a life beyond, but to abolish so far as possible this

* For an intriguing account of the consternation and havoc that might result from the elimination of natural death see Iris Barry's novel, *The Last Enemy,* and Albert Cosella's play, *Death Takes a Holiday.* Cf. also this book, pp. 127-128.

type of death entirely. Writes one father who lost a most promising boy at the age of fifteen through a blister infection that at first seemed trivial: "Bacteria —the lowest order of life—had brought this tragedy. The lowest had triumphed over the highest! Here was a boy in perfect physical condition, vibrant with health, energetic and athletic—a boy with a superior mind and high ideals, wholesome, affectionate, fastidious, tenderly considerate of others. And here, attacking him, were these bacteria, having neither mental nor moral qualities."[297] This statement is only too true; but it does not call either for flight to a supernatural realm of compensation or for bitter pessimism and resignation. What it calls for, in addition to great fortitude on the part of the parents, is a more strenuous and effective campaign against bacteria and all the other brute, amoral forces which are able to snuff out so abruptly the life of man.

It remains to be said, however, that in the shock of personal loss we are frequently fair neither to life nor to death. The tragedy of some fine character's dying in youth or in the prime of life sometimes seems so great that it overshadows the consideration that, after all, this person did live happily and usefully for a number of years. We allow a fateful and unhappy conclusion to cast a gloom over all that has gone before. But unless we accept the perverse philosophy that a value can be a value only if it lasts forever, this procedure is not justified. Life can be very short, but at the same time it can be very sweet. The old Greek saying, "Whom the gods love die young," is not without its wisdom. The fifteen-year-old boy mentioned above enjoyed his life to the utmost while it lasted and contributed a high and joyous quality to the life of others. Death could not alter this fact; for however death may affect the future, it cannot touch the past.

Most parents would prefer the experience and

pleasure of having had healthy and happy children, no matter at what early age they perished, to having had no children whatsoever. What Plutarch wrote to his wife after the death of their little daughter is as pertinent today as in the first century A.D. "Let us call to mind," he said, "the years before our little child was born. We are now in the same condition as then, except that the time she was with us is to be counted as an added blessing. Let us not ungratefully accuse Fortune of what was given us, because we could not also have all that we desired. What we had, and while we had it, was good, though now we have it no longer."[298]

2. *The Meaning of Death*

In justice to death it must be stated that the fate of those who die, whether early or late, is not really very dire. For if we are right in calling immortality an illusion, the dead have no consciousness that they are missing life or that the living are missing them. They cannot grieve over being parted from those whom they love. After life's fitful fever they sleep well; nothing can touch them further, not even dreams. The grave, as Job said, is a place where the wicked cease from troubling and the weary are at rest. Those who have passed on prematurely or in any other way can experience no sting, no sorrow, no disappointment, no remorse, no anything. As Epicurus pithily summed up the matter three hundred years before the birth of Christ: "When we are, death is not; and when death is, we are not."[299] Only if there is a future life need we worry about the dead or need the dead worry about themselves. Only immortality can disturb their eternal peace.

If death is the end, we can feel sorry for ourselves that we have lost a dear friend and for our country or humanity in general that it has lost a man of distinguished abilities; but we cannot rationally feel sorry for the departed person himself, since he is non-existent and can know neither sorrow nor gladness. We cannot be sorry for him as dead, but only for him as dying and as dying unwillingly, conscious that he was leaving this life prematurely with much of his rightful human experience being denied him. We can continue to regret that he as a living person was not able to go on enjoying the goods of existence; we can wish intensely that he were alive again so that he could share our pleasure in this or that. But it is unreasonable to transfer these wishes and regrets to the departed *as dead*, because as dead he is as completely insensible to all such things as any piece of earth or non-living matter. He is just exactly as non-existent as he was before birth and conception.

It is the living, not the dead, who suffer when death has done its work. The dead can no longer suffer; and we may properly praise death when it puts an end to extreme physical pain or distressing mental decay. Without pretending that the dead can in any sense enjoy their release from the vicissitudes of life, we can be glad that a deceased person is no longer subject to the trials and tribulations which may have afflicted him. And it is surely legitimate to use euphemisms like *sleep* and *rest* in reference to the departed. The familiar expression, "May he rest in peace" (*Requiescat in pace* in the traditional Latin), is a poetic sentiment that can be used without any connotation of supernaturalism.

It is, however, misleading to talk of death as a "reward," since a true reward like a true punishment entails conscious experience of the fact. To him, then, who sacrifices his life for some ideal and goes forever into the blank silences of oblivion, death is hardly a reward. While some men surrender up their lives on behalf of their fellows feeling sure of attaining eternal bliss thereby, there are many others who do so in the full knowledge that death means their absolute end.

No higher type of morality exists than to make one's death count in this fashion. There may come a time in the career of any man when to die will prove more effective for his central purposes than to live; when through his death what he stands for will become more clear and convincing than in any other way. The great unyielding martyrs of the past, men like Socrates and Jesus, have established this point beyond cavil. And many lesser persons—the unnumbered, unsung heroes of history and everyday existence—have likewise demonstrated their contempt for death in the name of life or of love or of some other supreme commitment.

It has usually been assumed that death as such is a very great evil and the worst enemy of man. Now certain specific ways in which death has manifested itself throughout human history, constantly striking down individuals and indeed multitudes in the prime of life and appearing in innumerable ugly forms, are correctly to be classified as evil. Yet death in and of itself, as a phenomenon of Nature, is not an evil. There is nothing mysterious about death, nothing supernatural about it, that could legitimately lead to the interpretation that it is a divine punishment inflicted upon men and other living creatures. On the contrary, death is an altogether natural thing and has played a useful and necessary role in the long course of biological evolution.* In fact, without this much-maligned institution of death, which has given the fullest and most serious meaning to the survival of the fittest and thus has rendered possible the upward surge of organic species, it is clear that the animal known as man would never have evolved at all.

Man could not exist, either, were it not for the helping hand of death in making available the most basic means of human living. Man's fuel, food, clothing, shelter, furnishings and reading materials all depend to a large extent upon the operation of death.

* Cf. pp. 71-73.

Coal, oil and peat originate in decomposed organic substances; wood for fuel, building, furniture and the manufacture of paper comes from dead trees; the death of plant life provides man with food in the form of vegetables, grains, cereals and fruits, and with clothing in the form of cotton, flax and rayon; the death of animal life brings him not only birds, fish, fowl and meat to eat, but also fur and wool for clothing and leather for shoes.

Living and dying, birth and death, are essential and correlative aspects of the same biological and evolutionary processes. Life affirms itself *through* death, which during an early era of evolution was brought into existence *by* life and derives its entire significance *from* life. In the dynamic and creative flux of Nature the same living organisms do not go on indefinitely, but retire from the scene at a certain stage and so give way to newborn and lustier vitality.

The novelist Anne Parrish enlarges upon this thought. Each one of us, she writes, "must die for the sake of life, for the flow of the stream too great to be dammed in any pool, for the growth of the seed too strong to stay in one shape. . . . Because these bodies must perish, we are greater than we know. The most selfish must be generous, letting his life pour out to others. The most cowardly must be brave enough to go."[300] So it is that death opens the way for the greatest possible number of individuals, including the descendants of our own families, to experience the joys of living; and in this sense death is the ally of the unborn generations of men down through the untold ages of the future.

Of course there are living forms like trees, far more simply organized than human beings, that endure for centuries and tens of centuries. In his novel, *After Many a Summer Dies the Swan*, Aldous Huxley, in satirizing the desire for immortality, stresses the ability of certain species of carp to live on for hundreds of years.

He pictures an English lord attaining a hideous, sub-human prolongation of life beyond two hundred years, by means of eating the intestinal flora of this fish. The point is that apparently one price of the organic complexity and specialization, including the valued assets of mind and sex love, that make man's career so exciting, so many-sided and so vividly self-conscious is death for the personality at the end of a relatively brief time span.

"The individual has, so to speak, made a bargain. For the individual comes out of the germ-plasm and does and lives and at length dies for the sake of life. It is a bit of the germ-plasm which has arisen and broken away, in order to see and feel life instead of just blindly and mechanically multiplying. Like Faust it has sold its immortality in order to live more abundantly."[301] For me, at least, one of the best antidotes to the thought of personal extinction is to undertsand fully the naturalness of death and its indispensable place in the great life-process of evolution that has given rise to increasing individuality and finally to the uniqueness and splendor of man himself.

Another consideration that may help to counteract the prospect of oblivion is that every man carries literally all eternity in his being. I mean by this that the ultimate elements of the body, as the Law of the Conservation of Mass implies, have always existed in some form or other and will go on existing forever. The indestructible matter that makes up our physical organisms was part of the universe five billion years ago and will still be part of it five billion years hence. The infinite past comes to a focus in our intricately structured bodies; and from them there radiates the infinite future.

The *social* meaning of death also has its positive aspects. For the occurrence of death brings home to us the common concerns and the common destiny of all men everywhere. It draws us together in the deep-felt

emotions of the heart and dramatically accents the ultimate equality involved in our ultimate fate. The uni-
versality of death reminds us of the essential brother-
hood of man that lies beneath all the bitter dissensions
and conflicts registered in history and contemporary
affairs. John Donne phrases it perfectly; "No man is an
Iland, intire of it selfe; every man is a peece of the
Continent, a part of the *maine;* if a *Clod* bee washed
away by the *Sea,* Europe is the lesse, as well as if a
Promontorie were, as well as if a *Mannor* of thy *friends*
or of *thine owne* were; any mans *death* diminishes *me,*
because I am involved in *Mankinde;* And therefore
never send to know for whom the *bell* tolls; it tolls for
thee."[302]

When we attain the realization that death finishes
the story, we know the worst. And that worst is not
really very bad. It is, in fact, relatively so far from bad
that traditional Christianity and other religions have
always insisted that for us sinful humans to escape
with mere extinction at the end of our lives would be
a terrible violation of justice and would throw grave
doubts on the existence of cosmic morality. To understand that death is the necessary and inevitable conclusion of our personal careers enables us to look this
fateful event in the face with dignity and calm. Such
understanding provides an invaluable stimulus towards
that high art of dying which should be an aim of all
mature and civilized men.

Today in the world large numbers of persons find
themselves in a state of unhappy suspense over the
idea of immortality. They are unable either to believe
or disbelieve. They feel that personal survival is a
rather doubtful proposition; yet the possibility of it
continues to haunt them. A definitive settlement of the
issue cannot but be for them a psychological gain. And
there can be no question that their resolute acceptance
of the fact that immortality is an illusion would be all
to the good. It is best not only to disbelieve in immor-

tality, but to *believe in mortality*. This means not only to believe positively that death is the end, but also to believe in the worth-whileness of human life on this earth and in the high intrinsic value of men's ethical and other attainments during that life.

Those who possess such a philosophy and who implement it by devotion to some significant work, profession or cause are best able to rise above the emotional crises engendered by death. Bertrand Russell gives good advice: "To bear misfortune well when it comes, it is wise to have cultivated in happier times a certain width of interests. . . . A man of adequate vitality and zest will surmount all misfortunes by the emergence after each blow of an interest in life and the world which cannot be narrowed down so as to make one loss fatal. To be defeated by one loss or even by several is not something to be admired as a proof of sensibility, but something to be deplored as a failure in vitality. All our affections are at the mercy of death, which may strike down those whom we love at any moment. It is therefore necessary that our lives should not have that narrow intensity which puts the whole meaning and purpose of our life at the mercy of accident."[303]

Where the impact of death may be lessened for many is in a change in the accepted manner of disposing of dead bodies and in the customs of mourning. In these matters we are still to a large extent barbaric. The sombre, silent cities of the dead have grown hand in hand with the crowded, restless cities of the living. Already it becomes a serious problem to find sufficient space for graveyards; already the dreary reservations of the departed, ever-present reminders of ever-present death, constitute a heavy economic burden. Cremation would appear to be a far more rational and healthy method of disposing of the dead than burial beneath the ground. For those who wish it, the ashes may always be preserved in an urn and the urn put in a suitable place. Those, on the other hand, who like to think of their bodily elements commingling with the active forces of Nature, can leave instructions for their ashes to be scattered over some favorite sector of land or body of water.*

There can be no doubt that cremation would do much to weaken those unpleasant and morbid associations that inevitably arise when the dead body is preserved intact and put in a visible coffin and a visitable grave. In this connection it might be wise to discourage the viewing of the corpse by relatives or anyone else. As for mourning, while individuals will here always follow out their own particular bent, the more extreme and public displays are clearly to be deplored. And it is much to be hoped that the wearing of black, which is a hold-over from primitive superstition, will in due course disappear. That simplicity and dignity should prevail in the matter of funerals is also devoutly to be wished. Today vulgarity and costliness frequently go together. The high cost of dying is only too well-known and only too often implies a financial exploitation of death which should not be tolerated. If a husband or father dies, it is bad enough for the family to lose its chief provider without bankrupting itself in giving him an expensive funeral and burial.

The proposal, however, to do away with funeral services entirely does not seem sound. Regardless of the religious and philosophical views of the deceased, his family and his friends, some final gathering and ceremony would appear appropriate and wise. A socially-minded community, keenly aware of the value of

* For instance, the ashes of George Bernard Shaw, after his death in 1950, were mingled with those of his wife and scattered in their garden at Ayot St. Lawrence. This was done in accordance with Shaw's will. We cannot approve, however, of the aviator, Captain Eddie Rickenbacker, carrying out literally the instructions in the will of Damon Runyon, the American writer, and dropping his ashes from an airplane over Times Square in New York City.

the individual, will wish to do honor to its dead, to show its compassion toward them, or at least to give all who die, no matter how slight their earthly achievements, the democratic recognition implicit in a funeral or memorial service. Also those who loved the departed must have a chance to express their feelings and to participate in a kind of last farewell. And if they have that familiar sense of unreality about the loss of a person whom they have known well, they should be given an opportunity fully to convince both their conscious and subconscious minds that death has actually occurred. Neither dignity nor psychological wisdom calls for suppression of the emotions in the face of death. The normal expression of grief is not inconsistent with reasonable self-control and can serve as a healthy release and purge of emotional tension. What is to be definitely deplored is the expansion of sorrow over a loved one's dying into a little cult of perpetual mourning.

Rituals concerned with death are a form of art and should embody the quality of beauty. In my opinion they ought to stress man's fundamental kinship with Nature and the deep social ties of experience; they ought to avoid sentimentality, showiness and sombreness. Funerals or memorial services need not, of course, be connected with any church or conducted by a clergyman. Various individuals and groups have already developed funeral ceremonies in harmony with the belief that there is no immortality and devoid of all supernatural references.[304]

Yet whatever improvements we make in human customs, to whatever extent we cut down the ravages of premature death, however intrepid and mature we become in our philosophies, however calmly we face the prospect of our own individual end, the loss of our near and dear will always deal a heavy blow, particularly if it is sudden or untimely. It would be mere shallowness to desire or pretend otherwise. When Jonathan Swift heard that Stella, the love of his life, was dying he wrote in a letter: "I am of the opinion that there is not a greater folly than to contract too great and intimate a friendship, which must always leave the survivor miserable."[305] It is understandable how Swift, distracted by grief, could give expression to such a sentiment. But as a serious suggestion it is not to be entertained; we cannot consider surrendering the highest human relationships simply in order to avoid the cruel partings of death. Between human beings there will always be the most ardent feelings; and where these prevail, it might as well be recognized once and for all that death can never be nonchalantly accepted with a shrug of the shoulder. Intense love, when death comes to force a separation, inevitably means intense sorrow. And men and women who are unafraid of the deeper experiences of life will not choose to evade the emotional consequences of mortality.

"Love-devouring death" is one of Shakespeare's aptest phrases. When a parent loses a son or daughter in the full flush of youth, or a lover a wife or husband in the prime of life, all the philosophies and religions in the world—whether promising immortality or not—cannot offset or veil the poignant tragedy. It is only possible to suffer and endure; to be, so far as strength allows, an unflinching Stoic. It is true that gracious Time will gradually soften the shock of death. It is true that wide interests and deep loyalties beyond the circle of friends and family can do much to cure the hurt. All this is true. But the tragedy remains. The sting of death may be tempered, but it cannot be removed.

3. Conclusion

Unsurpassed among the glories of man is his mind. This it is that enables him to know that there is such a thing as death and to reflect upon its meaning. The

animals cannot do this; they do not consciously foresee that some day they will perish. When their time
comes, they simply lie down and die. There is no problem or tragedy of death for them. They do not discuss
the resurrection and eternal life. Men can and do. And
it is a high privilege. That the outcome of that discussion and reflection should be the recognition that this
life is all does not make the privilege less. "Man alone
knows that he must die; but that very knowledge raises
him, in a sense, above mortality, by making him a
sharer in the vision of eternal truth. . . . The truth is
cruel, but it can be loved, and it makes free those who
have loved it."[306]

The truth about death frees us from both debasing
fear and shallow optimism. It frees us from self-flattery
and self-deception. To say that men cannot endure this
truth is to abdicate to the weaker elements in human
nature. Not only can men endure it, but they can rise
above it to far nobler thoughts and acts than those
centering around everlasting self-perpetuation. It is
said that the denial of immortality leads to a philosophy of "Eat, drink and be merry; for tomorrow we
die." We hope that men will always be merry; but
there is no reason why at the same time they should
not be intelligent, courageous and devoted to the welfare of society. If this earthly existence is our one and
only chance to have a good time, it is also our one and
only chance to lead the good life; or, better still, to
combine good time and good life in one integrated
whole. If it is our one and only chance to enjoy personally the fruits of existence—and why should we not
enjoy them?—it is also our one and only chance to
establish a high and honorable record among our
friends and fellow-men. There will be no second
chance; no fresh opportunity in some immortal realm
to redeem ourselves and alter the irreversible imprint
of our lives. This is our only chance.

Finally, the knowledge that immortality is an illusion frees us from any sort of preoccupation with the subject of death. It makes death, in a sense, unimportant. It liberates all our energy and time for the realization and extension of the happy potentialities of this good earth. It engenders a hearty and grateful acceptance of the rich experiences attainable in human living amid an abundant Nature. It is a knowledge that brings strength and depth and maturity, making possible a philosophy of life that is simple, understandable and inspiring. We do not ask to be born; and we do not ask to die. But born we are and die we must. We come into existence and we pass out of existence. And in neither case does high-handed fate await our ratification of its decree.

Yet between that birth and death we can live our lives, work for and enjoy the things that we hold dear. We can make our actions count and endow our days on earth with a scope and meaning that the finality of death cannot defeat. We can contribute our unique quality to the ongoing development of the nation and humanity; give of our best to the continuing affirmation of life on behalf of the greater glory of man.

NOTES

Chapter I

IMPORTANCE OF THE PROBLEM

1. William James, *The Varieties of Religious Experience*, Longmans, Green, 1910, p. 524.

2. Miguel de Unamuno, *The Tragic Sense of Life*, Macmillan, London, 1926, p. 5.

3. A. Avery Gates (ed.), *My Belief in Immortality*, Doubleday, Doran, 1928, p. xii.

4. Quoted in Radoslav A. Tsanoff, *The Problem of Immortality*, Macmillan, 1924, p. 245.

5. Quoted in A. Seth Pringle-Pattison, *The Idea of Immortality*, Oxford University Press, 1922, p. 184.

6. I Corinthians xv, 14 and 19.

7. Quoted in James T. Addison, *Life Beyond Death*, Houghton Mifflin, 1932, p. 159.

8. *Catholic Encyclopedia*, Vol. X, p. 23.

9. Quoted in a present-day Catholic funeral service.

10. Ludwig Feuerbach, *The Essence of Christianity*, Blanchard, 1855, pp. 225-226.

11. Harry Emerson Fosdick, *The Assurance of Immortality*, Association Press, 1926, pp. 100-102.

12. George A. Gordon, *Immortality and the New Theodicy*, Houghton Mifflin, 1897, p. 17.

13. James B. Pratt, *The Religious Consciousness*, Macmillan, 1928, p. 253.

14. George Lawton, *The Drama of Life after Death*, Holt, 1932, pp. 35-36.

15. Benedict Spinoza, *Ethics*, Fourth Part, Prop. LXVII.

16. F. C. S. Schiller, *Humanism*, Macmillan, London, 1912, p. 327.

17. John Baillie, *And the Life Everlasting*, Scribners, 1933, pp. 36-38.

18. John H. Randall, Jr., *The Making of the Modern Mind*, Houghton Mifflin, 1940, p. 49.

19. John Dewey, "A Recovery of Philosophy," pp. 30, 34 in Dewey and Others, *Creative Intelligence*, Holt, 1917.

20. *New York Herald Tribune*, Jan. 9, 1933.

21. See Julius F. Hecker, *Religion and Communism*, Chapman & Hall, London, 1933, p. 32.

22. Letter from Mrs. John Masefield, Aug. 20, 1929.

23. Sir Arthur Keith, "What I Believe," *The Forum*, April 1930.

24. C. D. Broad, *The Mind and Its Place in Nature*, Harcourt, Brace, 1925, p. 511.

25. Schiller, *op. cit.* (above, note 16), p. 320.

26. Mary Austin, *Experiences Facing Death*, Bobbs-Merrill, 1931, back of jacket and p. 55.

27. Morris R. Cohen, *Reason and Nature*, Harcourt, Brace, 1931, p. 369.

CHAPTER II

THE FUNDAMENTAL ISSUE

28. G. W. Leibniz, *Die Philosophischen Schriften*, Gerhardt, Berlin, 1875, iv, 300.

29. Lucretius, *On the Nature of Things*, translated by Cyril Bailey, Oxford University Press, 1926, Bk. III, lines 880 *ff*.

30. Genesis ii, 7.

31. Ecclesiastes ix, 5-7, 9-10.

32. *Ibid.*, iii, 19-20.

33. Psalms xc, 3, 5-6.

34. *Ibid.*, xxxix, 13.

35. Job x, 20-22.

36. Homer, *The Odyssey*, xi, 489.

37. Plato, *Republic*, Bk. III, 386.

38. Pratt, *op. cit.* (above, note 13), p. 249.

39. Matthew xxviii, 6.

40. Luke xxiv, 39.

41. John xx, 27.

42. Mark xvi, 19.

43. I Corinthians xv, 50.

44. Augustine, *The City of God*, Bk. xxii, Ch. 20.

45. Thomas Aquinas, *Summa Theologica*, Part III (Supplement), Q 79, Art. 1.

46. Dante, *Divine Comedy:* "Purgatory," Canto XXV, vv. 87-108.

47. *Catholic Encyclopedia*, Vol. 7, p. 211.

48. Bishop B. F. Wescott, *The Historic Faith*, Macmillan, London, 1890, p. 136.

49. Bishop Charles Gore, *The Creed of the Christian*, Gardner, Darton, London, 1895, p. 92.

50. W. R. Matthews, "The Destiny of the Soul," p. 200, *The Hibbert Journal*, Vol. xxviii, No. 2, Jan., 1930.

51. Streeter and Others, *Immortality*, Macmillan, 1922, pp. 102-104.

52. Harry Emerson Fosdick, *The Modern Use of the Bible*, Macmillan, 1924, p. 98.

53. Harry Emerson Fosdick, *Adventurous Religion*, Harpers, 1926, p. 199.

54. Fosdick, *Modern Use of the Bible, op. cit.* (above, note 52), p. 102.

55. William Adams Brown, *The Christian Hope*, Scribners, 1915, pp. 94-95.

56. *Ibid.*, p. 172. Italics mine—C. L.

57. S. D. McConnell, *Immortability*, Macmillan, 1930, pp. 83-84.

58. Robert Norwood, *His Glorious Body*, Scribners, 1930, p. 38.

59. *Ibid.*, pp. 30-31.

60. James De Wolf Perry as reported in *New York Times*, April 9, 1934.

61. William T. Manning, Easter Sermon, as reported in *New York Times*, April 6, 1931.

62. George Santayana, *Reason in Religion*, Scribners, 1926, p. 245.

63. Sir Oliver Lodge, *Why I Believe in Personal Immortality*, Doubleday, Doran, 1929, p. 14.

64. Eugene Crowell, *Primitive Christianity and Modern Spiritualism*, G. W. Carleton, 1874, Vol. I, p. 403.

65. John Goddard, *Right and Wrong Unveilings of the Spiritual World*, New-Church Board of Publications, New York, 1912, p. 69.

66. Lucretius, *op. cit.* (above, note 29); Bk. III, lines 626 *ff*.

Chapter III

THE VERDICT OF SCIENCE

67. Aristotle, *De Anima*, 412b.

68. Walter B. Cannon, *The Wisdom of the Body*, Norton, 1932.

69. Lucretius, *On the Nature of Things* (Charles E. Bennett, trans.), published for the Classics Club by Walter J. Black, New York, Bk. III, lines 446 *ff*.

70. Garrett Hardin, *Biology: Its Human Implications*, Freeman, 1949, p. 289.

71. Robert S. Woodworth and Donald G. Marquis, *Psychology*, 5th ed., Holt, 1948, p. 251.

72. C. Judson Herrick, *The Brains of Rats and Men*, University of Chicago Press, 1926, pp. 8-9.

73. Lucretius, *op. cit.* (above, note 69), Bk. III, lines 475 *ff*.

74. See William H. Blake, *A Preliminary Study of*

the Interpretation of Bodily Expression, Teachers College, New York, 1933.

75. John Donne, *An Anatomy of the World,* II, 244 *ff.*

76. Under artificial experimental conditions, when stereotyped reactions are not prevailing, non-Orientals find plenty of expression in Oriental faces. See Elizabeth B. Field, *A Study of the Judgment by American White Students of the Facial Expression of Chinese and White Men Students,* Columbia University, 1933.

77. This diary was published in J. A. L. Singh and R. M. Zingg, *Wolf-Children and Feral Man,* Harpers, 1942.

78. Arnold Gesell, *Wolf Child and Human Child,* Harpers, 1941, pp. 38-39.

79. Henri Bergson, *Mind-Energy,* Holt, 1920, p. 73.

80. Hans Driesch, *The Crisis in Psychology,* Princeton University Press, 1925, pp. 254-255.

81. William McDougall, *Modern Materialism and Emergent Evolution,* Van Nostrand, 1929, pp. 65-66.

82. Cannon, *op. cit.* (above, note 68), Ch. XIV.

83. William McDougall, *Body and Mind,* Macmillan, 1911, p. 356.

84. *Ibid.,* p. xiii.

85. Houghton Mifflin, 1898.

86. Lucretius, *op. cit.* (above, note 29), Bk. III, lines 799 *ff.*

87. Santayana, *Reason in Religion, op. cit.* (above, note 62), p. 240.

88. John Bunyan, *Pilgrim's Progress,* Oxford University Press, 1912, p. 366.

89. Proceedings of the American Society for Psychical Research, Vol. IX. See also Morton Prince, "The Problem of Personality: How Many Selves Have We?" p. 245 in *Psychologies of 1925,* Clark University, 1926.

90. James Gordon Gilkey in Gates (ed.), *op. cit.* (above, note 3), p. 21.

91. Plato, *Phaedo,* 86.

92. John Dewey, *Philosophy and Civilization*, Minton Balch, 1931, p. 302.

93. *Ibid.*, p. 303.

94. Baillie, *op. cit.* (above, note 17), p. 303.

95. John Locke, *Essay Concerning Human Understanding*, Clarendon Press, Oxford, 1894, Vol. 2, p. 193.

96. *Enchiridion*, Chs. 85-87.

97. Edwin A. Burtt, *Principles and Problems of Right Thinking*, Harpers, 1928, p. 425.

98. In Cassirer, Kristeller and Randall (eds.), *The Renaissance Philosophy of Man*, University of Chicago Press, 1948, p. 280.

99. A. H. Douglas, *The Philosophy and Psychology of Pietro Pomponazzi*, Cambridge University Press, 1910, p. 90.

100. John H. Randall and John H. Randall, Jr., *Religion and the Modern World*, Stokes, 1929, p. 67.

101. Owen A. Hill, *Psychology and Natural Theology*, Macmillan, 1921, p. 106.

102. I have mislaid the source of this statement and have been unable to trace it. *Cf.* John Fiske, *Life Everlasting*, Houghton Mifflin, 1901, p. 64.

103. Tertullian, *De Carne Christi*, Ch. 5.

CHAPTER IV

THE ENVIRONMENT OF HEAVEN

104. Jonathan Swift, *Gulliver's Travels*, Part III, X.

105. Quoted from Elie Reclus' *Primitive Folk* by V. F. Calverton, *The Passing of the Gods*, Scribners, 1934, p. 76.

106. Quoted in Randall, *The Making of the Modern Mind*, *op. cit.* (above, note 18), p. 33.

107. Philip Cabot, *The Sense of Immortality*, Harvard University Press, 1925, p. 5.

108. Pratt, *op. cit.* (above, note 13), pp. 246-247.

109. J. Helder (ed.), *Greatest Thoughts on Immortality*, Richard R. Smith, Inc., 1930, p. 55.

110. Fosdick, *The Assurance of Immortality, op. cit.* (above, note 11), p. 116.

111. Charles R. Brown in Sydney Strong (ed.), *We Believe in Immortality*, Coward-McCann, 1929, p. 106.

112. I John iii, 2.

113. I Corinthians ii, 9.

114. Harry Emerson Fosdick in William L. Stidger (ed.), *If I Had Only One Sermon to Preach on Immortality*, Harpers, 1929, p. 69.

115. Henry P. Van Dusen, *In Quest of Life's Meaning*, Association Press, 1926, p. 139.

116. Lyman Abbott, *The Other Room*, Outlook Company, 1904, pp. 94-96.

117. Brown, *op. cit.* (above, note 111), pp. 169-175. This citation covers the quotations from Dr. Brown on both pages 134 and 135 of this book.

118. Milo H. Gates, sermon as reported in *New York Herald Tribune*, Jan. 2, 1933.

119. Streeter, *op. cit.* (above, note 51), pp. 155 *ff.*

120. L. P. Jacks, "The Theory of Survival in the Light of Its Context," p. 615, *The Hibbert Journal*, Vol. XV, No. 4, July 1917.

121. Pringle-Pattison, *op. cit.* (above, note 5), p. 205.

122. Georgia Harkness, *Conflicts in Religious Thought*, Holt, 1929, pp. 305-306.

123. Plato, *Phaedo*, 114.

124. Santayana, *Reason in Religion, op. cit.* (above, note 62), pp. 243-244.

125. Quoted in Lawton, *op. cit.* (above, note 14), p. 52.

126. Lodge, *op. cit.* (above note 63), pp. 139-142.

127. Matthew xxii, 25-30.

128. Thomas Aquinas, *Summa contra Gentiles*, Part IV, 88.

129. C. J. Keyser, "The Significance of Death," p. 890, *The Hibbert Journal*, Vol. XII, No. 4, July 1914.

130. George Santayana, *Soliloquies in England*, Scribners, 1923, p. 99.

CHAPTER V

THE FAILURE OF EVIDENCE AND ARGUMENTS

131. David Hume, *An Enquiry Concerning Human Understanding*, Open Court, 1927, p. 121.

132. See Harry Houdini, *A Magician among the Spirits*, Harpers, 1924.

133. H. G. Wells, *The World of William Clissold*, Doran, 1926, Vol. I, pp. 46-47.

134. Broad, *op. cit.* (above, note 24), p. 540.

135. See Joseph B. Rhine, *New Frontiers of the Mind: The Story of the Duke Experiments*, Farrar and Rinehart, 1937.

136. See Joseph Jastrow, "ESP, House of Cards" in *The American Scholar*, Winter, 1938-39, pp. 13-22.

137. J. B. S. Haldane, *Possible Worlds*, Harpers, 1928, pp. 218-219.

138. William James, *Collected Essays and Reviews*, Longmans, Green, 1920, pp. 438-439.

139. Leonard Huxley, *Life and Letters of Thomas Henry Huxley*, Appleton, 1900, Vol. I, p. 452.

140. *The Journal of Philosophy*, Vol. VI, No. 15, July 22, 1909, p. 413.

141. Minot Simons, Easter Sermon, as reported in *New York Herald Tribune*, April 1, 1929.

142. Clarence C. Little, Strong (ed.), *op. cit.* (above, note 111), p. 10.

143. Immanuel Kant, *Critique of Pure Reason*, Preface, xxx.

144. Kant, *Critique of Practical Reason*, Bk. II, Ch. 2.

145. Kant, *Metaphysic of Morality*, Section II.

146. This and the subsequent quotations from Kant are from the *Critique of Practical Reason*, Bk. II, Ch. 2.

147. Brown, *op. cit.* (above, note 111), p. 174.

148. Quoted from Fichte in Edgar S. Brightman, *Immortality in Post-Kantian Idealism*, Harvard University Press, 1925, p. 42.

149. William Ernest Hocking, *The Self, Its Body and Freedom*, Yale University Press, 1928, p. 178.

150. J. Estlin Carpenter in Helder (ed.), *op. cit.* (above, note 109), p. 49.

151. E. G. Evans, "William James and His Wife," *Atlantic Monthly*, Sept., 1929.

152. Fosdick, *Assurance of Immortality*, *op. cit.* (above, note 11), pp. 88-92.

153. John Haynes Holmes, Easter Sermon, as reported in *New York Times*, April 21, 1930.

154. Fosdick, *Assurance of Immortality*, *op. cit.* (above, note 11), pp. 61-62.

155. J. Y. Simpson, *Man and the Attainment of Immortality*, Hodder and Stoughton, London, 1922, p. 295.

156. *Ibid.*, p. 296.

157. Tsanoff, *op. cit.* (above, note 4), p. 242, quoted from Petavel-Oliff, *Le problème de l'immortalité*.

158. Fosdick, *The Assurance of Immortality*, *op. cit.* (above, note 11), pp. 8-9, 14.

159. Charles F. Dole, *The Hope of Immortality*, Houghton Mifflin, 1906, p. 24.

160. Ralph Waldo Emerson, "Threnody."

161. William James, *The Principles of Psychology*, Holt, 1923, Vol. I, p. 348.

162. Brown, *op. cit.* (above, note 111), p. 160.

163. Harry Emerson Fosdick, *Spiritual Values and Eternal Life*, Harvard University Press, 1927, p. 4.

164. Fosdick, *The Assurance of Immortality, op. cit.* (above, note 11), pp. 10-11.

165. *Ibid.*, p. 16.

166. Shakespeare, *The Tempest*, Act IV, Scene 1.

167. I have mislaid the source of this quotation.

168. A. E. Taylor, "The Belief in Immortality," pp. 149-150, in *The Faith and the War*, F. J. Foakes Jackson (ed.), Macmillan, London, 1916.

169. Robert A. Falconer, *The Idea of Immortality and Western Civilization*, Harvard University Press, 1930, p. 53.

170. Louis De Launay, *A Modern Plea for Christianity*, Macmillan, 1927, pp. 220-221.

171. Taylor, *op. cit.* (above, note 168), pp. 149-150.

172. Fosdick, *The Assurance of Immortality, op. cit.* (above, note 11), p. 17.

173. Quoted in Randall, *The Making of the Modern Mind, op. cit.* (above, note 18), p. 564.

174. Fosdick, *The Assurance of Immortality, op. cit.* (above, note 11), p. 11.

175. *Ibid.*, p. 100.

176. F. W. Farrar, in Helder (ed.), *op. cit.* (above, note 109), p. 5.

177. William R. Alger, *A Critical History of the Doctrine of a Future Life*, W. J. Widdleton, 1871, p. 51.

178. Emil F. Kautzsch, in Helder (ed.), *op. cit.* (above, note 109), p. 62.

179. The believers in conditional immortality, who postulate no hell but do not guarantee heaven to everyone, are an exception.

180. Tsanoff, *op. cit.* (above, note 4), p. 239.

181. W. Somerset Maugham, *The Summing Up*, Doubleday, Doran, 1938, p. 275.

182. Ralph Waldo Emerson, "Immortality," p. 10.

183. Bliss Perry (ed.), *The Heart of Emerson's Journals*, Houghton Mifflin, 1926, p. 270.

184. Strong (ed.), *op. cit* (above, note 111), p. 56.

185. Kant, *Critique of Practical Reason*, Bk. II, Ch. 2.

186. Santayana, *Soliloquies in England, op. cit.* (above, note 130), p. 116.

187. Aristotle, *Nicomachean Ethics*, Bk. I, Ch. 4.

188. Fosdick, *The Assurance of Immortality, op. cit.* (above, note 11), p. 19.

189. Sidney Hook, *The New Leader*, Oct. 22, 1949, p. S-8.

190. Fosdick, *The Assurance of Immortality, op. cit.* (above, note 11), p. 88.

191. Sir James Jeans, *The Universe around Us*, Macmillan, 1929, pp. 83-84.

192. William James, *Pragmatism*, Longmans, Green, 1925, p. 106.

193. William W. Fenn, *Immortality and Theism*, Harvard University Press, 1922.

194. Quoted in John Haynes Holmes, *Is Death the End?*, Putnam, 1915, p. xv.

195. Unamuno, *op. cit.* (above, note 2), pp. 111, 91, 114.

CHAPTER VI

MOTIVATIONS AND SYMBOLISM

196. W. E. H. Lecky, *History of European Morals*, Appleton, 1927, Vol. I, p. 211.

197. Thomas Aquinas, *Summa Theologica*, Part III (Supplement), Q. 94, Art. 1.

198. Quoted in Alger, *op. cit.* (above, note 177), p. 515.

199. Quoted in Chapman Cohen, *Essays in Free-thinking*, Pioneer Press, London, 1928, p. 26.

200. Jonathan Edwards, Sermon, "Sinners in the Hands of an Angry God," Application.

201. President Edwards, *Works*, Isaiah Thomas, Worcester, 1809, Vol. VIII, p. 167.

202. Quoted in Pringle-Pattison, *op. cit.* (above, note 5), p. 233.

203. Quoted in James H. Leuba, *The Belief in God and Immortality*, Open Court, 1921, p. 298.

204. Pringle-Pattison, *op. cit.* (above, note 5), p. 133.

205. Leuba, *op. cit.* (above, note 203), pp. 254 ff.

206. *Ibid.*, p. 256.

207. Quoted in Ilya Metchnikoff, *The Prolongation of Life*, Putnam, 1908, p. 127.

208. Quoted in G. Stanley Hall, *Senescence*, Appleton, 1923, p. 89.

209. *Ibid.*, p. 262.

210. Walter Savage Landor, "Dying Speech of an Old Philosopher."

211. Quoted in Pringle-Pattison, *op. cit.* (above, note 5), p. 131.

212. *Ibid.*, p. 132.

213. Unamuno, *op. cit.* (above, note 2), p. 268.

214. Dylan Thomas, "Do Not Go Gentle into that Good Night," *Collected Poems*, New Directions, 1946. (Copyright 1952, 1953 by Dylan Thomas. Reprinted by permission of New Directions.)

215. Huxley, *op. cit.* (above, note 139), Vol. II, p. 67.

216. Cited by Pratt, *op. cit.* (above, note 13), p. 235.

217. Plato, *Symposium*, 208.

218. Quoted in Chapman Cohen, *op. cit.* (above, note 199), p. 19.

219. William Osler, *Science and Immortality*, Houghton Mifflin, 1904, p. 19.

220. Santayana, *Reason in Religion, op. cit.* (above, note 62), p. 235.

221. William Hazlitt, "On the Feeling of Immortality in Youth."

222. Sigmund Freud, "Thoughts on War and Death," Vol. IV, *Collected Papers,* International Psycho-Analytical Press, 1924, pp. 305, 313.

223. *New York Times,* April 21, 1930.

224. Fosdick, *The Assurance of Immortality, op. cit.* (above, note 11), p. 30.

225. F. J. E. Woodbridge, *The Son of Apollo,* Houghton Mifflin, 1929, p. 231.

226. See Cassirer, Kristeller, Randall (ed.), *op cit.* (above, note 98), p. 11.

227. Quoted in Leuba, *op. cit.* (above, note 203), p. 317.

228. Quoted, *ibid.,* p. 316.

229. *Ibid.,* p. 315.

230. James, *The Principles of Psychology, op. cit.* (above, note 161), Vol. II, p. 308.

231. Robert G. Ingersoll, *Lectures and Essays,* First Series, Watts, London, 1926, p. 127.

232. See Lawton, *op. cit.* (above, note 14), pp. 425-426.

233. *Ibid.,* p. 424.

234. Quoted in Winifred Kirkland, *The New Death,* Houghton Mifflin, 1918, p. 9.

235. *Ibid.,* pp. 163-164.

236. See Ray H. Abrams, "War Brings a Revival of Religion," Chap. XII in *Preachers Present Arms,* Round Table Press, 1933.

237. *New York Times,* Feb. 26, 1934.

238. Bernard Bosanquet, *The Value and Destiny of the Individual,* Macmillan, London, 1913, pp. 274-275.

239. John Dewey, *Experience and Nature,* Open Court, 1926, Ch. II.

240. Horace Kallen in Dewey and Others, *op. cit.* (above, note 19), p. 434.

241. Karl Marx, *The Class Struggles in France*, New York Labor News Company, 1924, p. 112.

242. Taylor, *op. cit.* (above, note 168), p. 139.

243. Quoted in Chapman Cohen, *op. cit.* (above, note 199), p. 25.

244. Revelation vii, 16.

245. See Philip F. Waterman, *The Story of Superstition*, Knopf, 1929, p. 276.

246. Copyright, 1915, by Dodd, Mead & Co., Inc.

247. Plato, *The Republic*, Bk. ix, 592.

248. G. Stanley Hall, *Jesus, the Christ, in the Light of Psychology*, Appleton, 1923, p. 693.

249. William Blake, "Milton."

250. Irwin Edman, "The Pagan's Hell," p. 176 in Dean W. R. Inge and Others, *What is Hell?*, Harpers, 1930.

251. Sir James G. Frazer, *The Belief in Immortality and the Worship of the Dead*, Macmillan, London, 1922, Vol. II, p. 319.

252. Randall, *The Making of the Modern Mind*, *op. cit.* (above, note 18), p. 55.

253. Schleiermacher, *On Religion*, translated by J. Oman, Kegan Paul, London, 1893, p. 101.

254. Benedict Spinoza, *Ethics*, Fifth Part, Props. XXI-XXIII.

255. *Ibid.*, Prop. XXXIV, schol.

256. George Santayana, "Introduction" to *The Ethics of Spinoza*, Dent, London, 1925, pp. xvii-xviii.

257. Plato, *Timaeus*, 90.

258. Plato, *Republic*, Bk. VI, 486.

259. Aristotle, *De Anima*, Bk. III, Ch. 5.

260. Aristotle, *Nicomachean Ethics*, Bk. X, Ch. 7.

261. Abbott, *op. cit.* (above, note 116), pp. 101, 105-106.

262. Stidger (ed.), *op. cit.* (above, note 114), pp. 68-69.

263. John xvii, 3.

264. Luke xvii, 21.

265. John x, 10.

266. Matthew xvi, 24-26.

267. Letter LXXV, Spinoza to Oldenburg.

268. *Ibid.*, LXXVIII.

269. J. Middleton Murry, p. 352, *The Adelphi*, Vol. II, No. 4 (New Series), July, 1931.

270. Romans viii, 6.

271. D. H. Lawrence, *Pansies*, Knopf, 1930, p. 129.

272. Dr. Albert E. Ribourg, Easter Sermon, as reported in *New York Times*, April 21, 1930.

273. Rabbi Stephen S. Wise, Easter Sermon, as reported in *New York Herald Tribune*, April 21, 1930.

274. Hall, *Jesus, the Christ, in the Light of Psychology, op. cit.* (above, note 248), p. 411.

275. *Ibid.*, p. xiii.

276. Randall, *Religion and the Modern World, op. cit.* (above, note 100), pp. 71, 73-74.

277. John Dewey, *Experience and Nature, op. cit.* (above, note 239), p. 70.

Chapter VII

LIFE WITHOUT IMMORTALITY

278. Quoted in the *Encyclopedia Britannica*, 11th Edition, Vol. XIV, p. 339.

279. The Rt. Rev. William T. Manning as reported in *New York Times*, April 2, 1934.

280. Albert Einstein, "What I Believe," *The Forum*, Oct. 1930.

281. *Encyclopedia Britannica*, 14th Edition, 1929, Vol. VI, p. 239.

282. *Ibid.*, Vol. IV, p. 326.

283. Quoted in *The Hibbert Journal*, Vol. II, p. 725.

284. Leuba, *op. cit.* (above, note 203), Ch. IX.

285. James H. Leuba, "Religious Beliefs of American Scientists," *Harper's Magazine*, August, 1934.

286. Translated by Alfred E. Zimmern, *The Greek Commonwealth*. Oxford University Press, 1924, p. 207.

287. Santayana, *Reason in Religion, op. cit.* (above, note 62), p. 247.

288. Huxley, *op. cit.* (above, note 139), Vol. I, p. 237.

289. Kirsopp Lake, *Immortality and the Modern Mind*, Harvard University Press, 1922, pp. 21-23.

290. Quoted by Irwin Edman in *The Uses of Philosophy*, Simon and Schuster, 1955, p. 153.

291. See Corliss Lamont, *The Philosophy of Humanism*, Frederick Ungar, 1965.

292. See Sellars, McGill and Farber (eds.), *Philosophy for the Future: The Quest of Modern Materialism*, Macmillan, 1949.

293. See Y. H. Krikorian (ed.), *Naturalism and the Human Spirit*, Columbia University Press, 1944.

294. Don Marquis, "Transient," by permission of Bernice M. Marquis. First published in *The Saturday Review of Literature*, Oct. 22, 1932.

295. Harlow Shapley, *Of Stars and Men: Human Responses to an Expanding Universe*, Beacon Press, 1958, pp. 74, 144.

296. *The Journal of Philosophy*, July 22, 1909, p. 415.

297. Edwin M. Slocombe, "Lantern in the Storm," *Atlantic Monthly*, Vol. 151, No. 5, May, 1933, p. 552.

298. Quoted in Holmes, *Is Death the End?, op. cit.* (above, note 194), p. 345.

299. Diogenes Laertius, *Lives of Eminent Philosophers*, Putnam, 1925, Bk. X, 125.

300. Anne Parrish, *Golden Wedding*, Harpers, 1936, p. 343.

301. H. G. Wells, Julian Huxley and G. P. Wells, *The Science of Life*, Doubleday, Doran, 1938, p. 551.

302. John Donne, *Devotions upon Emergent Occasions*.

303. Bertrand Russell, *The Conquest of Happiness*, Liveright, 1930, p. 230.

304. See F. J. Gould, *Funeral Services without Theology*, Watts, London, 1923, and Corliss Lamont, *A Humanist Funeral Service*, American Humanist Association, 1962. Also the funeral ceremonies of the Ethical Culture Societies are well worth studying.

305. Quoted in John Morley, *Recollections*, Macmillan, 1917, Vol. II, p. 114.

306. Santayana, "Introduction" to *The Ethics of Spinoza, op. cit.* (above, note 256), p. xix.

INDEX

Abbott, Lyman, 133-134, 135, 246
Acheron, 61
Achilles, 36-37
Adam, 17
Aeneid (Virgil), 40, 240
Africa, 24, 129
After Many a Summer Dies the Swan (Huxley), 270-271
Ahasuerus, the Wandering Jew, 128
Alexander the Great, 148
Alice in Wonderland, 48
Allah, 14
Almighty. *See* God
Amala, 89
Ambrose, St., 4
America, American (s), 2, 20, 23, 26, 37, 38, 49, 50, 58, 92, 116, 129, 149, 202, 217n. 232, 255, 274n. *See also* United States
Anglo-Saxon (s), 144
Apostles' Creed, 43
Aquinas, St. Thomas, 44, 47, 121, 143-144, 201, 241
Arabia, Arabian (s), 254
Aralu, 33
Aristotle, 28, 29, 44, 62, 130, 181, 240, 245-246, 254
Army, U.S., 261
Asia, 24
Athens, Athenians, 256
Augustine, St., 3, 44, 45, 47, 115, 247
Aurelius, Marcus, 254
Austin, Mary, 20
Australia, 156
Averröes, 254

Babylon, Babylonian (s), 33, 37, 216

Baillie, John, 14, 112
Barry, Iris, 265n
Beethoven, Ludwig van, 181
Bergson, Henri, 92, 93, 97
Berkeley, George, 119
Bible, 34-36, 133, 164, 167, 246, *See also books of; see also* Old Testament, New Testament
Blake, William, 56, 57, 138, 236
Blau, Joseph L., 254
Book of Common Prayer, 12
Bosanquet, Bernard, 225, 254
Brains of Rats and Men (Herrick), 75
Britain, British, 192. *See also* England
British Association for the Advancement of Science, 19
Brittany, 4
Broad, C. D., 20, 154
Brooke, Rupert, 234
Brooks, Phillips, 259
Brown, Charles R., 133
Brown, William Adams, 54, 134, 135, 136, 145-146
Brutus, Marcus Junius, 241
Buddha (Gautama Buddha), 255
Buddhism, Buddhist (s), 23, 116, 137, 178, 198-200, 262
Bunyan, John, 101
Burbank, Luther, 254
Burma, Burmese, 129

Caesar, Julius, 147, 217, 254
California, 192
Calvin, John, 202
Cambridge University, 20
Canine Cemetery, Hartsdale, N.Y., 116-117

Books Edited by Corliss Lamont

Dialogue on John Dewey, Horizon Press, New York, NY, 1981. (Write Author)

Dialogue on George Santayana, Horizon Press, New York, NY, 1981. (Write Author)

Man Answers Death, Philosophical Library, New York, NY, 1954.

Collected Poems of John Reed, Lawrence Hill Books, Brooklyn, NY, 1985.

The Trial of Elizabeth Gurley Flynn by the American Civil Liberties Union, Horizon Press, New York, NY, 1969.